SURVIVAL OF THE FITTEST

Total Quality Control and
Management Evolution

SURVIVAL OF THE FITTEST

Total Quality Control and Management Evolution

A. Richard Shores

ASQC Quality Press
American Society for Quality Control
310 West Wisconsin Avenue
Milwaukee, Wisconsin 53203

SURVIVAL OF THE FITTEST

Total Quality Control and Management Evolution

A. Richard Shores

Acquisitions Editor: Jeanine L. Lau
Production Editor: Tammy Griffin
Cover Design: Lori L. Schmidt
Set in Garamond by DanTon Typographers. Printed and bound by BookCrafters.

Published by ASQC Quality Press • Milwaukee

ISBN 0-87389-040-X

Printed in the United States of America

ACKNOWLEDGMENT

Many outstanding contributions have been made to the subject matter of this book in recent years. My knowledge of management and quality has been synthesized from reading the works of those in the vanguard and from my own practical experience. I have attempted to be precise with footnoting and acknowledging the sources of my thinking; try as I may, however, there may be some that I have missed. The passage of time may have melded my reflections with the thoughts of others.

There are also many contributions made by people with whom I work at Hewlett-Packard Company. Many of these contributions are also difficult to trace and acknowledge. To them, I also apologize and thank for the time we spent talking in the halls or over coffee, since the challenges they presented helped clarify my thinking on sometimes clouded issues.

Some people contributed directly in the research, the writing, and editing process. To them, I give special thanks and recognition. All contributed many hours away from their families to help make this book possible. Jim Rabins, TQC Trainer and Facilitator, contributed to the research and writing of three chapters (Chapters 8, 9, and 10) on quality teams, vendor participation, and employee suggestion systems. HP statisticians, Greg Kruger and Sudha Saletore; and TQC Manager and Support, Steve Hurd and Doug McCrea, contributed to the material in two chapters (Chapters 11 and 12) on process analysis and statistical quality control. Other contributions were made by Donalee Edwards, illustrations, and a very special group of technical writers at HP, in the editing cycle. I especially want to thank Jeanne Willard, my regular full-time secretary, and her family for the many hours she spent after work reading and editing my transcripts to make up for my sometimes poor choice of words and improper grammar. Without her keen eye and professional ability, the quality of this book would have suffered greatly.

Lastly, but most importantly, I thank my own family — my wife, Paula, for her patience and help through many months of obsessive self-indulgence; and my stepdaughters, Laura and Autumn, for the many (paid) hours they spent at the word processor helping to correct my rough drafts.

As you can see, this book was a genuine team effort and I sincerely thank everyone for their help.

TABLE OF CONTENTS

INTRODUCTION

Japan is a nation of 100 million people in a country roughly the size of California. It is a country historically short of resources, a country that had little influence from the outside world until the last 100 years. It holds a people born with hardships and deficits that ultimately influenced their religious beliefs, a people with a strong hierarchical society who respect one another's social position, be it high or low. This is the country that has emerged as the preeminent economic power in the world, a country that has the economy of other world powers reeling from its success. Japan: a nation that stated its objectives and achieved them.

During the depression of the United States, the Japanese-Americans were considered to be the best farmers in America. Working 12-hour days at great personal sacrifice, the immigrants from Japan toiled in the earth to bring in larger and better crops than American farmers. Their style of living was most meager while they saved money to buy their own land. Born of a country where tenant farmers had to give 80 to 90 percent of their crop to the landlords, the Japanese farmers found no discomfort in this style of living. The opportunity to own their own land was reward enough.

In Japan a similar story was being told — not a story about the Japanese farmer, but about the Japanese military. They were building a military arsenal that would dominate Far East Asia. The Japanese culture that contributed to their success as farmers would make an equal contribution to Japan as a military power. The farmers would sacrifice high percentages of their crops to support the *Zaibatsus* who were the economic power in Japan. The *Zaibatsus* controlled the government and industry and supported the military expansion to further enlarge their wealth.

The Japanese were chronically short of resources like metals and oil, and found it necessary to import these products. As a people they were accustomed to shortages and had developed methods of efficiency that carried through every aspect of their lives. These efficiencies allowed them to do more with less than anyone else in the world.

When war finally came between the United States and Japan, many speculated that it would not last more than a year or two; instead, the war lasted four years. The Japanese were able to prolong this war because of their ability to obtain maximum production from limited resources. Their discipline, loyalty, and efficacy proved to counterbalance the technology of the West.

1

After the war, the Japanese mounted a new offensive. They took direct aim at the economic domination of the world. They were poised with the same abilities that made them successful in farming and strong at war; they had the need, the desire, and the determination to be successful. All they needed was to be shown how to achieve efficiency in the complex industrial world; the advisors who later came to Japan would provide that knowledge.

Japan would spend the next 40 years climbing the ladder of success. The Japanese would learn how to eliminate waste through quality. They would learn how to improve management effectiveness through planning and review. They would learn how to utilize their people resource to the utmost through teamwork. They would learn how to use statistics and structured analysis to improve their processes — and all these things they would learn from America.

In the meantime, Americans were oblivious to the changes around them. We couldn't see the value of the new methods. We had just won a war; our businesses were thriving; our economy was stronger than it had ever been. Why question success? We did not realize that the world economy was changing more rapidly than before; we did not realize that the demands on management would increase, requiring more responsive methods; we did not know that our inefficient use of resources would leave our economy prey to those who were more efficient. In short, we were suffering from a chronic lack of leadership.

This is the same leadership that has allowed us to build a budget deficit that threatens our very livelihood; the same leadership that allowed us to get into and out of the Vietnam War without gain and at huge loss of life and money; the same leadership that now places us in jeopardy around the world with military involvement, aid, and support to politically unfriendly nations. This country is suffering from a shortage of leadership in every aspect of its existence.

Government, business, and education each has a need to improve its leadership effectiveness, because leadership is the only avenue through which any size organization can improve its efficiency. And efficiency is the only way we can build a future. In the world economy of today and tomorrow, we will compete for our market share and our economic well-being on the basis of the efficient utilization of resources — not on technology.

Technological growth has been the mainstay of competitive success during the last 100 years, but today technology is becoming a commodity to be bought and sold around the world. Japan's success is a clear example of this fundamental principle. They proved unquestionably that they could win an economic battle by improving the utilization of resources while making no significant contribution to the development of technology.

Japanese leadership is responsible for this unerring approach to economic success. Throughout Japan's economic development, leaders have maintained a clear focus on quality and efficiency. Quality, defined in its broadest sense, is the absence of defects. The Japanese apply this definition to everything they do, not just to their products and manufacturing processes. They work to eliminate defects in planning, communication, motivation, material, equipment, and yes, people.

Efficiency is the by-product of quality — the absence of defects. By eliminating defects in planning and communication, the Japanese not only improve management efficiency but also resource efficiency. When they eliminate defects in material and equipment, they not only improve equipment and material efficiency but also labor and management efficiency. Viewed in this context, quality becomes imperative to every organization and process.

American business has a long way to go to catch up with the Japanese. Our leadership is inadequate to compete on a national scale with the efficiency that will be required in the future. My experience with managers suggests there is a strong reluctance to accept this fact. They still believe that discussions on quality, total quality control, and Japanese management are frivolous. There is still a strong, not-invented-here syndrome that pervades American manufacturing. Government and education still don't see how these things apply to them. Changing these attitudes is part of a leader's job and is an essential element to catching up with the Japanese.

The leader's role is to create an environment that focuses on quality and efficiency as the means for improved competitive performance. When quality has become imperative for every process and every organization, we will be in a position to fight back. This book will provide the leaders with insight to identify and manage the changes that are necessary to the future of their organizational systems.

CHAPTER 1

JAPANESE CULTURE — ITS HIDDEN STRENGTH

The business culture in which we work is only a subculture of the environment in which we live. In our country, as in Japan, our culture defines our needs and the manner in which we satisfy them. Our culture is reflected in the way we live, dress, eat, learn, and apply our artistic talents. We could say that our culture is the synthesis of all that we have learned and have wanted to become.

In business we carry this culture with us; we nourish it, we enhance it, and we let it guide us as we manage our resources. Our policies about people reflect our culture. The way we manage technology, the way we manage our finances, and the way we manage our people reflects our culture. Each and every thing we do as managers is a reflection of our culture.

Japan has existed for over 1,800 years and, except for the last 100 years, has been relatively free of Western influence. The Japanese have carefully cultivated a homogenous society — a society in which every citizen is exposed to a common culture. Their needs and wants are clearly understood. Their relationships to one another are without question. Their willing self-sacrifice to preserve the harmony of their group and their environment is a major element of Japanese heritage. Their culture is unusually well suited to a competitive environment — an environment where teamwork, self-discipline, and a harmonious relationship with one's surroundings are the ingredients for success.

Japan's present position in the world economy clearly represents a success story unparalleled in modern history. Rising from a starving, shattered nation in 1945, Japan has rebuilt its factories, its cities, and its wealth to become one of the strongest economic powers of the world. Because the Japanese imported much knowledge from us, many people in the United States take credit for Japan's success. Too much credit, however, is given to this imported knowledge; Japan's real strength comes from the motivation provided by its culture.

5

We Learned it from America

In 1986 I helped develop and teach a workshop for a group of quality managers. The topic was *Hoshin* — a structured planning and review system that many Japanese companies use to set and maintain the direction of their businesses. Attending this conference were two managers from Japan with considerable *Hoshin* experience. I was somewhat confused on the roots of *Hoshin,* so I asked one of them how it originated. He was astonished that I asked this question, and his reply surprised me. He said, "We learned it from you: America!" He went on to explain that it was copied from what we call Management by Objectives (MBO) and the Deming Plan-Do-Check-Act (PDCA) cycle was applied to it. Many Japanese companies have been using it for years. Many Japanese people have made contributions to the development of *Hoshin,* but by and large the concepts are from America. The only thing Japanese about it is the rigor applied by using the Deming PDCA cycle (Deming, 1982), which is also American.

Though unexpected, his reply underscored what I had come to learn about other aspects of Japanese management. In short, most elements of Japanese management are somehow tied to ideas developed in the United States, but are more rigorously applied in Japan. Why, I wondered, did the Japanese adopt and apply these ideas so successfully while these same ideas went unnoticed in the United States? Were Japanese needs different? Was their culture? In time, I became convinced that the Japanese culture was a primary impetus for their motivation to adopt the principles of quality management systems.

My interest began in 1983 when, for the first time, I seriously addressed the full implementation of total quality control (TQC). There were many books on the market describing PDCA and statistical quality control (SQC), but it was impossible to find anything that gave a comprehensive explanation of the entire quality management system. As a quality manager, I would lose credibility with my general manager and my peers if I asked them to adopt and apply the tools of TQC simply because the Japanese were using them. We'd done this too much in the past, and management responded with anti-Japanese sentiment. TQC had a stigma attached — one that prevented managers from embracing TQC concepts. Many managers gave it lip service, but in the end, they thought it was just another Japanese management tool. "Who needs it?" they asked. I realized that if I couldn't understand TQC and provide the proper motivation for implementing it, I would be wasting my time. Quality people were always telling workers that the sky was going to fall on them, but this was not sufficiently motivating.

I needed to better understand Japan. Surely there was more to TQC than met the eye. Copying Japanese methods was not enough — too many people had done this without being effective. If I could understand why the Japanese so eagerly adopted TQC methods, I could better motivate American managers. I needed to look deeply into their culture to determine why the Japanese managers were more receptive than the American managers to TQC.

In 1984 I took a trip to Japan. Along with our division's manufacturing manager, I visited a sister division of Hewlett-Packard Company. Two years previously the Yokogawa division had won the prestigious Deming Award — an award given annually by the Japanese Union of Scientists and Engineers (JUSE) in recognition of companies that distinguish themselves in the application of the Deming principles. Yokogawa HP was praised and admired for this success. While Yokogawa was not necessarily typical of Japanese companies, its implementation of Deming's principles was consistent with that of other Deming Award winners.

Japan 1984

What an adventure! Visiting Japan for the first time, I wondered what surprises awaited me. I didn't have to wonder long. My first surprise was the taxi ride to Tokyo: $85.00 in American money! The ride, though, held more interest than the rather expensive fare. I was intrigued by the brand new, luxury Toyota sedan, and I was impressed with the taxi driver's impeccable dress and manners. He wore a suit and tie, white gloves, and a small hospital-type mask. The mask, he explained, was to protect his passengers (he had a cold and did not want to spread it). I wondered if all Japanese were so considerate of their neighbors.

Our hosts at Yokogawa HP planned every detail of our trip. They even arranged for one of their employees — who had to catch the train south of Tokyo — to stop by our hotel each morning, escort us to the train depot, and then ride with us to the Yokogawa HP plant north of Tokyo.

Japan's train system is second to none. It is the major form of transportation for most commuters. Our escort said that the average Japanese worker spends one and a half hours commuting each day. Japan has a shortage of space and housing, so once found, most people are content with their housing. Rarely is it convenient to where they work. This surprised me because I'd been told they generally work for the same employer all their lives. Every evening throngs of people pour out of the businesses in Tokyo, filling the train stations for hours. At 10:00 one evening, as we returned from dinner, the common routes to the station were still packed with people returning home.

My strongest impression of the Japanese is that they are the most polite people on earth. Even in crowded train stations, we never had trouble finding someone to help us with directions. People usually would see that we were lost and would approach us, offering assistance. Only once did I doubt their politeness — when we boarded a very crowded train and everyone was mashed together with little regard for individual comfort.

That many Japanese people work long hours was nothing more than a rumor before my visit to Japan; however, I observed this work ethic to be true. A level of dedication exists that was beyond my Western understanding. The family orientation of business and lifelong employment also exists in Japan. The respect and trust that people show for each other exceeds my experience in America; employees trust their employers to meet their needs and the employers do not betray this trust.

We had our first view of a Japanese electronics manufacturing company at Yokogawa HP. Outward appearances provided nothing beyond what you would see at the most progressive American companies — volleyball courts, tennis courts, and soccer fields. All were used frequently for intramural sports. What we saw however, inside the company doors, provided us with a new perspective.

The first obvious difference was the entirely closed-off manufacturing area, an area that was completely static free. Everyone, including the manufacturing manager, wore static-free uniforms. People entering from other areas were required to cover their clothes with special slippers and smocks. The entire floor was painted with conductive paint to bleed off static charges. These precautions exemplify the extreme application of static protection, something most American companies approach only halfway. The benefits include lower failure cost in manufacturing and better product reliability for customers.

Additionally, Yokogawa HP had implemented a just-in-time (JIT) manufacturing system to cut down on inventory requirements and space. The process from start to finish took six days — one tenth the time and one tenth the inventory required using traditional batch systems. Reportedly, the JIT system was not in place when they won the Deming Award. This came later, after sufficiently improving the quality of their process to run a JIT system without costly shutdowns.

Yokogawa HP reported that while inventory reductions and quality improvements are important benefits of JIT, a big motivation for Japanese industry is space savings. Space in Tokyo is in short supply and very expensive. It is essential to find more space-effective ways of manufacturing products. With a one-time reduction in inventory, they might save $1 million. That, in turn, may avoid lease expenses of thousands of dollars each month — and that's thousands of dollars saved every month.

Yokogawa HP used the structured planning and review process, referred to as *Hoshin*, throughout the organization. *Hoshin* provides the direction for the business and sets the focus for Yokogawa HP's quality circles. It was clear that everyone and every process had a purpose that was tied to the driving force of the business. They focused constantly on their customers' needs and held regular reviews to evaluate performance. Goals and metrics were assigned to every process; statistics were used to analyze any variation.

Before returning from Japan, we visited several other companies, including Toyota. We found these companies to share many management philosophies with Yokogawa HP. All were team oriented, quality conscious, extremely clean, well organized, highly disciplined, and space efficient. We were satisfied with the additional knowledge we gained on Japanese quality management systems. We returned to the United States and designed a new and comprehensive TQC system.

It would be nice to say that everyone in our organization accepted this new system and supported it, but this simply wasn't the case. Many middle managers were still reluctant to embrace TQC concepts. Most of the real enthusiasm for TQC came from the quality assurance people. This was true for HP and for other companies with whom I associated as well. Middle managers readily acknowledged the rationale for TQC, but they could not bring themselves to fully adopt the practices. It was too risky — TQC was countercultural.

Suspicion of TQC has existed in all the companies with which I have been associated. The culture of our country supports the technological answer: more automation, more personal computers, more of the "we can beat them with our next new product" stance. Our culture supports a fairly loose attitude about the concept of quality: "Prove to me that it is affecting orders, and we will fix it," or "All that stuff about customer satisfaction is motherhood and apple pie," or "I'll start paying attention to these things when my boss does." These familiar quotes reflect the attitude of most middle managers in this country. The reward systems simply don't support the needed changes. Americans still believe that we can beat the Japanese with our technology. In the meantime, the Japanese move steadily ahead in quality and productivity.

We've all read enough about the cost of quality in American industry to know that 25 to 30 percent of the cost of doing business in this country is due to process inefficiency or to the cost of poor quality. Compare this with Japan's 5 to 10 percent cost of quality. Overall, this gives Japanese businesses a 20 percent productivity edge when using similar technologies. A 20 percent productivity advantage represents a 15-year technology advantage. This is because the U.S. gross national product per capita has grown 1.6 percent per year over the last 80 years and this growth is attributed to technology (Gill, 1980). That's quite an incentive to reduce waste.

Understanding this advantage would seem reason enough to adopt the methods of TQC, but there are still many leaders who have yet to understand this need. I say this because most top management emphasis is still on quarterly profits and technological improvements. Maybe they don't understand the nature of our competition or maybe they don't understand our own culture. The trip to Japan helped me to see the cultural differences that contribute to Japan's success in business. American managers need to understand these cultural advantages and begin to cope with them. To better understand and explain these differences we must look back to Japan's not-so-distant past, to a time of strength before Japanese companies used TQC management methods.

Japan 1941

How could Japan — a country with limited resources, approximately the size of California, and a population of 70 million people — attack the United States in an act of war and expect to win? This question has been asked and answered many times in the last 45 years. Unquestionably, Japan was a strong military power. It spent large amounts of its gross national product on military equipment and supplies. Its subsequent military prowess proved even greater than its arsenal suggested. A war that many speculated would last one to two years persisted for four long years.

Did the Japanese ever doubt their capacity to win? Did military pride allow them no alternatives? Were they so enamored of their principles and self-righteous military expansion in Asia to have no choice when the United States and others applied economically crippling trade sanctions? Were they so dependent on outside resources to feel that war was their only alternative — and that they could win with a surprise attack? Surely the answer must be yes. If we examine history, we find similar circumstances at the root of many conflicts — conflicts both bloody and costly or conflicts only contemplated.

In 1941 Western society considered the Japanese people to be resourceful, disciplined, frugal, loyal, and enduring. Cultural intoning, some speculated, would allow the Japanese army to defeat, man for man, any technologically equal wartime opponent. The United States ultimately overwhelmed Japan with both economic and technological superiority. The atomic bomb provided the final destructive act.

In the 1930s, an American named John Patric studied and wrote about Japanese culture. In 1936 Patric spent several months in Japan, living as a common citizen and traveling over 7,000 miles. In 1943 he published an account of Japan's strength in a book entitled *Why Japan was Strong*. Patric's original goal was to understand the contribution of Japanese culture to the success of Japanese-American farmers in prewar America. I was as obsessed about Japanese success in business as Patric was about their success in farming. He later concluded that the same cultural traits that made them successful farmers also made them strong soldiers (Patric, 1943). They are the same traits that make Japan successful in business today.

Japan has always been short of resources. There was never enough tillable land to produce enough foodstuff to provide more than the basics of some grains, rice, and fish. Meat was not a normal part of the Japanese diet, so cattle was not raised. The food value in a pound of meat was less than the food value of the grain it took to raise the animals. Other resources, like scrap metal and oil, were imported to meet their needs for steel and energy. The people of Japan have lived with these conditions for hundreds of years, and enduring these shortages has become a part of their culture (Varley, 1973).

Patric told a story that illustrates the cultural adaptation to these shortages. He saw a man eating a bowl of clear soup with only a few grains of rice and some vegetables in it. He asked the man why the Japanese do not eat creamed soups or blend their flavors. The man explained that creamed soups would leave a coating of food on the sides of the bowl that would be inedible. Over the period of a few weeks this would accumulate to an amount that could feed a child for several days. Since they do not have enough food to go around as it is, all forms of waste must be eliminated from their cooking and eating habits. He continued to explain why all parts of a fish are eaten and how the leftover bones and gristle are used to manufacture other needed items (Patric, 1943).

Another story involved a starving dog in the park. The dog was tied helplessly to a tree. It seemed to be nothing more than a skeleton wrapped in skin. Patric was painfully aware of the dog's condition; he approached the dog to give it food from his sack. When he offered the food, the dog snapped hungrily at his hand, puncturing it badly. By now, people gathered around him, laughing at Patric's situation for being such a fool — a fool to waste food on an animal that someone else had abandoned. Only a foreigner would be so foolish. Later, Patric noted the creatures with whom the Japanese find so much pleasure and comfort such as the singing crickets that sound so beautiful but eat so little (Patric, 1943).

Food shortages were exacerbated by the military buildup before World War II. Traditionally farmers were accustomed to keeping only 10 to 20 percent of their crops, the rest kept by the landowner. This system accumulated wealth in the hands of the great financial combines called *Zaibatsu* (Varley, 1973). The *Zaibatsu* exploited the masses in all sectors of the economy. To increase access to more resources and more wealth, they provided funding for the military to expand in Asia. The average Japanese citizen was in some ways as much a victim of this military and economic expansion as were people of other nations invaded by imperialist Japan.

Economic expansion through military action is an alternative many countries have chosen in the past. There is always someone with something you want. Primitive instincts have guided nations to war to seize desired commodities, such as gold, oil, grain, and other raw materials. Since World War II, it would seem that Japan has learned a more civilized alternative for getting what it wants from other nations.

The Japanese entered World War II with a high level of self-discipline and self-control, possibly stemming from their Shintu and Zen heritage or from their environmental and agricultural hardships. Their self-control and endurance gave them the ability to wage war under conditions that most Westerners could not comprehend: long periods without food or shelter; transport ships packed with thousands of soldiers when Americans would place only hundreds. Their ability to endure such discomforts enabled them to wage the war for as long as they did.

Finally, the practice of *kamikaze* flights illustrated their win-or-die attitude that reflected a Japanese commitment to their country and heritage. Kamikaze was an honorable form of *hara-kiri* — a ritual suicide to save face. To the young flyers who piloted the kamikaze planes, there was no alternative. It was an honor to die for one's country and failure to do so would have left them unbearably shamed for the rest of their lives.

The Japanese also developed a hierarchy of respect that entered every aspect of their lives. At the family level the hierarchy established everything from the order of the bath to the order of succession in the father's business. This was true even in the industrial sector. Workers were held in a paternalistic servitude by their employers. The people of Japan had almost total trust for the established order — they would comply with the discomforts and apparent disparate distribution of goods with little complaint. This was, they accepted, the natural order of things and the way it would continue to be (Varley, 1973).

These circumstances were somewhat unique at the time. Traditionally, Japan had been isolated from the rest of the world; for over 1,500 years, a powerful dynasty had ruled continuously. Internally fought wars had little impact on the commoner — the wars were fought by the *samurai*. The common citizens were left alone to harvest their crops. With this in mind, it's easy to see why the Japanese people developed extreme reverence for an order that protected them, though it exploited them at the same time.

Post World War II

After the war, Japan faced many changes. Early in his book, Patric speculated about the war and the future of Japan:

> And though Japan be — as she will be — decisively defeated after a long war, her people cannot be resigned to the peace that follows; a peace that inevitably will be but the beginning of preparation for another war unless one of three things happens:
>
> (a) The Japanese can be convinced that they are an inferior people and that they do not deserve an economic prosperity equal to that of the Americans, Canadians, British, Australians, or the Dutch in the Indies. This can never be so long as the Japanese remain a people highly literate, sensitive, and proud.
>
> (b) Our economic level is brought down to Japan's. This may happen at the end of a long war of blood and sweat and tears, for it is easier to cut down a high standard of living, such as America's, than to cut a lower one still lower.
>
> (c) The Japanese level is brought nearer to ours. This could be and should be accomplished at the war's end. I think partly by completely disarming Japan and averting all her accustomed military expenses to the ways of peace — to raising the economic level of the people — but to make it effective would require a large measure of free trade with the rest of the world.

History substantiates Patric's uncanny foresight. In fact, the United States did implement a recovery program that followed the counsel of Patric's recommended third option. Some of Japan's immediate restructuring was aimed at governmental and industrial hierarchy in order to help control the economy. The emperor was reduced to a dignitary of state. A more democratic government was established. The *Zaibatsus* were purged of all influence in government and industry. Labor unions were permitted and modeled after American-style bargaining units. These sweeping reforms were to establish a more equitable distribution of wealth and power, preventing future recurrence of the conditions that led to the military buildup of World War II (Halberstram, 1986).

After the U.S. occupation forces left Japan, most of the reforms remained intact. However, some withered or changed with time. One such example is the labor union. After gaining a powerful start, the labor unions were engaged in frequent and disruptive strikes. This power struggle eventually eroded, and the unions took on a more cooperative relationship with management (Halberstram, 1986). Both labor union and company management believed it inconceivable to coexist in total opposition. They realized each depended on the other for survival.

This new relationship was to be a major factor in Japan's future economic success, particularly in the auto industry. Labor and management were mutually dependent on business success. Allowing a system where labor or management benefits from the other at the expense of long-term success would be economic *hara-kiri*.

After the war, Japanese culture still retained elements of efficiency and discipline, the hierarchical support of authority (and conversely, the paternalistic accord to subordinates). Japan was now poised for an undeniable rise to the top. The *Zaibatsus* were no longer accumulating all of the wealth of the country and squandering it on military expansion. Industrial income now would be distributed more evenly among the people and would be invested in domestic industry. The Japanese, accustomed as they were to the ascetic life, would save a large portion of their income, creating a rich source of capital to finance industrial growth.

To compete in world markets, Japan would have to overcome two major obstacles. One was a reputaton for cheap goods and poor quality (Morita, 1986); the other was a shortage of resources that caused the Japanese to pay higher prices for goods than did their offshore competitors. Japan's major advantage was an abundant resource of hard-working, educated people. This pool of low-cost, literate labor provided them with an advantage over other, more technologically developed countries.

An economist, however, might project that, over time, Japanese economic growth would catch up with itself. The economy would grow, inflation would take its toll, and a time would come when economic equilibrium would take place (Heilbroner, 1972). The cost of labor would reach a parity with other countries, and the labor cost would cease to be an advantage. To some extent this has happened. Japan is now moving some of its manufacturing efforts to countries where wage rates are lower.

The cost of producing resources also increases with economic growth. More developed countries must look to less developed nations for lower cost resources. Let's take oil, for an example. As the price to find and produce oil in the United States grew, we increased our imports from the Middle East. This allowed the United States to maintain stable energy costs for many years. This worked well until we became too dependent on foreign oil. In 1972 the oil-producing countries found it easy to get together and fix the price. The increased oil prices forced all importing countries to find internal supplies. In the meantime, the Middle East countries profited enormously from this windfall. This income, however, caused their economies to grow and inflate — they would experience financial difficulties when the importing countries found alternative fuel supplies or reduced their oil demand through higher efficiency.

Now let's look at Japan's situation. Japan was importing a lot of resources, including oil. By using these resources more efficiently, Japan surpassed its competitors and more than offset the cost of imported raw materials by exporting a larger number of finished products. Its efficient use of oil was especially advantageous when oil prices went up. Quite simply, Japan was less affected by increased oil prices; in fact, its auto industry was better positioned to take advantage of the need for more efficient cars (Halberstram, 1986).

Japan's economic situation improved and the yen gained strength; the relative price of imported resources went down as Japan's economy grew stronger and faster than the economy of the supplying nations. By limiting imports exclusively to necessary ones and by maximizing exports, Japan was able to create a growing trade surplus — and that fueled its economy even more. The trade surplus and high savings rate gave Japan a growing cache of capital. When invested in technology and capital goods, it provided an even greater advantage over its competitors — competitors from whom Japan was seizing the market share.

We might speculate that this would put Japan in an upward growth spiral. Japan could stay well ahead of other nations, as long as it continued to do three things:

1. Buy as many basic resources as possible from less economically developed countries at a cost equal to or less than competitors pay.

2. Be more efficient than its competitors in the use of resources.

3. Invest trade surplus wisely in technological/capital investments.

Other nations with equal technology can only recover by better use of resources for improved efficiency, assuming that they do not unite against Japan in a war of trade restrictions and price controls. Such actions, however, are being contemplated in the United States today.

This presents an ominous picture for America. Faced with huge trade deficits and a declining source of capital for investments, our economic growth has slowed. We call it a recession. We expect it to be cyclical, as recessions in the past have been — with good times just around the corner. All the while, our cultural tolerance of waste is taking its insidious toll. Instead of the economic growth we found normal in the 1960s and 1970s, much of America's industry is in an extended slump. CEOs nervously wait for the next new product introduction to save them, only to find that sales aren't as large as anticipated. These are the symptoms of economic decay with which Americans must contend. We must contend with them as other countries, like Japan, progressively enter our markets with more cost-effective products.

Fortuitous circumstances probably surrounded Japan's post-war rise to the top. It is improbable that anyone could have foreseen the scenario to unfold after World War II. The Japanese recognized their country's immediate needs; because of desperation, they sought new methods to improve the quality and efficiency of their processes. It was obvious to their economic advisors that they needed guidance to begin overcoming the resource shortage problem. It was time to consult advisors from American industry and American educational institutions.

Immediately following the war, American advisors began to arrive in Japan. W. Edwards Deming brought Japanese industry new techniques for improving quality and efficiency. The Japanese didn't need to learn the importance of eliminating waste; this was already part of their culture. But they needed to learn how to identify waste, measure it, and reduce it. Henceforth, Deming became a hero to a country in desperate need of his knowledge. Conversely, American industries paid mere lip service to Deming and others of his field. We in America were rich in resources, prosperous, and undisciplined. Who cared if Deming's techniques could reduce waste? We didn't need it.

Given the events of the last 35 years, we have come to witness what John Patric observed before World War II: "Provided technological and economic equality, the Japanese could win a war against any foe" (Patric, 1943). It looks like they have. We have provided them with the technology and the methods; we have helped them eliminate the need for military expenditures, while expanding our own. Now, after 40 years, their culture is proving to be an indomitable, competitive advantage.

This is not unlike the competitive advantage of the lean and mean athlete who possesses the motivation and technical tools required for training. The athlete will always win against competitors who are overweight, undisciplined, and undertrained and who lack the motivation and commitment required to be competitive. American business is analogous to the untrained athlete: overweight with inventory and inefficient processes; too much organization fat and underutilized assets. There is a complacency with the status quo, a reluctance to commit to the required disciplines. This attitude is not unlike a man's approach to middle age when facing health issues seriously for the first time. He may find it difficult to discipline himself to lose weight, to drink less, to quit smoking, and to get plenty of exercise. He may yearn to be young again and wish things to be as they were when he was youthful and healthy. His choice is twofold: He can either go on living the way he had and die a premature death or develop the discipline to practice moderation. American business has the same choice: We can continue to live with the excesses we have come to enjoy, or we can change our ways and live a longer and healthier life.

The differences in our cultures may, in fact, have contributed to Japan's competitive success over these last 40 years. This, however, should not stand as an excuse in the future. America has demonstrated many times that it can meet any challenge in a time of crisis. We may have to compromise gratification of our cultural needs, but we still have the ability to respond with disciplined management practices. Given that America recognizes this challenge, I am certain we can succeed.

References

Deming, W. Edwards. *Quality, Productivity, and Competitive Position.* Cambridge: Massachusetts Institute of Technology, 1982.

Gill, Richard. *Economics and the Public Interest,* 4th ed. Pacific Palisades, Calif.: Goodyear, 1980.

Halberstram, David. *The Reckoning.* New York: Morrow, 1986.

Heilbroner, Robert L. *The Making of Economic Society.* Englewood Cliffs, N.J.: Prentice-Hall, Inc., 1972.

Morita, Akio. *Made in Japan.* New York: E.P. Dutton, 1986.

Patric, John. *Why Japan was Strong.* New York: Doubleday, 1943.

Varley, H. Paul. *Japanese Culture: A Short History.* New York: Praeger, 1973.

CHAPTER 2

THE CHANGING ENVIRONMENT AND THE MANAGEMENT SYSTEM

Do you remember when the newspapers referred to "the big four automobile manufacturers"? When Westinghouse, General Electric, and a few others had the domestic household electronic market sewn up? That was not so long ago, yet it seems a lifetime away. Today, there are twice as many competitors in many U.S. markets as there were 20 years ago. In the automobile industry, there are now several major competitors that didn't exist in 1965; in household appliances, the list of manufacturers now reads from A to Z. Many of these new products come from foreign countries; the expanding world economy has created new industries in areas that previously had none.

The expanding world economy and the ensuing growth of competitors have increased the rate of technological changes and customer expectations for product performance. The lost market share of U.S. businesses has gone to the foreign competitors who have made greater improvements to product performance, productivity, and quality. These changes pose new challenges for the management systems used by American industry.

The advent of more competitors in a given market has subtle implications for the way a business is managed. More competition means more contributors to the growth of technology and products, thus increasing the rate of change. Given more choices, customers will become more discerning; products will have to be of higher quality, greater utility, and lower cost (higher value). The increasing changes in technology, products, and product value challenge the management systems of industry to become more efficient. Efficiency improvements come from the reduction of waste in scrap, rework, and underutilization of resources and must be achieved in every aspect of the business. This is the driving force for quality as a strategic weapon in the world's economic future.

For example, let's assume a business is not growing with its industry. It may view manufacturing efficiency to be the key to future success; yet, improving manufacturing efficiency does nothing to help it introduce the right product at the right time. It may spend more money in research and development, only to find later that R&D's effectiveness was limited by its inefficiency. Further investigation might reveal that R&D incurred high levels of rework cost and project cancellations because of poor product definitions at the start of the product design. The next tendency would be to spend more money in marketing — the competitive environment could justify more investment here. The problem this business faces is that all of the processes are inefficient. Spending more money in any or all of the departments to overcome these inefficiencies won't help. The business will fall further behind because its competitors are improving efficiency and thus lowering the cost per unit rate of change. The successful competitors are not haggling over where to spend their money while their business fails; they are eliminating waste — improving the efficiency — in every process of the business, thereby improving their competitive fitness.

Competitive Fitness

A business' success is dependent on its fitness relative to its competitor's fitness — survival of the fittest. Organisms, animals, and men have been in a competitive environment for millions of years; hence, the world has experienced many arenas of competition. Some were natural, as in the struggle of biological species to survive amidst limited resources; and some were manmade, as in athletic competition and business. An abundant supply of analogies exists to help assess the common elements of competitive fitness for business.

There are two ways to improve the productivity of a business: the first is by evolving the physical attributes of a business through capital investment in technology and the second is by improving the efficiency through waste elimination. Competitive fitness measures how effectively the assets are utilized, such as the improved use of technology applied to our products/processes or how material and labor relate to waste. While business has been effective in utilizing technology, it has not been effective in minimizing waste. The analogy of a competitive runner illustrates this point.

The world record for the mile has improved by 20 percent since 1880. In 1880 the approximate record stood at four minutes and 35 seconds; today, the record is approximately three minutes and 43 seconds. This improvement has occurred with little benefit from human physical evolution. The changes that contributed to this improvement were due to asset utilization. At the turn of the century, the competitive runner was 10 to 15 percent heavier, and trained only five to 10 miles per week compared to the 70 to 100 miles per week of today's runner. More times than not, they ran because they just happened to be good at it, as opposed to being part of a dedicated training program. Today's competitive runner has trained the body to be more efficient by reduction of body weight and the amount of fuel and oxygen needed to maintain speed. There have been no major technological improvements to the physical form — runners have improved their efficiency through training.

The discipline to commit oneself to the rigors of a full-time training program requires a high level of motivation to succeed. For the runner, the motivation may come from the financial rewards or the worldwide recognition conferred to gold medal winners at the Olympics. Success requires the coaches to be knowledgeable of the best training methods and the runner to have confidence in the coach's ability.

For continuous improvement, the individual must be cognizant of the achievements and goals of others. The ingredients of competitive fitness and success are established by looking to future performance expectations, by being motivated to excel, and by subscribing to a disciplined training program.

The Management System

The competitive runner and the competitive business share in the need for fitness. To achieve and maintain a position of leadership, both share a common need for a management system that provides an understanding and orderly implementation of the objectives and strategies. The management system is responsible for the processes that lead to competitive fitness. The definition of this management system becomes more critical as the complexity and rate of change in our environment progresses. A brief review of the mechanics of our environment will clarify this point.

The world economic environment is a complex system with many elements: customers, investors, vendors, people, governments, and businesses. Competitive fitness is defined by how effectively a business utilizes its resources to meet its customers' needs (Figure 2.1).

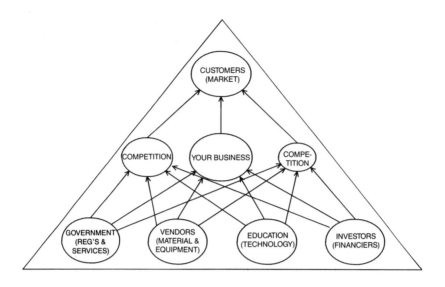

Figure 2.1   The Economic Environment

In this environment the customers are the primary focus of the business. It is through customer satisfaction that the business receives the revenues necessary to satisfy the needs of the other elements of the environment. The business must show profit to ensure its continued growth and to pay shareholders a return on their investment. A portion of the profit pays taxes to support the government in preserving the environment in which we do business. A business' overall success will be determined by comparing how effectively it satisfies the needs of the environment compared to its competitors.

Business is a subsystem of the environment that can be illustrated by its inputs, processes, and outputs (Figure 2.2). Its subsystems are comprised of many different processes from each of the functional areas. The processes serve to receive the resources from the environment, perform a function on them, and deliver the product to the customers. The management system is the means of control for the inputs, outputs, processes, and other linkages within the business. As the control element, the management system provides for the proper balancing and timing of the flows within the business to ensure that resources are used to the highest levels of efficiency. The management system can be efficient or inefficient in this service.

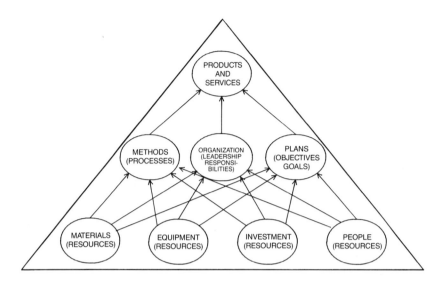

Figure 2.2   The Scope of the Management System

Because the environment is constantly changing, business must also continuously change. The element of control is never perfect; therefore, differences always exist between the needs of the environment and the state of the business. The needs of the environment are referred to as the "desired" state, while the state of the business is referred to as the "present" state (Simon, 1973). The business is always attempting to change from its present state to the desired state. The differences that exist between these two states represent the inefficiency of the management system. This inefficiency is the result of an absence of quality in the performance of the processes that contribute to the changes of the business.

Business success in this environment is dependent on three factors:

1. *Strategic Planning.* The methods the business uses to identify and plan for the present and future needs of the environment.

2. *Productivity.* The cost effectiveness with which the business uses its resources to meet the needs of the environment.

3. *Adaptability.* The efficiency of the business' ability to change and improve toward its goals.

23

Strategic planning includes setting the direction of the business by stating objectives and developing strategy. Planning is traditionally divided into long-term and short-term strategies. Long-term strategy is applied to environment expectations five, 10, or more years in the future. Short-term strategy refers to the needs of the environment today. In the ideal business system, the strategic planning process involves articulating the desired state of the environment with a statement of mission, vision, objective, and strategy. If a business is effective at interpreting the future needs of the environment, it can better define the changes that need to be made.

Productivity is a measure of the cost effectiveness with which business utilizes resources. Business resources include material, equipment, technology, people, and money. Strategies define the resources needed to meet the environment's needs. The function of the business is to combine its resources to achieve a product or service which satisfies the environment at the lowest possible cost.

Adaptability is a measure of the business' ability to move from the present state to the desired state. The complexity of the business and the changing environment combine to create an innumerable set of possible changes. These changes exist as problems or deviations in the many processes separating the present business state from the desired business state. These problems can relate to product strategy, product quality, or resource utilization. Continued success for the business is directly influenced by the effectiveness of the processes responsible for reviewing, analyzing, and implementing corrective actions. The resulting changes will transform the business from what it actually is to what it wants to be.

The management system has the responsibility to assure that planning, productivity, and adaptability are combined and controlled to provide the highest levels of competitive fitness. Therefore, it is the management system that we must continuously strive to improve if we are to improve our competitive fitness.

The Leadership Process

An important part of the management system is the leadership process. In the dictionary, *leadership* is loosely defined as the ability to lead; to *lead* is to guide, orchestrate, or direct the actions of others to a desired conclusion or objective. In a business environment think of leadership as the ability to foresee or visualize a future need, plan for its provision, and create the necessary motivations to make it a reality.

In his book, *Management,* Peter Drucker said, "Performance requires that each job be directed toward the objectives of the whole organization. In particular, each manager's job must be focused on the success of the whole. . . . If these requirements are not met, managers are misdirected and their efforts are wasted." In today's environment most of us realize that this is also true of the business' nonmanagement employees. To create an environment wherein managers are directed to a common goal, Drucker added, "Management by objectives must be made the living law of the entire management group."

Management by objectives has been used to help American industry provide leadership for a number of years. As indicated in Chapter 1, the Japanese have adapted the principles of MBO to the *Hoshin* process, which is their form of leadership. The Japanese have evolved MBO to a more disciplined process, however, to accommodate the accelerated changes in the environment. The evolution of the MBO process began thousands of years ago, long before a formal name existed for this process. The MBO process began when people first understood that leadership was needed to work together on organized projects.

The great Cheops Pyramid was built in Egypt around 2560 B.C.; it exists today as one of the oldest standing examples of the process we know as management by objectives. This example explains the importance of each of the elements used in the MBO process.

Elements of the MBO Process

(1) Statement of Objectives

The *Encyclopedia Britannica* tells us that the Cheops Pyramid, the greatest of all pyramids, stands 481 feet tall and is 755 feet wide on each of its four sides. This enormous structure is said to be perfect in lateral proportion and has a perfect north-south alignment. The architect who designed this structure undoubtedly had been given a clear set of building objectives from the Pharaoh. These construction plans must have been well documented to maintain the focus of the 100,000 men it took to build this pyramid over a 20-year period.

The business environment requires that our organizations also must have a clear vision and statement of their objectives. Without objectives, the success of our organizations would take on the appearance of chaos, just as if 100,000 Egyptians had gathered to build an unplanned pyramid. The responsibility for creating, documenting, and communicating business visions and objectives belongs to its leadership function.

(2) Standards of Implementation

It is reasonable to believe that the Egyptians had been given clear standards of implementation by which to gage the size and shape of each of the 2.3 million blocks, weighing 2.5 tons each, before setting the stones into place. This would have ensured that the quality of each block made a contribution to the ultimate perfection of the whole pyramid. These standards would have specified the surface smoothness and the exact size and shape of the different blocks. No doubt the standards were documented in such a way as to make them accessible to the leaders and thousands of workers.

Modern businesses have hundreds of processes, each building separate blocks of what will ultimately become the whole, and the standards of implementation are just as important to ensure that business objectives are achieved. The creation and propagation of these standards is also the responsibility of the businesses' leadership function.

(3) Motivation

The Egyptians also had a system of motivation. Contrary to what many people may believe, historians tell us that slave labor was not a big factor in building the pyramids. It is now believed that labor may have been donated for two reasons: either religious devotion to a Pharaoh who they held to be divine, or seasonal work by the regional farmers while their fields were flooded from the Nile. Some historians believe that the laborers were paid in grain to sustain them through the flooding season until they could replant and harvest their crops.

The motivation system is an important element of any project requiring continuous effort. Motivating an individual or group to keep working toward the objective has always been a fundamental responsibility of the leadership process.

(4) Measures and Review

Certainly the Egyptians had measures by which to determine their progress. Regular reviews were made to ensure that errors were corrected. Methods such as leveling techniques, height measurement, and angularity tests had to be a continuous part of the process to ensure the reality of the perfection we see today.

Progress measures and regular review are also needed in today's business environment and are a fundamental part of the leadership process; but, depending on the group's visions and the objectives, each set of measures will be different.

MBO Today

Many managers use the elements of this leadership process to ensure that businesses stay on track. Unfortunately, some people have not figured out how to implement some of the fundamental elements of this process. The fundamentals that every manager must learn are to state clearly defined objectives, create standards of implementations, provide motivations for desired actions, and conduct regular reviews of success measures. The timely and efficient documentation, communication, and implementation of the elements of this process is the secret of the Japanese success with *Hoshin.*

The Japanese tell us that the purpose of the *Hoshin* process is to provide the entire company with direction. This guidance process requires constant correction as deviations occur. James McDonald, president and chief executive officer of General Motors Corporation, says that this process is error driven — that it's like guiding a missile through a changing environment (McDonald, 1986). After the missile is launched, there are an infinite number of variables that can accumulate as errors. Unless they are compensated for these errors can cause the missile to miss its target. In this case, the control system that detects and compensates for these errors is electronic. This is more than a split-second time process; errors are compensated for in microseconds, allowing for the missile to achieve precision accuracy.

Another relevant analogy exists in the computer industry. Improvement in computer technology efficiency has been of great magnitude over the last 50 years. Computer hardware and software capability has progressed as rapidly as technology. More memory, faster processors, and larger networks have posed new challenges for the designers of operating systems. In some cases the basic architecture of the computer hardware has remained the same for several years, but new operating systems were introduced to improve the efficiency of the system and to keep pace with competition. In the computer, the operating system is the management system; it is responsible for the control process which directs the other functions within the computer.

Business has a similar need to improve the efficiency of its management systems. Over the last 50 years, business hardware has changed as much as the computer; for example, business has more information, increased automation, faster processes, more complex markets, and better educated employees. Together these changes present the need for improved management systems, just as the changes in the development of the computer presented the need for improved operating systems. The management system in business is analogous to the operating system in the computer and becomes more so as business evolves toward higher levels of automation. In the meantime, people still handle the controls and do not react well to electronic impulses. Business must therefore continue to depend on the manager's equivalent — referred to as MBO or *Hoshin*.

The Systems Approach to Management

The preceding analogies of MBO and electronics control systems can be of particular advantage to an engineer. Assuming that the engineer is now a manager and has responsibility for designing a management system, he or she could be particularly effective at putting all the important elements in place. The systems approach to management would appear to be a natural course of action for Japan, but observers say that Japan's educational system does not teach management as part of its curriculum. Students are graduated from the universities in engineering or other technical fields and develop their business acumen only through on-the-job experience. This engineering orientation is a primary contributor to the evolution of their management system. Dr. Chalmers Johnson of the University of California at Berkeley tells us that the Japanese don't manage their institutions, they engineer them (Johnson, 1986). To this end, the Japanese have used systems engineering techniques to design a management system that ensures business will operate in better harmony with its environment.

American management has been reluctant to accept many of the cybernetic metaphors for business. The systems approach has found reader interest, but not much more; the need to change business philosophy simply did not occur. As John Naisbitt pointed out, "Until recently Americans considered changing the corporation analogous to reinventing the wheel" (Naisbitt and Aberdeen, 1985). Today, Americans are just beginning to understand the need for change. The changes that are being made vary from industry to industry and from business to business, depending on the boss' interpretation of the need. Sadly, few changes are reflected where they are needed most — in the management system.

Use Technology on our Side

A systems approach to management offers an opportunity to beat our worldwide competitors at their own game. After all, the United States has the world's greatest wealth of human resources, business experience, and industrial technology. By using system technology to improve the use of our resources, competitive gains can be made that go beyond anyone's vision. This strategy, however, requires a vision of the goals toward which business is evolving. From this vision, the future needs of the management system can be defined; then, the path from a business' present situation to its future goals can be defined.

The Factory of the Future

Creating a Vision

Rosabeth Moss Kanter explained that creating a vision and sharing it throughout the organization is an essential prerequisite to effecting change of any nature (Kanter, 1983). The vision serves as the target or objective for which all strategies, goals, and standards are established. A shared vision of the factory of the future brings the elements of the needed strategies into perspective and helps to understand the value of many of the management tools associated with Japanese management practices.

The Vision

Driven by the evolution of technology, business is developing toward a future that has progressively higher levels of automation. Eventually, factories will be totally automated. In this environment people will not be needed to perform the basic processes because robots will be used with other forms of automation. The factory will be an automated system, in perfect harmony with its markets and suppliers. It will have a radar-like sense of market changes and will be efficient and flexible enough to provide products that meet those changes ahead of its competitors. This system will be intolerant of poor quality input from all sources, including design, marketing, and suppliers. By considering the nature of this business, the changes that need to be made to the management systems today can be better understood.

System Operating Characteristics

By the very nature of its robotic and computer design, this system will be limited as to how fast each process can be operated. Attempts to run the system faster than its designed speed will cause defects in data transfers and parts fabrication. The defects will lead to system inefficiencies caused by delays, rework, scrap, resets, and other problems. Additionally, many obscure process errors will go undetected, and will not become evident until they are manifested as defects or failures to customers. Subsequently, valuable computer system capacity will be used for defect analysis and decision-making processes to correct these problems. Preventing these types of inefficiencies is the responsibility of the management system's designer; it is his or her responsibility to ensure that each process will never be operated faster than its ability to maintain optimum quality and efficiency.

People in the System

Assume that the system is in place and working as designed. After a while, the design center introduces a product that requires some processes that have not yet been automated, but it will take a couple more years to design the robots needed to do the job. This forces the use of people in the processes; people, however, don't have probes attached to their heads, so computer control is out. People are also notoriously inconsistent and unreliable when it comes to quality. Using this archaic form of labor, how is the system going to work?

In place of the robots, people will perform part of the processor tasks. Each individual will bring unique skills to the task that cannot be controlled by direct line to the computer. It will be necessary to train all people in their tasks extremely well and ensure that they understand that quality is more important than speed at each step of the process. The management system must therefore be programmed to understand each individual's speed limitation within quality standards and never increase the system speed beyond that limit. The added cost of training will be rationalized as part of the system preventative maintenance costs.

People are similar to robots in many ways. For example, let's examine the function of memory in both instances. A robot may have a repetitive task process stored in local memory, in readiness for activation by the operating system. People also keep much of the process knowledge in their brains. If the task is highly repetitive, they probably never need to refer to the master computer for input; but, if the task increases in scope, or the time between operations increases, both people and robots may need to refer back to master documentation. This requires that the system provides access to accurate, complete documentation as needed.

Maintenance is another example of people's similarity to robots. Robots require regular feedback on their quality, which may result in recalibration of the system; people need regular feedback for the same reason. Robots require an occasional squirt of oil to keep them functioning smoothly; people need periodic breaks, time off, and vacations. People also need financial compensation in the form of pay and benefits to provide for their care and well-being.

People are also very different from robots; they have feelings and needs that go beyond even very sophisticated machinery. People have a need for social belonging at work as well as at home. They have a need for security, recognition, accomplishment, and respect. These characteristics are human nature elements for which the management system should provide. Some of these needs, like employment security, can be provided by the system through its success. Other needs, like recognition and respect, can only be provided for by other people.

These needs surface early after people are introduced into the system. Their social nature encourages them to talk about their jobs at coffee breaks. In these discussions they start to learn what others are doing, and they begin to wonder why some people have more process problems than others. One person may know how to do something that another doesn't understand; or an individual or a robot may not be providing their function, thus causing a process shutdown. The management system will motivate the immediately affected team of people to get together and solve these problems. These teams will eventually take on a formal part of the process improvement task and provide the peer pressure and recognition that individuals and groups need to be successful.

The need for supervisors and managers hasn't been discussed. So far the tasks have been assigned by the management system, the instructions are provided by the system, and the work groups meet to solve local problems and to keep the system running efficiently. Why are supervisors needed? Look at how supervisors presently spend most of their time.

In today's environment, supervisors spend time scheduling people's work; in the ideal environment, the management system would do this. Supervisors spend time chasing down parts that didn't arrive on time because of system quality problems. This is something that wouldn't occur in the new system.

They spend time going to meetings to solve process quality problems that keep people from doing their jobs. They spend time writing evaluations and relating them to elaborate merit pay systems that motivate people to work beyond their quality limits. In summary, today's supervisors do little that adds value to the product. They spend most of their time fixing the quality problems that the system encourages people to create. When quality problems are eliminated from the system, relatively few supervisors and middle managers will be required. The managers that would be needed in the new system will spend their time understanding and planning for the organization's future goals and objectives.

The Design Center

In the factory of the future, the design and specification information will be downloaded from the design center computer to the manufacturing computer. This information will represent all of the up-to-date deliverables that the design function provides to manufacturing and will include computer-controlled machining instructions, test procedures, assembly procedures, and job specifications.

It will be absolutely necessary that the design be complete before being released to manufacturing. Failure to meet this criteria would be very costly. This would be reflected in the additional engineering support required to sort out the manufacturing design problems; in inefficiencies caused by the manufacturing process starts and stops; and in the movement of resources required to work around these problems. Throughout this transition period, considerable customer product dissatisfaction would be generated. These problems would motivate the inclusion of necessary safeguards to ensure that the design is complete before release to manufacturing.

Marketing

The marketing center provides the close environmental interface required of an adaptive business system. This includes current and up-to-date market and competitive strategies that will signal the need for change. It also includes a sensitivity to the technological developments that might trigger the need for new products and/or provide opportunities for competitive entry. The market research information should be well documented and maintained in data bases for easy access and reviewed as part of the long-term and annual planning activities in the business.

Another part of the marketing organization is the marketing communication function. This includes advertising, promotion, trade shows, and other forms of customer communication to create customer awareness. The business should maintain data base information on all advertising media available, including the breakdowns of the market segments reached for each method of communication. Metrics will be maintained for the customer attention achieved per dollar invested. Spending decisions will be based on the statistical merits of an alternative as opposed to the emotional merits.

Accurate records will be kept of the sales effectiveness in terms of the customer contacts, the purchase orders, the reasons for order loss, etc. Businesses will know the levels of customer satisfaction achieved by using various performance measures, i.e., on-time delivery, warranty failure rates, and surveys.

The marketing center of the future will read the environment as easily as reading a book. The influencing factors will be understood and quantified in such detail that the R&D center will be able to translate that information directly into a product definition. This responsibility will be a key part of the leadership role in the business.

Leadership and Management System

The business will be capable of functioning indefinitely without leadership. It could continue to supply the same products, using the same technologies, as long as a demand exists and the motivations are self-sustaining in the management system. If these motivations are not self-sustaining, the system will slowly deteriorate because customer problems will not be handled and failing equipment will not be replaced. In time, the system will cease to be competitive and will eventually die.

The motivations that keep the system running will be maintenance related. The system must provide the maintenance service required by the equipment. If people are involved, they must be provided with the financial and human-oriented maintenance needs. These are the hygiene factors that Herzberg described — not the big motivators to excel, just the minimum to keep the system running (Herzberg, 1968). The maintenance factors, as discussed earlier, are the elements that must be self-sustaining in the system on an equitable basis; these should be considered part of the management system.

If this system is to be adaptive to the changes in the environment, leadership must be provided. The leadership would (1) identify the elements of change in the environment that need adaptations, and (2) provide the guidance and motivation needed to change the business system. Change requires that a business has resources dedicated to analyzing the environment. This is normally the responsibility of marketing, but R&D would also contribute by staying in the forefront of technology. Business leaders would analyze the information available to them and draw conclusions about the implications for future success. They would then conceptualize any future product business state required to survive the coming changes. These visions may change with time as the requirements to meet the needs of the environment also change. The business may be operating as efficiently as possible; therefore, the vision may be limited to the next family of products. On the other hand, the business may have all the right product strategies and still be uncompetitive because of cost and efficiency. The vision guides the business into the future; if the vision is ambiguous, the future of the business is doubtful.

When it has been suitably articulated, the vision will be integrated into the system. The leader will require that all system functions develop plans and goals that directly support it. The leader will require a coordinated effort to ensure that each tactic makes a measurable contribution to the objective. When this plan has been linked throughout the system, it will require regular review to ensure that continuous progress is being made and that resources are being allocated appropriately. This is the contribution that leadership should make to the system. Without this kind of leadership, the business would be confined to a charter of maintenance until the environment changes sufficiently to make the business obsolete.

Summarizing the Future Management System

(1) Create the Vision

The successful business system will operate in harmony with the business environment. It will grow more rapidly than the market as long as there is room for growth. It will continuously sense and analyze change; it will deliver needed products faster than the competition; and it will use its resources more efficiently than the rest of the industry.

(2) Define the Organizational Responsibility

Each of the major contributors to revenue (i.e., marketing, R&D, and manufacturing) will be individually responsible for the quality and the efficiency of its processes. A quality assurance function will not be needed. All functions, including personnel and finance, will view each activity as a process and will work for continuous improvement through customer evaluation.

(3) Provide the Leadership

The leadership of the business will focus on understanding the customer's needs, defining goals and measures, planning goal achievement, providing motivation, and following up with reviews. The reviews will provide insight into the deviations and will result in changes within the system to meet the required goals.

(4) Define the Performance Measures

The business will have a set of well-defined organizational measures. The measures will relate to the product attributes, customer interface, process performance, and business capacity (to be defined in Chapters 5 and 6).

(5) Institutionalize the Proper Motivations

The management system will provide the necessary training, document-ation, and reward mechanisms to ensure that the quality of each process will conform to the established specifications. All motivations will be removed that cause the processes to operate at rates exceeding their ability to meet quality standards. The appropriate response to a process not meeting system speed requirements will be to (1) fix, redesign, or replace the process or robotics, or (2) repair the disability, or retrain or replace the employee.

The management system will motivate the work group to use problem-solving techniques in handling interprocess deviations, thus encouraging peer support and peer recognition. The groups will use statistical tools to analyze variations and will use a common form of structured analysis to understand the deviations, assign causes, and recommend corrective actions. The management system will ensure that all people are treated with mutual respect and are given recognition for contributions. The management system will ensure that individuals assume full ownership for the quality of their processes. Defects will not be allowed into the system from any internal or external source. The management system will provide for equitable hygiene-maintenance factors:

- All salary and benefits will be equal within a structured level of contribution.

- Merit increases in salary will be used to reflect an individual's consistent contribution to work group flexibility, necessary retraining to sustain quality and flexibility, and work group contribution.

- Exceptionally valued contributions will be recognized through an employee suggestion system and other reward systems designed to exceed an individual's normal pay level.

- Profit sharing will be equitably administered, based on the individual's total company salary.

- Participation in business ownership will become the norm as fewer people are needed to perform the processes.

(6) Manage the Assets Productively

As dictated by the changing business environment, the management system will ensure sufficiently flexible assets to enable redeployment. If the employees, the cash balance, the fixed assets, and the current assets are disproportionate or obsolete, then the system will not be adaptive. Consider the people in this new system. The wrong balance of skills could create huge entrance barriers to developing markets. As the environmental changes progress, people skills will become more important. This will cause increasing pressures on the business training systems. Eventually we will find that people cannot be retrained fast enough to keep up with the pace of the changing environment.

The new system will view reliable material suppliers as assets and will provide special financial incentives for good quality and timely delivery. We have already seen businesses that refer to their supplier and customer relationships as "partners in business"; this will begin to take on a more formal nature — as it has in Japan.

Conclusion

Today's environment demands that managers be cognizant of the environmental changes taking place. Managers must understand the evolutionary aspects of the economy and the ensuing dynamics of the business system. The concepts of leadership, quality, and competitive fitness must be fully integrated to ensure future economic survival. New management systems will emerge out of this integration process and will define better management tools. These tools will encompass both the philosophies and the methods required to exist in an environment where the evolutionary axiom is still *survival of the fittest.*

The management tools developed by the Japanese are part of this answer. TQC represents a set of management tools aimed at improving today's management system as it evolves toward higher levels of automation. In today's environment, people are still an important and inescapable part of the process. Managers must ensure that their contribution to the system is an asset to efficiency rather than a liability. Many businesses today promote their people as being their most important asset when, in fact, the cross motivations of their management system cause them to be a liability. The correction of this anachronism is the fundamental contribution of TQC.

References

Drucker, Peter F. *Management.* New York: Harper and Row, 1974.

Herzberg, Frederick. "One More Time: How Do You Motivate Employees?" *Harvard Business Review,* Jan./Feb. 1968.

Johnson, Chalmers. "How to Think about Economic Competition from Japan." Presentation, Dec. 5, 1986, Seattle, Washington, at the Japan-America Society of the State of Washington Seminar.

Kanter, Rosabeth Moss. *The Change Masters.* New York: Simon and Schuster, 1983.

McDonald, F. James. "The Quality Guidance System." *Quality Progress,* Oct. 1986.

Naisbitt, John and Patricia Aberdine. *Re-inventing the Corporation.* New York: Warner Books, 1985.

Simon, Herbert A. "The Architecture of Complexity." *Readings in Managerial Psychology.* Chicago: University of Chicago Press, 1973.

CHAPTER 3

TOTAL QUALITY CONTROL
AND THE MANAGEMENT SYSTEM

What do you want, quantity or quality?

I can still remember asking this question 20 years ago; it was my first supervisory position and my boss at the time answered quickly, "I want both, of course." Since then, I have heard this question asked many times by those looking for managerial approval to put more emphasis on quality. The sly boss inevitably will avoid making that choice for the individual. He or she knows that the motivations of the management system have already made that choice; God help the person who chooses quality over quantity if it causes a missed schedule.

Unfortunately this is a sad commentary that applies to many U.S. companies. The reward systems, such as the merit pay increase system, are usually based on the most obvious process measures. These measures normally will relate to the schedule or to quantity. On the other hand, quality is talked about, quality posters are hung, and quality slogans are written to present the impression that it is important. The employee, when faced with a decision of quantity or quality, will always make a choice based on the company's reward system.

Employees are faced with this decision every minute of their working day, and each employee will decide differently between quality and quantity. Every group of employees is composed of people with varying degrees of skill. When everyone is asked to meet the same quota or time standards, the main variable becomes quality. The most capable people will easily meet or exceed quantity standards without compromising the group's standards for quality. However, the employees with lesser skills will find it necessary to work slower to achieve the same quality. If the people of lesser ability are told that they will not be given raises because their *quantity* is not large enough, they will cut corners on *quality* to optimize their speed and pay. This fundamental principle of human nature will prevail regardless of quality slogans or the supervisor's instructions.

The advent of stockless production, called just-in-time (JIT) production, carries with it some hidden benefits for quality. In a JIT system there is little or no inventory of parts; everything is manufactured and delivered just as it is needed for the production process. This saves many

39

of the costs related to keeping an inventory, but JIT systems also require defect-free processes for proper functioning (Schonberger, 1982).

If each process creates defects and passes them on to the next process, workers will spend most of their time correcting other people's mistakes, thereby preventing the system from operating the intended way. JIT systems are designed to be run at a constant rate to properly balance the load at each station in the process. Quality work is mandatory to achieve JIT performance for two reasons: (1) the system rate is fixed, based on optimum balancing of the work load at each workstation, and (2) the system does not tolerate a rework stop at one station, since the entire process must then be stopped.

Because of the characteristics of JIT production, individual efforts to speed up the process do not work. Individual ideas contributed through the efforts of the team, however, can be of major impact. Quality teams become the forum for individual contribution; to the extent that a merit pay system exists, it can be based on an employee's contribution to quality and to the team.

All managers, regardless of specialty, need solid understanding of the principles of TQC; the delegation of this knowledge will not be adequate preparation. The emphasis given to the individual team contribution is overwhelmingly stronger in Japanese reward systems (especially those known for TQC) than in most U.S. businesses. Profit sharing, quality circles, and employee suggestion systems are part of this reward system and comprise major elements of TQC. Along with the reward system, there are many other elements of TQC that are sometimes elusive to U.S. managers; they collectively provide significant contributions to the effectiveness of the management system. All managers will need to firmly grasp these contributions to be competitive in their business environments.

Total Quality Control

TQC has been evolving in Japan since World War II when many American advisors were sent to Japan to help the Japanese restart their economy. Deming, one of the more notable advisors, taught them the value of a structured approach to quality and process improvement. Through the years Deming's methods have permeated every aspect of Japanese business. Market analysis, structured planning and review, process analysis, and employee involvement all reflect the fundamentals of Deming's teachings.

In 1983 Myron Tribus, Massachusetts Institute of Technology, studied six Japanese companies that had won the prestigious Deming Award. His paper, entitled *Reducing Deming's 14 Points to Practice* (1983), provides an excellent background for what the Japanese refer to as CWQC and for what Americans have come to know as TQC. The common elements of TQC, as practiced by these companies, will be the focus for understanding the contribution that TQC makes to business.

The six businesses shared the following TQC key elements:

- Each CEO decided to implement a TQC system because of survival problems.

- Every level understood that the only way to increase productivity and reduce cost was to improve quality.

- Each business was reorganized from top to bottom to implement Deming's 14 points (Deming, 1982).

- Each company provided TQC training programs.

- Each company had an annual presidential quality audit.

- Each company used quality circles.

- Everyone in each company was familiar with the seven statistical tools and a common problem-solving method called Plan-Do-Check-Act or PDCA.

- All maintained that TQC is not just a program; it is a way of life.

(1) Survival

The common reason for changing their basic operating system was the most signficant of all the elements shared by these companies. Each CEO recognized that his business had a survival problem and that fundamental changes were required to fix it. These companies were losing their markets; in each case, it was obvious that the environment in which they were doing business had changed or was changing. Some changes were due to technological advancements; other changes were due to direct competition and an expanding world economy. Nonetheless, it became a matter of survival. The decisions made by the CEOs of those companies suggest that they also recognized that being "one up" on their competition today would not guarantee their survival tomorrow.

Rapidly growing technology and a competitive situation ensure an increasing demand for change and therefore require a business system that continuously adjusts to these changes.

(2) Productivity through Quality

In classical economics, productivity is defined as the per capita output of the economic system (Heilbroner, 1972). Throughout history productivity gains have resulted from capital investment. A classic example is agriculture, where productivity has multiplied many times during this century through investment in new machinery, modern methods, and fertilizers. In factories, automation and the development of new technologies have provided a continuous source of ideas for productivity improvements. The output per capita has constantly increased, and technology has been its driving force.

In the first half of this century the United States owned many of the leading technologies and abounded in natural resources. These prize possessions were protected by an economy that operated mainly at a national rather than a world level. Our learning institutions led in the development of technology. Limitations in communications prevented other countries from copying our developing ideas. A lack of transportation prevented massive international exchanges of national resources. This situation provided the United States with many competitive advantages.

As the U.S. business economy took on more global proportions, we watched many of our previous competitive advantages disappear. More countries could now afford to invest competitively in capital equipment for manufacturing; the increasing world exchange of raw materials eliminated many of the geographical advantages the United States once held. More countries were reaching parity in science, education, and communication, thereby reducing the opportunity and advantage of the United States to be first with new technology and to make it readily available on world markets.

These factors began to create competitive equality throughout the world by minimizing many of the traditional U.S. advantages. Other countries began to make inroads into our markets without making any significant contributions to technology; their incremental productivity gains were achieved through a focus on quality. Since then, quality has become their primary competitive weapon.

For the Japanese companies in Tribus' study, people at all business levels understood that the only way to increase productivity was through quality improvements. In his book, *Quality, Productivity, and Competitive Position,* Deming states that, "Failure of management to plan for the future and to foresee problems has nurtured waste of manpower, materials, and machine time, all of which raise the manufacturer's cost and the price that the purchaser must pay for the product." Throughout his book, Deming pursues the methods required to be aware of problems, to analyze them, and to fix them. These methods are fundamental to the Japanese companies that have instituted TQC as their business system. This philosophy, when taken to its extreme and applied to every process in the business, is TQC.

TQC can be divided into two parts: philosophy and methods. Its philosophy is the underlying belief that customer satisfaction is the key to business success and that the only means to achieve total customer satisfaction is by emphasizing quality improvements in all of the business' processes. Focusing on customer satisfaction provides the best prioritizing system that businesses can use to direct company planning and measure job performance. Focusing on customer needs also ensures that everyone in the organization is working toward the right objectives.

The TQC methods include those activities that improve the business processes and achieve the objective of customer satisfaction through a quality emphasis; examples are SQC, problem solving, and quality circles. Figure 3.1 shows a typical TQC model and illustrates the relationship that exists between the objective, the philosophy, and the methods that are needed to bring about total customer satisfaction.

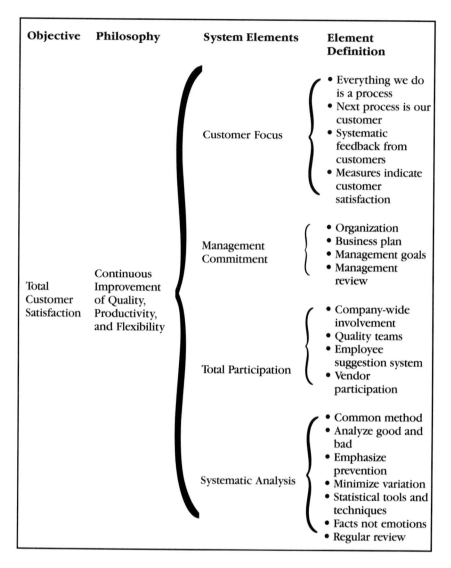

Objective	Philosophy	System Elements	Element Definition
Total Customer Satisfaction	Continuous Improvement of Quality, Productivity, and Flexibility	Customer Focus	• Everything we do is a process • Next process is our customer • Systematic feedback from customers • Measures indicate customer satisfaction
		Management Commitment	• Organization • Business plan • Management goals • Management review
		Total Participation	• Company-wide involvement • Quality teams • Employee suggestion system • Vendor participation
		Systematic Analysis	• Common method • Analyze good and bad • Emphasize prevention • Minimize variation • Statistical tools and techniques • Facts not emotions • Regular review

Figure 3.1 Total Quality Control Model

Quality, Efficiency, and Productivity

The benefit of quality on productivity is derived from efficiency. Efficiency increases output by reducing waste or loss in the process. Efficiency is defined as the ratio of the total output to the total input of the system, as a function of the losses. Assume a system produces 100 units per day, and the input required — due to losses in the process

— is the same as might be required for 130 units if there were no losses. The potential exists to raise the output to 130 units by reducing losses. The efficiency of this system would be:

$$\frac{\text{Output}}{\text{Input}} = \frac{100}{130} = 76\%$$

If process changes are made to improve the quality and eliminate the losses, the efficiency is improved by 33 percent. Efficiency should be viewed relative to all resources, including material, labor, equipment, and money.

Figure 3.2 shows the empirical basis for efficiency. Efficiency is expressed as the ratio of output to input, or $\frac{X^2}{X^1}$ as a function of X^3.

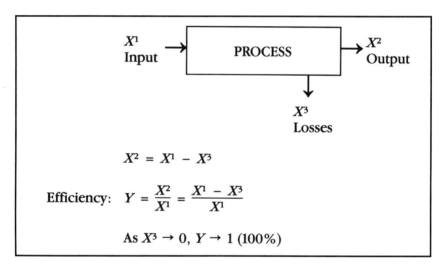

$$X^2 = X^1 - X^3$$

Efficiency: $Y = \dfrac{X^2}{X^1} = \dfrac{X^1 - X^3}{X^1}$

As $X^3 \rightarrow 0$, $Y \rightarrow 1$ (100%)

Figure 3.2 Efficiency

In a manufacturing process, the total cost is equal to the combined cost of the resources, which includes waste (losses due to imperfect material, equipment, labor, or procedures). Since waste can only result from poor quality, quality becomes the only variable for efficiency.

There are two tools to influence productivity; the first is the capital investment of classical economics theory, and the second is efficiency. As efficiency increases, so does output per capita, thereby increasing productivity. Since quality is the only variable for losses (and therefore efficiency), quality becomes the tool for competitive advantage when there are no discernible advantages in the application of technology.

Flexibility through Efficiency

One of the principal advantages in businesses that achieve a high degree of efficiency is that they become more flexible. Flexibility can be defined as the ease with which the output of the business can be adjusted.

Quality in all of the processes helps to make a business more flexible or better able to adapt to the environment. If the marketing and the R&D processes are efficient, a business will be in tune with its customers' needs and provide timely products to meet those needs. The most efficient production processes are able to adapt the business' production capabilities to provide products and services with the least waste, and this results in the lowest final cost. The more efficient these processes, the more readily a business can sense the need for change and implement that change.

Yokogawa HP won the Deming Award for the application of Deming's principles and for the improvements they were able to show in quality, productivity, and customer satisfaction. Very little is said of their flexibility improvements; but their inventories went down, production and R&D cycle times went down, and their ability to respond to a changing market went up considerably. They had become more flexible. Since then, they have been able to change their factory to include a JIT production system, which has brought about even greater improvements in productivity and flexibility. All of their management staff agree that none of these achievements would have been possible without the focus they put on quality.

Market Leadership through Efficiency

The industries of mass-produced products have already lost their market share to the better efficiency of many Japanese companies. Some American industries, however, still have a technological advantage that is beginning to disappear as the Japanese move up the technology ladder. These companies realize that it is only a matter of time before the Japanese leverage themselves into the markets with higher levels of investment and efficiency. Figure 3.3 shows a general chronological time line over which the Japanese have progressed up the technology scale. The difference between the efficiency lines of Japan and the United States at each stage is based on the differences we see in the cost of quality.

46

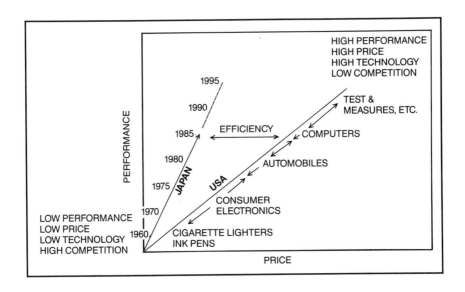

Figure 3.3 Competitive Position through Efficiency

Cost of Quality

One figure of merit used by many businesses in their attempts to measure efficiency and quality improvements is cost of quality (COQ). COQ has been defined as the cost of appraising, fixing, and preventing quality problems in the system. Estimates of COQ for some American businesses, like IBM and Hewlett-Packard, have been reported as high as 25 to 30 percent of sales (Byman and Young, 1983). The Japanese businesses that have been successful with TQC have reportedly achieved COQ levels of between 5 and 10 percent of sales. This would imply that the efficiency of Japanese business is 90 to 95 percent, while the U.S. efficiency is only 70 to 80 percent. This difference represents a significant competitive advantage for Japanese business and explains the efficiency advantage shown in Figure 3.3

The preceding discussion of quality and productivity demonstrates that quality in every process leads to productivity improvements. This does not reduce the need for gains through technology. The competitive advantage will be obtained by those businesses with the highest focus on technology and quality. Figure 3.4 illustrates the connection between quality, productivity, and customer satisfaction.

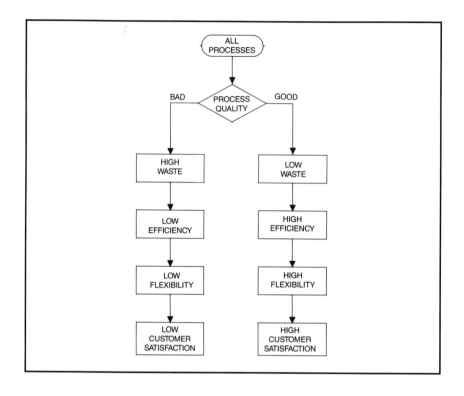

Figure 3.4   The Quality Connection

(3) Tops-Down Approach

The tops-down approach and emphasis on TQC were fundamental to the success of the companies in Tribus' study group. The need for this system was recognized as a matter of survival by the CEO; therefore, the emphasis on it was driven relentlessly from the top. Undoubtedly, the middle managers of these organizations had done everything possible when the company found itself in trouble. For a company to successfully adopt a completely new operating culture, it is mandatory that the CEO understands and guides the process. As Deming stated in his book, *Quality, Productivity, and Competitive Position,* "It is not enough that top management commit for life to quality and productivity. They must know what they are committed to — i.e., what they must do. These obligations cannot be delegated."

The consequence of not starting at the top will be a lack of the necessary commitment, measures, and rewards required for success. This can be seen in many American organizations today; the middle managers of these organizations sit on the fence with one foot firmly planted on traditional management methods and the other lightly placed on TQC methods. The CEOs of these companies have proclaimed that the elements of TQC must be adopted if a business is to be successful, yet they permit middle management to cling to old ways. The CEOs have not recognized that the old reward system is a roadblock to implementing TQC.

This paradox implies that many of the elements of TQC run against the motivations of traditional management. The resolution of this problem is crucial to the ongoing success of a business in the present environment. Let's compare some of the basic differences between traditional management methods and TQC methods, as used by the Japanese.

Traditional Methods Rely on the Individual

Model American managers are often viewed as corporate superpersons. So they can be easily recognized by others, we give them a special title and pay them a large salary to use their skills on the important problems. In essence, we place the success of our business in their hands; we call them the chief executive officers or general managers.

These managers select and promote people with abilities similar to their own. Each business has a select few of these highly talented people who constitute the power hierarchy in the organization. When problems arise, their job is to cut through the red tape and resolve the problems as quickly as possible. Other people in the organization are considered important to accomplish the daily tasks of business but are not trusted with important decisions, and they are left to compete for economic rewards at a level entirely different from that of upper management. They receive the basic rewards accorded them by their employing business or industry, but they seldom have an opportunity to contribute to or be compensated beyond that level.

The problem-solving mode in which most American managers operate provides scant encouragement for employees to focus on anything more than short-term projects. The reward system of this management approach usually compensates short-term results and consequently tends to be reactive in nature. When individuals view their rewards as derived from solving problems, they direct their energies toward the problem-solving process. Since most problems are viewed as stumbling blocks to goals, this system tends to degenerate into the management-by-crisis syndrome.

The real opportunity for contribution exists in doing things right the first time, which requires a greater emphasis on planning and teamwork. Making the shift from problem solving to planning and prevention requires a conscious change in how the individual prioritizes his or her time. Unless this change is made, the organization will perpetually waste time and materials and may never achieve the levels of efficiency required in a competitive environment.

The Japanese business' management system motivates people toward prevention rather than reaction. The TQC methods they employ utilize the combined wisdom of the entire organization to prevent problems instead of emphasizing the abilities of a few employees. Preventing problems through teamwork requires many "little" people, functioning in a disciplined, well organized manner to achieve operation consistency and smoothness. Individual superpersons are not asked to solve these problems because their approach destroys the teamwork and orderliness of the group's efforts. Such behavior in Japan is considered counter-productive and is frowned upon by the management system. In fact, most Japanese businessmen attempt to avoid any form of distinction.

In this environment, individual success takes longer to achieve. Promotion comes from being a major contributor to a series of successful team situations, but this may take years to become apparent. This success is more lasting, however, and commands more respect from one's peers. The focus for the individual is on the success of the group, and the focus for the group is on the success of the future. The pressure for short-term rewards diminishes because of the importance of the longer term view.

Changes in the culture and the reward systems can take place only with the conscious effort of the organization's highest level. Businesses that believe in the competitive advantages of teamwork, participation, and discipline must recognize the need to change the reward system. To this end, the rewards for the individual must be based on personal contribution to the team and quality; this, of course, must start at the top corporate level.

(4) Training

The emphasis given to training in the Japanese business culture is different than that in American companies. Skills training is one such example; Japanese companies provide a great deal more training before putting employees to work in a real process. Under the guidance of an instructor, they learn everything needed for good quality production before becoming responsible for making an item a customer will see. If they change jobs, they are retrained in the new job before entering into the process (Goalstone and Okada, 1984). Contrast this with American industry where employees are usually hired with only some academic skill relating to a job. They are immediately put into the process to learn as they go. Scrap costs are high and quality is low during this on-the-job educational phase.

Next, consider management training; here the comparison works exactly the opposite way. In Japan, managers are offered little classroom training. Individuals are expected to learn about management techniques from their superiors and job environment before they are promoted. Promotions are slow to come but effectiveness is fast. In the United States, most of our training money is spent on managers. We hire promising young candidates, promote them, and then send them to supervisory and management classes to learn how to manage. Throughout their learning experience they make a lot of mistakes and cost the business a lot of money.

All the Japanese businesses in Tribus' study had training programs directed at the principles of TQC. This training is a necessary part of the culture change that Japanese businesses are trying to achieve. The *Hoshin* planning process, PDCA, and SQC are fundamental elements of this new business culture, and formal training programs are necessary to ensure that they become a way of life.

Employee training is an important opportunity for the United States to develop people as assets. Minimal or delayed employee preparation costs this country billions of dollars every year; if trained people could be capitalized, as investments in equipment are capitalized, all managers would provide more training programs.

(5) Presidential Review

Japanese management systems that utilize TQC contain a presidential review process. This review is intended to assure that continuous progress is made throughout the company toward the implementation of Deming's 14 points. The companies that won the Deming Award had good reasons for using this process; each felt that the employees needed a common goal. Having a presidential review also allowed them the opportunity to provide recognition for individual achievement and constructive feedback to those who needed help. The goals of the review process may be stated as follows:

- To ensure that performance plans and goals are achieved by using a common method such as TQC.

- To ensure that the performance of the process is being controlled with the aid of SQC tools and techniques.

- To reveal the strengths and weaknesses of the system for improving the quality of the product or service.

- To ensure that performance measures and goals are realistically set to reflect current problems and issues.

In structuring their organizations for presidential reviews, the Japanese demonstrate that each detail in the hierarchy has significance to the mission of the business. They use detailed planning systems to ensure that every goal and measure is connected to the next level in the hierarchy. People in the organization are not allowed to waste resources on issues that do not specifically relate to the mission of the business and the objectives. The presidential reviews are specifically designed to provide the visibility and recognition required to guarantee that all resources focus on the mission of the business.

American managers often find this level of detail and regimentation undesirable. Their attitude toward detailed planning and review is oriented more toward results achieved than methods used. Specific plans seem to get put aside and are rarely reviewed in the same context as prepared. Extenuating and unforeseen circumstances always seem to render the plan obsolete before it is three months old. The minimal rewards associated with this type of planning have been very demotivating to American managers.

The Japanese, however, have made their detailed planning systems rewarding for the manager. They make certain that the plans, objectives, and mission are coordinated throughout the organization; short-term setbacks are willing to be incurred if long-term gains offset them. Japanese reviews emphasize the methods used as well as the results achieved; they make certain that the planning process does not waste resources. Tops-down participation is emphasized throughout the company, from the board of directors down, to implement and report on progress; this systematic approach ensures that resources are not wasted.

(6) Quality Circles

Quality circles (QCs) are used extensively in Japan as a means to gain employee involvement in the problem-solving process. QCs started in Japan in 1962 and by 1984 expanded to 160,000 circles with 1.5 million members. QCs in Japan are comprised of coworkers who share responsibility for the quality of a process. QCs offer an opportunity for employee involvement in the problem-solving process. Japanese managers recognize that workers are the closest to the process and therefore most familiar with its operation and problems. Getting them involved instills pride and responsibility for their work.

QCs also serve another purpose. In a business environment having many interconnecting processes, it is impossible for a small number of managers to monitor all the control parameters, analyze the deviations, and take corrective action. Allowing the process workers to participate in these activities increases their supervisors' control and productivity; it also increases everyone's sensitivity to variation and reduces their response time.

As American companies have struggled with the implementation of QCs, they have learned many lessons. In many cases, American managers quickly decided that quality circles were a waste of time. They abandoned them as a cultural anomaly of Japan. Persistent companies have learned that QCs warrant considerable merit, if managed correctly. Still, there is much controversy among American managers about the value of QCs. The controversy exists because of the bad experiences many have had, compounded by industry-wide naivete about the contribution QCs make to the organization. Few American managers recognize the structured approach of QCs to a more participative style of management and teamwork.

Evolution of Management Style

During the last 25 years, some American companies have moved toward a more participative management style. Leadership style has taken on a new appearance with MBO and, more recently, management by walking around (MBWA), coffee talks, and other forms of communication. Providing employees with flexible working hours, more holidays, increased benefits, and pleasant working conditions has improved employee job attitude. All of these advances speak highly of American management's good intentions, but none of them provides the significant motivational benefits available from real participative management and teamwork.

Many theories on the benefits of participative management have been presented by organizational behavior scientists since 1950. Americans, caught up in their own success in the 1950s and 1960s, ignored most of these as being impractical for use in the daily work of most employees. Conversely, the Japanese were very receptive to new ideas. They took advantage of many of the ideas that were given to them by American managers who were sent to help Japan after World War II.

Kenneth Hopper reported that much of what the Japanese learned about participative management came from the post-war Civil Communications Seminar taught by Charles Protzman, Homer Sarasahn, and Frank Polkinghorn (Hopper, 1985). These seminars and further teachings became the basis of Japan's philosophy to place quality first on their list of objectives.

The human relations aspect of this seminar was considered to be different from the more autocratic teachings of American business schools of that era. Japanese leaders were encouraged by Sarasahn to secure the respect and faith of those working for them, while Protzman argued strongly that participation must be achieved everywhere and at every level.

Early Leaders in Participative Management Style

The teachings of the Civil Communications Seminar may have differed from the teachings of the business schools in the late 1940s and 1950s, but they were quite consistent with the developing theories of behavioral scientists of the time. The experiments and results of Elton Mayo at Western Electric in the 1930s and 1940s gained influence in the United States. Further work by Edwin Fleishman and Rensis Likert demonstrated the value of the supportive supervisor and participative management style. As a manufacturing executive from Western Electric, Charles Protzman must have been well schooled in these theories when he traveled to Japan, as were Frank Polkinghorn from Bell Labs and his colleague Homer Sarasahn.

In 1957 Douglas M. McGregor introduced his classical Theory X and Theory Y model about people. In the opening lines of *The Human Side of Enterprise,* he points out the following challenge for business:

> It has become trite to say that the most significant developments of the next quarter century will take place not in the physical but in the social sciences, that industry — the economic organ of society — has the fundamental know-how to utilize physical science and technology for the material benefit of mankind, and that we must now learn how to utilize the social sciences to make our human organizations truly effective.

Progress toward Collegial Methods

During the last 25 years many American companies have moved away from the Theory X style of management, but they have yet to fully harness the potential of human energy. Using a model developed by Keith Davis for classification of management styles (Table 3.1), most of today's business styles can be classified as custodial or supportive (Davis, 1967). While many businesses have changed their styles from the autocratic to the custodial, and from the custodial to the supportive, few if any have changed successfully to the collegial. Even though most of the benefits of human energy are derived from collegial-style management, most American companies have viewed the collegial environment applicable only to professional environments and impractical for hourly workers. The Japanese have demonstrated validity of its application throughout their factories with the use of QCs.

	Autocratic	Custodial	Supportive	Collegial
Depends On:	Power	Economic Resources	Leadership	Mutual Contribution
Managerial Orientation:	Authority	Material Rewards	Support	Integration Teamwork
Employee Orientation:	Obedience	Security	Performance	Responsibility
Employee Psychological Result:	Personal Dependency	Organization Dependency	Participation	Self-Discipline
Employee Needs Met:	Subsistence	Maintenance	Higher Order	Self-Realization
Performance Result:	Minimum	Passive Cooperation	Awakened Drives	Enthusiasm
Moral Measure:	Compliance	Satisfaction	Motivation	Commitment to Task and Team

Table 3.1 Four Organizational Behavior Models
(Reprinted with permission of McGraw-Hill Book Company)

Many people in American industry believe that the high level of commitment, participation, and achievement of the Japanese people is culture-bound. It is proposed here that any business or culture willing to adopt the leadership style characterized by McGregor and Davis, as illustrated in the collegial model, will achieve the same results. The following is a discussion of participative management, as referred to in the collegial model developed by Keith Davis:

Collegial Model

1. Readily adapts to the flexible, intellectual environment of scientific and professional organizations, working in substantially unprogrammed activities which require teamwork. (Americans in 1967, when this article was published, presumably thought that the structure and regimentation of the factory workers precluded the need for teamwork.)

2. Depends on a feeling of mutual contribution among the participants in the organization. Employees must believe they are contributing something worthwhile; they must also believe that managers and others are contributing in order to accept and respect their roles in the organization.

3. Is orientated toward managerial teamwork, which provides an integration of all contributions. This manifests itself as:

   - Integrating power rather than commanding power.

   - Employee responsibility as the employee response.

   - Employee quality production from desire rather than command.

   - Self-discipline as the employee psychological result.

   The feeling of shared responsibility prepares the employees to discipline themselves for team performance.

4. The employees gain self-realization and fulfillment. The result is job enthusiasm. (Davis relates this to Herzberg's motivators: achievement, growth, intrinsic work fulfillment, and recognition.) Employee morale is measured by commitment to job task and quality team, because these are seen to be instruments for self-actualization.

QCs are vehicles for achieving a participative management style. By and large, American management has shied away from employee involvement on the production lines. Engineers are expected to develop the tooling, the technology, and the procedures for manufacturing the products. Production line employees are simply asked to follow the procedures, work as fast as possible, and minimize the mistakes. If problems arise, they are to bring them to the attention of their supervisor. Any other course of action is actively discouraged and suggestions are not always welcomed. It is understandable that these employees lack the enthusiasm to do any more than they are paid to do.

James S. Bowman makes an interesting point when he states, "The Japanese do not need quality circles" (Bowman, 1985). Although they benefit from quality circles when they are established, "such techniques are best understood as manifestations of employee-focused management, not an essential component of it." They are, however, the best techniques developed to date for moving toward a more participative management style. QCs, therefore, need not be considered an end in themselves, but the structure and discipline of QCs help to facilitate the learning process required to make this change (Mohrman and Lawler, 1985).

In a participative management system where the employees are asked to meet regularly with their supervisors to analyze processes for improvement, both levels participate in identifying and documenting the expectations of their processes. Everyone helps to identify the measures of performance and to establish goals which are consistent with the goals of the larger group. With the assistance of engineering, they measure their personal performances, analyze deviations, and then recommend and implement changes.

In this type of environment, people are constantly encouraged and supported by the management team. As changes occur in the satisfaction of needs, the motivations and the results begin to resemble those of the collegial model. The Japanese have developed utilization of human resources through their QCs. Americans have the same opportunity if they move toward participative management — with or without the use of QCs.

(7) Common Problem-Solving Method

Statistical Quality Control

A recurrent theme among TQC participants is SQC. Using statistical methods to measure and analyze performance is the accepted way to eliminate emotion from decision making. "Use facts — not emotions," is a common quote from manuals defining SQC procedures. SQC serves to increase a person's sensitivity to the process' variations. A control system would be unreliable if it were unable to detect all changes, good or bad. To measure variations, the use of reliable sampling plans, data collection methods, and control charts are essential to spot trends and problems, even when the changes are small or obscured by feelings. SQC thus becomes the mechanism for detecting and analyzing change in the control of the process.

PDCA — The Common Method

The PDCA cycle is derived from the science of systems analysis. Though PDCA is less complex, it possesses the common attributes of all analytical studies represented by the sciences of systems analysis and operations research. The significance of Japan's PDCA method demonstrates that quantitative analysis can be used by everyone in the company. Its use should not be limited to large investment decisions. On the contrary, by simplifying it and teaching everyone in the company to use it, businesses can solve the hundreds of operational problems that keep them from meeting their goals.

Plan

Within a Japanese company, the plan is divided into three parts:

1. Interpret the requests or expectations of higher management.

2. Generate a plan of action.

3. Identify the controlling points and parameters that are essential for high quality.

Do

After the plans have been made, reviewed, and accepted by higher management consensus, targets are set and implementation is begun. The implementation phase is the basis for any new, valuable activities to be introduced within the process.

Check

Information on the control parameters is continuously collected and reviewed by managers and people involved in the process and organized into QCs. Through the use of SQC techniques, explanations for all variations are attempted. This check is also extended to the annual management review, where accomplishments are compared to goals. In a control loop analogy, this check represents the comparison of the process results to the expected goals. The deviation is then analyzed in the next step.

Act

The last step of the cycle requires a variation analysis to be made, its causes to be assigned, and any corrective actions to be identified. Moving from here back into the planning phase brings you through a full cycle of planning for action, implementating plans, checking results, and analyzing and identifying needed actions.

The main goal of the PDCA cycle is to eliminate variation in the process. It is well understood that even favorable variations — if unexpected — must be analyzed, because they represent an opportunity to learn how to achieve better results. SQC represents a method for improving our sensitivity to variation; PDCA represents a method for improving the response to problems. Reducing the number and frequency of variations depends on how quickly a process deviation is recognized, how quickly it is analyzed, and how quickly controls are implemented. The cycle time in the PDCA loop is then characterized by how long it takes to detect and compensate for the cause of the deviation. This is an important measure, since time is quantity and quantity is cost.

Any business can introduce quantitative analysis to solve its daily operational problems, and PDCA is an excellent model from which to build. It is possible to improve on the Japanese accomplishments, however. The only prerequisite is a good understanding of the scientific methods of quantitative analysis. For a new method to be effective throughout a business, there are a few simple rules that should be followed. (These rules are the essence of Japanese success with PDCA.)

1. Keep the method simple and easy to learn. Most people in the organization are not analysts and cannot be expected to learn complicated problem-solving methods. Some may need to learn the more complicated analysis methods. In the interest of economics, however, they should be encouraged to use the simpler method when applicable.

2. Use a common method. This encourages the learning that takes place when everyone speaks the same language.

3 . Do not try to teach statistics to all your people. For people who have not gone to college, the average math ability is at about the eighth grade level. If they do not use math regularly, even college educated employees struggle with statistics. It is better to use graphic tools similar to those presented by Ishikawa (1982). These tools do not require the extensive knowledge of statistics. Teach statistics to the people who have the ability to learn; when difficult problems arise, use their knowledge to provide the statistical backup for analysis.

Once the decision is made to develop and use a common method, the objective is to turn everyone in the organization into systems analysts and to gain the leverage that numbers provide. There are no fundamental differences in logic among the various problem-solving approaches. The differences are in the methods used for problem solving and, to some extent, the emphasis. The emphasis in PDCA and SQC is quality, and quality is the means to improve efficiency. The basis of the traditional and scientific approach to problem solving includes the following:

- Formulate problem. Describe the problem, the objectives, the criteria, and the mission.

- Assemble facts. Collect the data relative to the measures and the objectives.

- Analyze. Apply the data to the problem-solving model and make a comparison of the results, the causes, and the effects.

- Draw conclusions. Recommend actions for change, decisions, and implementation.

The traditional approach to making large investment decisions ends here. Unless it is possible to construct a model and do an experiment, action is taken. With less significant problems, real-life experiments are feasible. For the iterative cycle, use the following steps:

- Implement the change. Design tooling, change documentation, etc.

- Monitor the results. Collect data and compare to objectives.

- Analyze the facts. As above, do traditional quantitative analysis.

- Make the decision. As above, decide the probable cause and propose changes.

This iterative loop is the basis for continued improvement to meet the changing objectives of the environment. The PDCA method directly parallels this approach.

(8) A Way of Life

TQC is not a program that is installed within the business system. It *is* the business system. The managers at Yokagawa HP, for example, think of a TQC review as their business review; the two are inseparable. The reward systems are institutionalized such that they motivate the individual to contribute to the group, and the group to focus on quality. The elements of TQC must become a part of the management system before they can become a way of life.

Total Quality Control and the Management System

The preceding discussions have elaborated on the history and function of the major elements of TQC. Collectively, the elements of TQC form the fundamental parts of the bridge that exists between quality and customer satisfaction. Managers who understand the architecture of this bridge will be able to improve the design and construction of their organization's ability to provide for customer satisfaction.

Total Quality Control Today

As TQC developed, each new aspect presented a new challenge. To understand these new challenges, we created labels and attempted to fit them into our system of understanding. This evolved into a model as previously shown in Figure 3.1. This model places each element of TQC into one of four categories: customer focus, management commitment, total participation, and systematic analysis. These are the essential functions of TQC that most managers have come to value.

This model has served us well, but it has some limitations. For example, it is still hard to view TQC as anything but another program, in spite of what we say. Nonquality-oriented managers view it as a foreign concept — they don't see how it fits in with traditional management methods and values. Managers find it difficult to visualize a total implementation — institutionalization — of TQC, therefore it is difficult for them to plan and prioritize. Quality consultants are good at describing where an organization is weak, but have trouble defining the ultimate plan and the motivations for implementation. In the end, they ask that you accept TQC on faith, because it has worked for others.

The view that TQC must be accepted on faith, tends to put it into a class with witchcraft — believe in it, and it will cure your ills. Similarly, TQC proponents are often perceived as wild-eyed zealots who conjure up tricks to gain the faith of others. Fortunately, managers don't have to accept TQC on faith, any more than they need to depend on witch doctors to heal their physical ills. TQC is a highly developed set of methods that enhance organizational effectiveness through the science of systems analysis and control. These mechanisms form the architecture that bridges quality to customer satisfaction.

Customer Satisfaction

Customer satisfaction is the key to business success. When customers are satisfied with what they hear, see, and feel they will come back for more. Another way to think about customer satisfaction, is that customers will be satisfied to the extent that their expectations and needs are met. These expectations are based on what they have been told and the experience they have had with your products and your competitor's products.

Businessmen have a sense about such things. They know that customers care about the product attribute set — function, usability, performance, reliability, and supportability. Customers also care about getting the best price and best availability. To be successful then, a business must have the right product, right price, and right availability. The level of customer satisfaction is based on what customers hear, see, and feel about these product attributes.

Organizational Effectiveness

An organization's effectiveness is measured by its ability to provide for customer satisfaction. Therefore, an organization's effectiveness is based on its ability to (1) provide the right product in a rapidly changing environment, which will require effective planning systems; (2) the ability to provide a product at the right price — productivity; and (3) the ability to provide the needed product at the right time and place — availability. These organization attributes — planning, productivity, and adaptability — are the primary elements of competitive fitness and hence the most important elements of organizational effectiveness.

Total Quality Control's Contribution

It would appear from this argument that all activities proposed to improve customer satisfaction should make a contribution to organizational effectiveness. TQC for example, has many elements such as SQC and PDCA. These activities must make a contribution to planning, productivity, or adaptability, or they have no value to the organization.

In the traditional context of TQC, quality makes a contribution to process efficiency by eliminating waste, and subsequently improves process responsiveness by improving efficiency; i.e., wasted material and labor inhibits a process' response to change. A similar relationship exists between the elements of organizational effectiveness and customer satisfaction. In fact, the elements of TQC, provide leverage to organizational effectiveness, and similarly, organizational effectiveness leverages customer satisfaction (Figure 3.5).

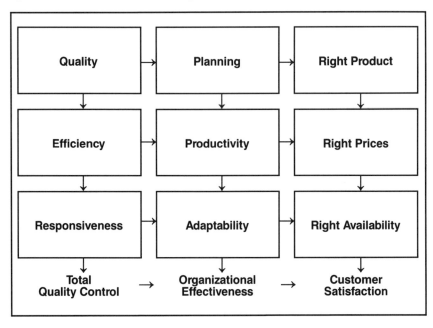

Figure 3.5 Relationships of TQC Organizational Effectiveness and Customer Satisfaction

For organizational effectiveness, the quality of planning will have a direct effect on defining the right product, and directing the people in the organization to work on the right things. This in turn affects productivity. Subsequently, when everyone is working on the right things with a high level of productivity, an organization will be more adaptable to meeting the needs of the environment.

For customer satisfaction, the features of the product have a direct effect on complexity and therefore price. Price is also influenced by productivity, which is provided laterally from organizational effectiveness. Subsequently, complexity, productivity, and adaptability have a direct effect on time to design and manufacture and, therefore, availability.

When the relationships in Figure 3.5 are integrated vertically and horizontally, the basic architecture that forms the linkage between quality, the fundamental element, and customer satisfaction — the highest order element of competitive success — is complete.

This view of the organization should be thought of as three-dimensional. Behind each of the blocks there are many methods that can be used to improve the system's effectiveness. These methods are made up of the elements of TQC and other management methods developed over the years. Some of them are more effective in what they contribute to quality, organizational effectiveness, and customer satisfaction. Managers choose methods to use based on their understanding of the method's effectiveness at providing for the functions of the management system.

The Management System

Business organizations behave according to the same principles that govern all systems; i.e., feedback, analysis, and control. In the "business system," the "management system" provides for this control. Through proper control, the management system ensures that the business is adaptive to the continuous changes it sees in the economic environment. By adapting to changing customer needs at a faster rate than competitors, a business assures itself of the highest level of customer satisfaction and financial success.

The management system facilitates the feedback, analysis, and control through five major functions that are described below. The titles of these functions have been chosen arbitrarily from the TQC model in Figure 3.1 for continuity.

1. *Management Commitment.* Management commitment must be present in the form of policies, organizational structure, investment, and individual responsibility and authority. Management commitment provides the organization with the *physical* and *organizational* realities of the business.

2. *Leadership.* Leadership is a process that exists in the form of visions, plans, motivation, and review of progress. Without leadership the organization would not make consistant progress in a chosen direction. Leadership is the primary function used to *control* the direction of the business.

3. *Customer Focus.* Customer focus provides for constant awareness of customer needs and success at meeting those needs. It is the source of the *feedback* needed by the system for analysis. Without customer focus a business would not know whose needs it was trying to satisfy.

4. *Total Participation.* Total participation ensures that the full genius and capability of the people resources are used. This provides for the harmonious workings of the internal parts of the organization. Without total participation a business would depend on the genius of a few and never gain the synergy that comes from total contribution of each element of the process. Total participation provides for the *synthesis* of the component parts of the system.

5. *Systematic Analysis.* Systematic analysis facilitates constant feedback, analysis, and control throughout the organization. It is through systematic analysis that deviations are *analyzed* and the knowledge is developed to decide when and where a compensating change must be made. Without systematic analysis the organization would be inconsistent in its response to change.

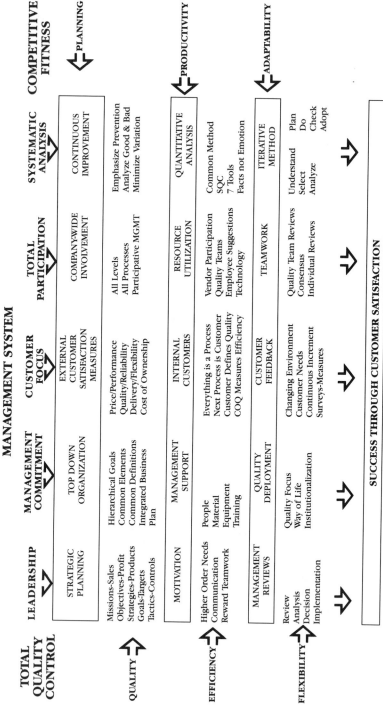

Figure 3.6 The Management System

Details of the Architecture

TQC and traditional management consist of many different methods. These methods contribute to organizational effectiveness through the functions of the management system. Some methods will be more effective than others at providing for feedback, analysis, and control. The individual effectiveness of a method can be measured by the quality and timeliness of the response it provides. This is a figure of merit that applies to all systems.

The TQC methods chosen by Japanese management are more responsive to change than many traditional methods. SQC, for example, ensures that random and nonrandom variation are understood. This understanding ensures that responses to variation only occur when there is an assignable cause. For this reason, SQC has led to the saying, "Respond to facts, not emotions." PDCA applied to every process also fits the feedback, analysis, and control model for systems. This form of systems analysis is simplified to make it easy to learn and use by everyone in the organization.

Figure 3.6 illustrates where TQC methods contribute to the management system and organizational effectiveness. This model is derived from Figure 3.5 and can be thought of as the third dimension discussed previously.

The Model

The columns represent the functions of the management system and are labeled as described previously. The rows represent the elements of organizational effectiveness and are labeled accordingly on the right. The methods of TQC are shown in lower case and are organized to show (1) where they contribute to organizational effectiveness by row, and (2) the function they provide to the management system by column.

Remember these methods integrate vertically and horizontally, and when combined, make the greatest contribution to customer satisfaction. For example, look at leadership: Quality planning through visions, objectives, and strategies make a contribution to the leadership process. Quality planning will ensure that everyone is working on the right things and thereby enhancing efficiency. Proper communication and rewards are part of the leadership process; they motivate the right things to happen and therefore make a contribution to productivity. Regular reviews are also part of the leadership process; they provide feedback on performance. By combining plans with motivation and review in a vertical direction, leadership is provided to control direction and thus contribute to customer satisfaction.

Leadership doesn't stand alone in its contribution to planning. The other methods shown laterally in the planning row are also necessary. The elements of management commitment, customer focus, total participation, and systematic analysis are just as important. Each of the methods represented in these functions must be present and responsive for the system to achieve optimum function.

Managers can use this model to conceptualize a total system and plan for the orderly implementation. They can look at pieces, like the planning structure, and choose the methods they want to use. They can evaluate policies to see how they contribute to planning effectiveness or motivation. Managers can identify missing pieces in the system and understand the criteria for selecting new ones. They can choose methods for synthesis and systematic analysis. Every need of the organizational system becomes more readily apparent when compared to this model.

This model also lends itself to measuring an organization's progress. For example, managers can measure the planning system by asking the right questions of the management system: Does it provide consistent missions, goals, and strategies? Are the plans hierarchical, with common elements? Do the plans have customer input and measures? Have all levels and processes been included in the planning process? Do all goals tie together? Is continuous improvement stressed and are plans developed to reduce variation? Progress can be measured by developing indices for the responses to the above questions.

When the design, construction, and implementation of the total management system are complete, and managers have eliminated the wasteful encumbrances to responsiveness, the business will be in the most competitive position possible. It will provide better products, at better prices, and at better availability than its competitors. When industry has accomplished this, TQC will have evolved from witchcraft, and will be viewed as an important element of management science.

A Summary of Total Quality Control and the Management System

Planning

Strategic planning provides direction for the entire organization. While there are many models of strategic planning from which to choose, success is determined by the effectiveness of model application. To be effective, the planning model must reach all levels and processes of the organization; it must be well defined and consistently communicated throughout the organization.

The Japanese use a basic hierarchical planning model, called *Hoshin*, to ensure that a common approach is used by everyone in the company. This disciplined approach to planning is typical of the way they approach all their business functions. The elements of their planning model are well understood at all organizational levels; each level knows its responsibility to long-term and short-term goals and strategies.

Long-term objectives and strategies are mapped out by top level management to provide the general direction for company progress. Middle level managers emphasize the strategies required to achieve the desired long-term results, while lower level supervisors work on the short-term goals and tactics (Goldstone and Okada, 1984).

The planning process is not finished until each level completes its contribution to the planning process. When the planning process is finalized, all plans are combined into an integrated business plan. This plan serves as the basis for the annual presidential review.

Planning and Leadership

Traditionally, management practices have been undisciplined in this area. Key business objectives may be communicated clearly throughout the organization at first, but the discipline of the planning model and its relationship to lower level strategies and goals become vague the further we get from top level management. Little effort is put into identifying the proper connection between the proposed plan and the desired goal.

70

Poor communication within the organization inadvertently allows lower levels to deviate from or not contribute to the business goals. Improving this situation is fundamental to improving business efficiency and is the responsibility of leadership.

Planning and Management Commitment

To implement a planning system in a diverse organization of independent-thinking managers, the required level of discipline is only possible if the company president is committed for the system to be followed by all. A great deal of time is needed for this accomplishment because each management level is required to spend many hours reviewing and revising subordinate goals and strategies until they correlate with company objectives (consensus).

Planning and Customer Focus

The Japanese emphasis on customer satisfaction objectives is a major contribution to the traditional planning process. Traditional goals and measures emphasize growth, profit, and other cost-related goals. While these measures are important to the business, they should not be its only focus.

Traditional measures of growth and profit may hide underlying business problems. During times of rapid economic growth and expansion, some companies may grow and achieve satisfactory profits even though their customer satisfaction measures are not high. Customer satisfaction problems that are not addressed in the planning process may prove to be a company's undoing when a recession sets in or other competitors enter the market. Identifying and monitoring measures of customer satisfaction eliminates an ambiguous position in the business environment.

Measures of customer satisfaction include price/performance ratios, usability, reliability, availability, functionality, and ownership cost. Integrating the customer satisfaction objectives with the traditional business goals is required to ensure that everyone's plans include the provisions to satisfy customers' needs.

Planning and Total Participation

The hierarchical nature of the business plan should ensure that it affects every process and every level of the business. This suggests that all people must be involved in setting goals and strategies for their processes. In Japan, middle level managers participate in developing goals and strategies with upper level managers until consensus is reached. This, in turn, filters downward throughout the organization, and results in a higher level of commitment and dedication to the goals of the organization.

Planning and Systematic Analysis

The strategy of the business should include an emphasis on prevention rather than reaction. Early recognition, while the investment is low, that certain plans may not work is far better than abandoning a project after large investments are made in time and money. The preventative approach analyzes the small market variations in order to predict changes in the environment.

The Japanese use the incremental strategy in marketing new products (Goalstone and Okada, 1984). This strategy uses continuous analysis of the environment and the results in smaller variations between the goal and the result. Analyzing the market and revising the strategy on a continuous basis supplies the data to track diverse and changing markets. Color preferences on cars, for instance, are constantly changing; therefore, continuous analysis of customer preferences must be made to prevent accumulating inventories of unpopular colors.

Larger, fundamental changes of business are not handled with the incremental approach. These changes, referred to as seed sowing, result in new businesses or new technology applications to provide compatibility with the long-term needs of the environment (Goalstone and Okada, 1984). Effective and systematic analysis of market and technology trends is the key to successfully growing new business.

Incremental strategy and seed sowing provide the continuous change and improvement to stay in the forefront of competition. To be effective in both approaches requires the effective use of systematic analysis tools.

Planning and Quality

Consistent with the view that quality affects the efficiency of all processes, the elements of planning must be integrated with high-level quality. Sloppy, unclear plans and ill-conceived objectives can only lead to confusion in the business; the success of the organization depends on quality planning as its foundation. Each of the previously discussed relationships exists to improve the quality of the information and the procedures used in the planning process.

Productivity

Productivity and Leadership

The traditional approach for improving productivity has been capital investment in new technology. The motivation of employees has long been viewed as a factor, but was of insignificant importance as long as people were kept busy and allowed to enjoy their work. In the past, emphasis has been toward replacing people with more productive machinery wherever possible.

Traditional management approaches have designed reward systems to motivate the individual to higher levels of achievement, resulting in ranking systems and personnel evaluations that place individuals in a competitive role for merit pay increases. This reward system is effective in motivating the individual, but it takes away from teamwork. The leadership of the business has the responsibility to ensure that the reward system motivates the individual to optimize the results of the team.

The structure of the reward system is a key part of leadership and motivation. Japanese reward systems are designed to encourage teamwork. The Japanese promotion rate is based on sustained teamwork skills and tends to be slower than that of U.S. companies. A high proportion of pay (45 percent) is based on profit-sharing, which inspires people to work together. Seniority earns a high premium in pay and retirement benefits; this encourages long-term employment. These factors combine to provide the incentives necessary to encourage the highest level of teamwork (Goalstone and Okada, 1984).

Productivity and Management Commitment

Management commitment means providing the necessary resources to get the job done. People, material, equipment, and training are necessary ingredients that managers must provide at the appropriate levels to ensure that the highest levels of quality and productivity are achieved. Withholding investment in new technology can be just as damaging as too much investment. Training that is insufficient or ill-timed costs a company millions of dollars in scrap and rework.

Many American companies invest heavily in formal training programs held outside daily work activities; the Japanese, however, provide training within job work hours. Because advancements come slowly, supervisors are expected to be knowledgeable in all aspects of their jobs. In turn, they are expected to provide proper training to their subordinates at all levels. This training style emphasizes the process skills, the teamwork elements, SQC, and process improvement. This type of training, combined with employee longevity, maintains high levels of process knowledge and efficiency.

Effective communication is difficult to achieve within a modern and diverse organization, but it is an essential part of productivity improvements. All levels must be open to receiving and sending information continuously, and interdepartmental communications must be barrier free. In America, managers have come to rely on several forms of communication: the open door policy, MBWA, coffee breaks, staff meetings, etc. The Japanese managers also use many forms of communication, most notably the communication that takes place on the golf course or during social drinking after work. These are not unlike many American methods of learning about underlying employee concerns.

Productivity is enhanced when communications are uninhibited. Every effort should be made by management to reduce the barriers of communication. The Japanese managers try to build very close interpersonal relationships among their people to enhance communication. This results in a family-like spirit, similar to that found in American companies such as HP. In their first weeks of employment, Japanese employees are often brought together for training and orientation; many even live together during this period of time. This type of high-level and close, informal communication enhances teamwork; and teamwork is the essence of productivity improvement.

In a business, employee reward systems, training programs, and communication processes are under the direct control of management. The extent to which they are used to enhance productivity is limited by management's commitment to a successful management system.

Productivity and Customer Focus

System productivity is directly related to the efficiency of all the processes in the system. Quality improvements that are made early in a series of processes have a significant impact on the cost of subsequent processes. The cost in the subsequent process is typically referred to as COQ and is commonly defined as the costs of appraising, fixing, and preventing the quality problems.

Because the next procedure of a process is on its receiving end, it is referred to as a customer of the previous stage. Hence, there are internal customers and external customers. Internal customers are those processes that are internal to the business, while external customers are those processes that are outside the business.

Customers are really the only ones who fully appreciate the cost of poor quality. They are usually the ones who must bear the burden of the rework or scrap that results from poor quality in the preceding process. This is independent of whether they are internal or external customers. It is, therefore, the customers' needs that determine the definition of quality.

Productivity and Total Participation

Reducing the COQ implies that the business system is utilizing all resources with the highest efficiency. Since material, equipment, and people are the primary resources, efforts to reduce the COQ should be emphasized here.

Vendors are the source of material and equipment, but the technological edge of modern materials and equipment is lost if high losses occur due to poor quality supplies from vendors. Including vendors in company efforts to improve overall quality is an investment that reduces COQ. The TQC approach relies on developing close ties with a few concerned and motivated vendors who are willing to work toward quality improvement of material and equipment. This willingness to participate should be a company's primary factor in selecting vendors.

People are human resources in a business and affect the productivity of every process. The Japanese approach to QCs is an effort to draw from the combined wisdom of all their people, and the manner in which QCs are managed significantly affects employee contribution. As a vehicle to participative management and teamwork, QCs provide huge benefits to worker quality, dedication, satisfaction, and motivation.

Another method of harnessing the knowledge of everyone in the company is through an employee suggestion system (ESS). The ESS provides process workers with the opportunity to benefit from the ideas of others who are outside the process. This method can be very productive, but it is probably not practical until the basic mechanisms for process improvement are established with quality teams throughout the organization. The number of suggestions would be unmanageable and probably would trigger defensive reactions among people usually responsible for process improvement.

Vendor participation, quality teams, and ESSs combine to provide the total participation required for improved resource utilization. When all competitors have the same technological information, a company's competitive edge can only be productivity through improved resource utilization.

Productivity and Systematic Analysis

Improving the many variables in the processes of a business system goes beyond man's intuitive judgment. Since the quality improvement of each of these processes is the key to efficiency improvement, a more accurate and efficient way to analyze process variation is required. Statistics, the study of variation, provides the necessary tools to understand the variables within a process.

The Japanese use a common method of process analysis, previously discussed as PDCA. Using a uniform method of analysis throughout the organization makes its own contribution to productivity by simplifying the training process. Better training results are achieved when everyone uses the same method analysis; thus, people can learn from one another.

SQC is the common method of quantitative analysis with which everyone in a modern successful company should become familiar. SQC focuses on the quality of the process; therefore, it provides the basis of analysis to understand the variables that affect resource efficiency.

Statistics can be overwhelming for most employees, depending on their mathematical abilities. For this reason, the Japanese have emphasized the use of an understandable basic set of tools. With a minimum amount of training, these fundamental tools can be used efficiently by everyone in the company, and they should be emphasized when teaching employees how to use SQC.

Productivity and Efficiency

The integration of the above elements with traditional methods of productivity improvement is part of the key to Japan's success. In most Japanese-dominated markets, success has not been through technological advantage. On the contrary — most of the time the U.S. was technologically superior, but the Japanese were able to combine the elements of efficiency to attain a position of productive leadership.

Adaptability

Adaptability and Leadership

Traditional change management methods tend to be like those adopted by the Japanese. The differences, where they exist, appear to result from the discipline used to achieve change and the focus for the intended change. American managers are very undisciplined; they look at profits and growth only at quarterly and annual reviews. They may cursorily review product strategies, but they seldom challenge middle management for statistical evidence to back up claims of potential market opportunity. They get a lot of good hits and they miss a few — but as long as the bottom line looks good, everyone is happy.

When major changes are required, decisions are reserved for those at the top. Consensus is achieved only to the extent it agrees with the thinking of the boss. After all the decisions are made and the method of implementation is pending, the appropriate managers are handed back the controls to implement the changes.

This portrayal of the American manager is probably unfair to many managers, but the system of review, analysis, decision, and implementation for changing the direction of a business is very slow, undisciplined, and erratic. This conflicts with the requirements of a successful business that operates in a complex and changing environment, where the change should come about swiftly, continuously, and smoothly. The Japanese contribution to change provides the elements to improve these components of adaptability. The leadership of a business has the primary responsibility to ensure that their change processes are efficient.

Management reviews should be of precise content and timing; focusing only on daily problems is not adequate. The business plan establishes the elements of the review for every organization level and should be used as a guide for establishing the review. Certain long-term objectives don't need to be reviewed as often as short-term objectives, but all objectives should be reviewed in several, short time increments if they are to be accomplished. This allows for the application of the philosophy of prevention rather than reaction.

Adaptability and Management Commitment

Product quality, customer needs, and improvement methods will not be given their deserved attention unless they are an equal part of the review process. Reviewing profits and product strategies is not adequate; care must be taken to review the results achieved as well as the methods used. Only in this way can a business converge on a common management system. When its reviews focus on the methods used to achieve improvements, management commits the organization to institutionalizing the improvement process. This is an essential part of making continuous improvement a way of life.

Adaptability and Customer Focus

Because the environment is constantly changing, businesses need to constantly monitor the state of the environment. The Japanese use incremental strategy as part of their response to the continuously changing environment; continuous customer feedback is required for business to make small incremental changes.

Internal feedback results when businesses monitor their own results from customer sales, warranties, and complaints. Constant monitoring of these indicators is necessary if total customer satisfaction is to be achieved. Sometimes, however, it is impossible to gage present or future trends and opinions unless customer polling is done; this requires some form of external customer feedback.

The Japanese and many others have been very successful in using surveys for this purpose. Surveys, however, are only as good as the questions posed and, therefore, should be constructed very carefully. Surveys should be used primarily to establish customer expectations and levels of satisfaction. They can be overdone, however; the time it takes to complete the survey may not provide the customer with a good return on his or her investment. Therefore, customers need to be confident that the product will improve as a direct result of the time invested in completing the survey.

Adaptability and Total Participation

Quality teams are key to the business' analysis and change process. As such, their effectiveness makes a major contribution to a business' adaptability. Management should review quality teams as rigorously as they review department results. The emphasis should be on the methods used to improve a process, as well as on the results. By providing the recognition and reward for a team effort, this motivates management to continue using a team approach. This approach is instrumental in offsetting competitors who are motivated by the merit pay system.

Some Japanese companies create a forum for quality team competition. Quality team reviews provide an excellent opportunity to measure the effectiveness of the training programs used for process improvement.

These reviews should be conducted on the basis of problem selection, teamwork, problem-solving time, solution implementation time, and problem-solving methods. Care should be taken to avoid too much emphasis on initially achieved financial results.

Individual reviews are also part of the adaptability equation. Individuals should be evaluated on their team contributions, cooperation, flexibility, and adaptability. When individuals are willing to work toward consensus of the needs of the team, the team is more responsive.

The review of these elements of total participation combines with the other elements to create a more flexible environment.

Adaptability and Systematic Analysis

The previously discussed common method of analysis must be an iterative process. All of the elements of successful management depend on continuous adjustment to a changing environment. Iterative methods, such as PDCA, provide continuous improvement as long as the environment requires. PDCA, however, has some limitations that have been remedied by USA-PDCA (Understand-Select-Analyze-Plan-Do-Check-Adopt). The USA-PDCA method allows the quality team to use it for both an iterative improvement of the process and a vehicle for planning.

Adaptability and Flexibility

All of the elements previously discussed in the traditional adaptability approach as well as the Japanese TQC approach can be integrated to produce a more adaptable business. When we combine planning and productivity in leadership, our business system is competitively positioned to realize success through competitive fitness.

Summary

We have discussed the competitive nature of our business environment and the elements of success required in that environment. The Japanese have demonstrated the effectiveness of their methods, referred to as total quality control, to improve the efficiency of their management system in this environment. The management system depicted in the preceding matrix is an idealized version of what businesses should be striving toward. The Japanese have made the most progress in the development of this model. The challenge to Americans is to close the gap in competitive fitness. This can only be done with a commitment and dedication to the discipline of a more efficient management system. Our task for the future is to build a management system that exceeds the achievements of Japanese management practices.

References

Bowman, James S. "Why Japanese Companies in the U.S. Don't Need Quality Circles." *Personnel Administrator,* Oct. 1985.

Byman, Ed and John Young. Speeches on IBM and Hewlett-Packard given at AEA Conference, Nov. 1983.

Davis, Keith. *Human Relations at Work: The Dynamics of Organizational Behavior, Systems, Organization, Analysis, Management: A Book of Readings.* New York: McGraw-Hill Book Co., 1967.

Deming, W. Edwards. *Quality, Productivity, and Competitive Position.* Cambridge: Massachusetts Institute of Technology, 1982.

Mayo, Elton. *The Social Problems of an Industrial Civilization.* Boston: Division of Research, Harvard Business School, 1945.

Fleishman, Edwin. *Leadership Climate and Supervisory Behavior.* Personal Research Board, Ohio State University, 1951.

Goalstone, Cliff and Haruo Okada, translators. *How Japanese Companies Work,* by a group of unidentified Japanese managers, July 1984.

Heilbroner, Robert L. *The Making of an Economic Society.* Englewood Cliffs, N.J.: Prentice-Hall, Inc., 1972.

Hopper, Kenneth. "Quality, Japan, and the U.S.: The First Chapter." *Quality Progress,* Sept. 1985.

Ishikawa, Kaora. *Guide to Quality Control.* Tokyo: Nordica International Ltd, 1982.

Likert, Rensis. *New Patterns of Management.* New York: McGraw-Hill Book Co., 1961.

McGregor, Douglas M. *The Human Side of Enterprise.* Proceedings of the Fifth Anniversary Convocation of the School of Industrial Management. Cambridge: Massachusetts Institute of Technology, 1957.

Mohrman, Susan A., Edward E. Lawler, and Edward E. Lawler III. "Quality Circles after the Fad." *Harvard Business Review,* Jan./Feb. 1985.

Schonberger, Richard. *Japanese Manufacturing Techniques.* New York: Free Press, 1982.

Tribus, Myron. *Center for Advanced Engineering Study.* Cambridge: Massachusetts Institute of Technology, 1983.

A Business Example of Just-in-Time Manufacturing

To stay competitive in its product markets, a business must merge its quality programs with a highly rationalized system of managing productive resources: people, materials, space, systems, tools, and information. The system is JIT production. Whether quality improvements are an effect of JIT or whether TQC really drives JIT, quality is affected positively by a JIT production process.

In printed circuit board (PC) assembly, all process development is focused on three major efforts: lot size reduction, buffer stock reduction, and space reduction. The desire in driving these three factors as low as possible is to achieve minimum cycle times. History has shown that a quality program can have only limited success if production lots stay large. By reducing lot sizes to only what the final assembly line needs (for example, rate per day production) large lot sizes of nonconforming material are avoided.

Many of the problems require the expert support from quality assurance, engineering, production control, purchasing, and other staff groups. These groups are forced to set priorities to support the production processes better. Any reduction in lot sizes causes problems to be exposed sooner, and this allows more real-time response in finding solutions to these problems. Reducing buffer stocks between operations also has similar effects on quality as do smaller lot sizes.

The goal for the PC is also to drive all operation buffer stocks, or *Queue*, to the minimum that is required to maintain continuous flow of material into all PC operations. This is managed in the PC by the use of tracks in all operations. These tracks are simple but effective tools that allow the *Queue* to be visible at all times. Whenever the *Queue* becomes too large, the input is shut off from the previous operation, and resources are moved to the operation with the large *Queue*. This operational load balancing will allow more emphasis on quality and teamwork and less on quantity control.

The objective is not to feed the next operation as fast as possible, but to feed the subsequent operation only what its capacity can support. This load-balancing strategy has been difficult to maintain at times, due again to the mentality of producing at the highest rate (below standard) with little concern for the capacity of the next operation.

82

With low *Queues,* quality problems must be handled immediately because of the lack of additional work orders for production capacity change. The gain in cycle time is significant because of the more rapid progress in lowering the buffer stock *(Queue).*

The reduction of production space requirements has been achieved in the PC by designing all processes with low *Queues* and short material movement. In evaluating material flow in the PC, the major goal was to reduce the amount of time the employees spent looking for and moving material to the workstation. The desire was to eliminate the need to look for any needed material by having it arrive at the workstation in readiness for employee use.

The combination of easy presentation and material delivery has already had an effect on quality results in the PC. In all the PC operations, space has been compressed so that there is no room to allow accumulation of work that is in progress. This also forces the reduction of buffer stock size. Since less time is spent between operations and less unfinished work is being handled, the task of finding and reworking problems is reduced. In other words, the discovery of defects equates to more real time; the operation where the defect occurred is easier to determine, and, hopefully, the cause of the problem is corrected sooner.

In all, the PC is trying to reduce the lot sizes, the buffer stock, and the production space to better support the total quality efforts that the manufacturing department is implementing. Process control, quality feedback, and process improvements are all positively affected as the PC production process moved into a JIT production environment.

CHAPTER 4

MANAGEMENT COMMITMENT AND QUALITY DEPLOYMENT

"It is not enough that top management commit for life to quality and productivity. They must know what they are committed to — i.e., what they must do. These obligations cannot be delegated."

(W. Edwards Deming, 1982)

These words should have special significance for the managers of companies faced with a dwindling market share in today's competitive environment. The changes that must be made in the way we manage for quality and productivity are a major departure from traditional methods. For example, we must change from a centralized responsibility for quality — the quality assurance department — to a distributed responsibility — individual ownership. We must also universally adopt the philosophy that quality is the primary measure of performance, and that without it we cannot expect to achieve customer satisfaction and competitive position. The impetus for achieving the organizational motivation to adopt these changes is the unqualified commitment of top management.

Myron Tribus' study focused on Japanese companies that changed management systems to ensure their survival. They provided top management commitment in each case, as emphasized by Deming. Subsequently, they made major turnarounds in their performance and competitive position. Today, we in the United States are beginning to see a few American companies that have adopted these same philosophies. They are also making major turnarounds in competitive position. Since there is much to be learned from them, we will look at two of these well known U.S. companies.

Harley-Davidson Motorcycle Company

In 1982 the Harley-Davidson Motorcycle Company appeared to be on its way out. Japanese competition was closing in on the last U.S. manufacturer of motorcycles; at that time, however, Harley-Davidson asked for and received protective trade tariffs for five years on large foreign motorcycles. It has since aggressively changed operations to improve the quality and productivity of its motorcycles. That effort has recently paid off: One year before their expiration date, Harley-Davidson asked that the tariffs on foreign motorcycles be lifted.

In March 1986, Harley-Davidson chairman Vaughn L. Beals reported that the tariffs were no longer necessary. The motorcycle company had been transformed into a financially viable business that is now a market leader. Ronald Reagan summed up the improvements made by Harley-Davidson at a press conference on May 6, 1986: "You [Harley-Davidson] cut work needed to make a motorcycle by one third. You cut inventory by two thirds. You tripled the number of defect-free machines you shipped. You kept price increases small and, on some bikes, even lowered prices" (*San Jose Mercury News,* 1987).

In an interview with *Quality Magazine* in 1985, Beals talked about many of Harley-Davidson's life saving actions (Beels, 1985). The first and foremost was an increased emphasis on quality. Beals reported that Harley-Davidson needed a new approach to quality: "The responsibility for quality had to rest with the machine operator, and management must provide the necessary tools to evaluate performance." To instill this new philosophy, Harley-Davidson instituted a training program from the top to the bottom of the company.

Specific actions included:

- Statistical process control (SPC) throughout the factory. This required a significant amount of training; some employees received 90 hours of statistical training.

- JIT production, which reduced inventory by 50 percent and saved $11 million in cash.

- Vendor SPC training for three full days.

- Quality circle implementation throughout the factory. Over 50 percent of the employees were actively involved in QCs.

For Harley-Davidson, the trade tariffs gave them breathing room to turn things around. The tariffs were time limited and, by themselves, did not guarantee a secure future. According to Beals, the five-year tariff on motorcycles was akin to giving a fighter an extra few weeks to train for a championship fight. The management commitment to train for that fight is finally what saved Harley-Davidson. The philosophy of "survival of the fittest" is still valid. In the end, it will make the final decision.

Chrysler Motor Corporation

In 1978 Chrysler Motor Corporation faced a similar survival crisis. Lee Iacocca, just hired as president, had the responsibility of turning Chrysler around. In his 1984 autobiography, Iacocca talks of many of the challenges he faced with quality, productivity and organizational effectiveness. These challenges were not unlike those of Harley-Davidson — or those of the Japanese companies in Tribus' study. Iacocca's response to the problems was also similar; he recognized that these problems were his responsibility, and it was through his commitment that they were turned around. Here are a few of Iacocca's observations (Iacocca, 1984):

- Chrysler needed a dose of order and discipline — and quick.

- Nobody at Chrysler seemed to understand that interaction among different functions in a company is absolutely critical.

- It wasn't only the style of Chrysler products that had a bad reputation. The company had also run into big problems with quality.

- Aspen and Volare were introduced in 1975, but they should have been delayed a full six months. The company was hungry for cash and this time Chrysler didn't honor the normal cycle of designing, testing, and building an automobile.

- The manufacturing guys would just build cars without ever checking with the sales guys. They just built them, stuck them in a yard, and then hoped that somebody would take them out of there. Chrysler ended up with a huge inventory and a financial nightmare.

These problems are symptomatic of most companies that are in trouble today. Poor quality, high warranty costs, high inventory, poor cash flow, high borrowing, poor communication, etc., are the indicators of a company in trouble. In Iacocca's situation, he saw what needed to be done and did it. Consider a few of the specific philosophies and some of the actions Iacocca took personal responsibility for:

- Iacocca made it clear to everybody in the company that quality was their top priority.

- Easy to manufacture — that's the key to quality.

- Quality doesn't stop with the engineer. It has to be part of the consciousness of the workers in the plants. Through the establishment of *quality circles,* Chrysler's plant workers have become far more involved than they used to be in the building process.

- Chrysler also set up a joint UAW — a Chrysler management quality program that says "look, we'll argue about everything else, but when it comes to quality we're not going to fight each other." Quality cannot get mixed up with other bargaining and be compromised by the usual adversarial relationship between workers and management.

Other specific actions mentioned by Iacocca include implementation of JIT production, which saved millions of dollars in inventory, and thinning out the management ranks and reducing the number of workers performing tasks that might have been avoided if the management system had been working properly in the first place. These actions, and many others taken at Chrysler, spell out the harsh reality of what must be done by management if it is going to turn around a business on the brink of failure. Again, the actions taken at Chrsyler are similar to those taken by Harley-Davidson. The common element of quality before anything else continues to be the winning theme. Iacocca repeatedly refers to the axiom "survival of the fittest" as the impetus for his actions.

In the cases of Harley-Davidson and Chrysler, both CEOs assumed personal responsibility for quality deployment. At Harley-Davidson, Beals commissioned his quality manager and provided the resources to achieve the deployment. The story was the same at Chrysler, where Iacocca did the same and more. Iacocca reported that he authorized the hiring of 250 quality professionals to help initiate the quality turnaround. He did this even though the company was overstaffed in other areas. The commitment and ensuing actions of both CEOs reflect the level of commitment necessary to turn around a business in today's environment. The results of both of these companies substantiate the value of this commitment.

Organizational Transition

As other American businesses start to make quality a strategic element of their competitive strength, they will face many challenges. A strong commitment from top management will ensure that these challenges do not become obstacles to success. The challenges to quality as a strategic focus will come during the implementation phase. Each functional area will battle over resources, responsibility, and ownership of the quality problems, but a carefully planned strategy for quality deployment can alleviate many of these problems. The following discussions describe a strategy for implementing quality as a strategic issue throughout the organization.

The Quality Assurance Function's Role

The quality assurance department in American business has traditionally been assigned the responsibility for ensuring customer satisfaction. This responsibility has been carried out by creating large quality assurance organizations that provide layer upon layer of inspection services. These services have been provided to the manufacturing organization, including qualification testing for the research and development laboratory and information systems for collecting defect information. Reducing this inspection activity presents a major opportunity to improve the efficiency of the business system. The key to improvement is to achieve a distributed responsibility for quality — sometimes called quality responsibility deployment.

This concept has far-reaching implications for all departments in a business. As the department with the most incremental resources dedicated to customer satisfaction, quality assurance is in a strategic position to influence this change; and in the process, it is the department that must change the most. The following discussion addresses the strategic and organizational issues that must be dealt with to effectively shift the responsibility of customer satisfaction from the quality assurance department to include every other employee in the organization. Toward this end, the quality assurance department's role will become one of facilitation and education.

The strategy to make this transition is focused on the following areas:

- *Awareness.* The entire business needs to be aware of the need to distribute the responsibility for customer satisfaction across every process and every employee.

- *Motivation.* Everyone in the organization must be provided the leadership and incentives to take responsibility for customer satisfaction.

- *Methods.* All employees must be trained in the methods for achieving the highest levels of customer satisfaction in the most efficient way.

- *Organization.* The organization is a reflection of the commitment of resources and must be adjusted to align the resources in the best interest of achieving and maintaining a distributed responsibility for customer satisfaction.

Awareness

The first challenge for an organization is to make sure that every individual is aware that each is responsible for the quality of his or her own work. Many people, through years of conditioning, have come to believe that quality can only be achieved by inspection at the end of the line. Asking individuals within a process to take responsibility for the quality of their own work can be a traumatic experience. They may fear that the additional time needed to produce good quality will be held against them. They may not believe that management really supports this philosophy. These factors combine against the acceptance of in-process quality control. These attitude-type problems must be overcome in the awareness phase.

Changing people's attitudes requires changing their beliefs. This is a fundamental part of the motivational theories of Maslow and Herzberg. A person's behavior is based on his or her attitude which, in turn, is based on his or her beliefs. People will be motivated to do certain things to the extent that they believe it will be intrinsically rewarding for them. In this regard, two concepts must be addressed. The first stems from McGregor's Theory X and Theory Y beliefs about people (McGregor, 1957). Theory Y proposes that people basically want to do good work and — provided the opportunity and the proper reward system exists — will perform to the utmost of their ability. Theory Y must be accepted and practiced throughout the organization if progress toward higher levels of quality is to be achieved.

The second concept that must be internalized by the organization relates to quality and productivity. The six Deming Award-winning companies studied by Myron Tribus shared the common philosophy that there can be no productivity improvements without first achieving quality improvements. This philosophy also has proven to be the essential ingredient of survival for Chrysler and Harley-Davidson; they believe this so strongly that quality is the primary determinant in measuring their performance. It is understood at all levels that productivity is the result of their focus on quality. This philosophy is captured and perpetuated through the application of TQC concepts.

TQC also reflects many Japanese businesses' beliefs about people. As discussed in Chapter 3, QCs are used as a means to use an individual's ideas on quality to improve team performance. Keith Davis' collegial model of organizational behavior (Davis, 1969) reinforces McGregor's Theory Y concept toward people and provides rewards of the highest order. This, in turn, provides the highest possible levels of motivation, commitment, self-discipline, and self-realization in the work environment. TQC, therefore, becomes the vehicle for a business to internalize these beliefs about the relationship between people and quality.

Changing peoples' beliefs requires training and reinforcement of these ideas. Reinforcement comes from management's commitment to these principles by (1) providing training budgets, and (2) defining measures of performance and reward systems.

The areas of focus for training are:

People and Motivation

- What are the real reward systems?

- What is participative management?

- What contributions do quality teams make to participative management and teamwork?

- How do we implement a collegial work environment?

Quality, Efficiency, and Productivity

- What is a process and how do we measure it?

- What effect does quality have on the efficiency of a process?

- How do we measure customer satisfaction of a process?

- How do we get synergy from quality in a process?

In-Process Quality Control versus End-of-Line Inspection

- How do you move ownership of quality to the people performing the task?

This training will provide the basic knowledge for employees in all areas of the organization to understand their relationships to each other and to their ultimate success. The objectives of the training should be to get each area to acknowledge (1) their individual contribution to the success of the business, (2) their individual measures of success, and (3) their individual responsibility for achieving that success. This might be viewed as a company-wide consensus of the following points:

- The R&D laboratory is independently responsible for design quality as products are released to be manufactured and shipped. This implies all costs and measures of customer satisfaction with product design.

- The marketing department is independently responsible for the quality of the market analysis information and the product's sales tools. This also implies acceptance of all costs and measures of satisfaction for the marketing services.

- The manufacturing department is responsible for the outgoing quality of the processes used in manufacturing to produce and deliver the product. This also implies responsibility for the costs and measures of customer satisfaction for the manufactured product.

Once a consensus for these responsibilities is achieved, the organization is ready to move forward, but there will be many tests and failures of the ownership issues before the transition is complete. For example, what will happen when pressure is exerted to release a new product that can contribute significantly to needed revenues? Will the R&D manager push to get it released even though it is not quite ready? Or will the manager say up front that it's not ready and refuse to release it? The answer to these questions will determine whether or not R&D has accepted true responsibility for customer satisfaction with the design. The same questions can be asked of manufacturing managers who are confronted with quality problems or marketing managers who want to ship products without adequate documentation.

Motivation

An awareness of and consensus about our responsibilities are only the beginning steps. The next step is to ensure that the motivations are in place to cause actual changes. The reward, recognition, and admonishment for customer satisfaction must be realigned to agree with the new responsibilities. For example, the general manager may agree that the manufacturing manager is responsible for the quality of the manufactured product, yet future inquiries about manufacturing quality still may be directed to the quality assurance manager. This pseudo-transfer of responsibility leads to an erosion of the previously made agreement. The quality assurance manager will continue to be motivated to do all of the inspection to assure customer satisfaction. Subsequently, the manufacturing organization will not do it because they will believe that the quality assurance department is responsible for it.

Transition in the Manufacturing Environment

The next example illustrates how well this transition can be made if the manufacturing manager and the quality assurance manager work together in transferring the ownership of manufacturing quality responsibility. In November of 1984, the manufacturing manager and I, the quality assurance manager, were in the process of introducing TQC. At the time, we were struggling with the concepts of TQC and were trying to define our future strategies.

When our efforts began, we were a traditional Hewlett-Packard quality assurance and manufacturing organization. Electronic instruments were manufactured in a traditional production environment and then passed on to quality assurance, where they were inspected according to a defect-driven, progressive sample plan designed to guarantee a 2 percent outgoing quality level. At this time the defect rate was causing us to inspect about 50 percent of all products being shipped, and it was not getting any better. This was the state of affairs when we began making changes.

We first introduced into the division a comprehensive TQC training program that was aimed at awareness, motivation, and methods. We assigned people in both quality assurance and manufacturing to facilitate training the people in the division. The training involved the philosophies of TQC, process improvement, SQC, and quality teams — all of which we believed were the necessary ingredients for customer satisfaction and productivity improvements. These activities were and still are an important part of our system. In retrospect, however, the contribution made by this early training primarily increased our awareness.

When we attained a level of training where we had confidence that most of our people understood what we were trying to achieve, we decided to gamble with the ownership of a customer satisfaction issue. An analysis of our warranty data revealed that a disproportionate number of failures was occurring in the first six weeks of operation. Further analysis demonstrated that by reducing the number of these early failures to the level of the longer term failure rate, we would reduce warranty costs by 25 percent and would make significant improvement in customer satisfaction.

We then visited a few customers who were high-volume users of our products. They reported that the cosmetics and overall reliability of our products were excellent, but they were concerned about the early failure rate on a few of our product models; i.e., after early failures were detected and fixed, the products were very reliable. They complained that the kinds of problems being detected seemed to be due to poor workmanship.

93

From the customer visits and our own data, we decided that the emphasis on quality assurance was misplaced. Our inspection time had been equally divided between the cosmetic/mechanical inspections and the electrical tests that were conducted under ideal factory conditions. These procedures uncovered a lot of problems, but they were not necessarily the same problems the customers encountered. Furthermore, the problems were not being given needed attention by engineering. We decided to establish a complete new set of quality assurance procedures.

The new procedures were designed to do the following:

1. Identify the types of customer problems and complaints.

2. Establish a system for assuring problem ownership and implementing remedies.

3. Reduce the quality assurance worker's responsibility to manufacturing's quality problems.

The new procedure would be a fixed-rate sample plan. We had already learned that the progressive sample plan was a filter, at best, and that as long as the production people measured their performance by the quality assurance defect rate and not by customer defects, quality assurance would be guaranteed jobs in the future. This, combined with the belief that most of the reported problems did not have a direct relationship to customer satisfaction, gives you a good idea of why little action was taken to fix them.

We wanted manufacturing to understand that quality assurance would no longer be a filter in the production process. We therefore set the sample rate to be 20 percent of our outgoing production, based on a random sample. The remaining 80 percent was shipped directly to customers from the production line.

The tests that we established did two things: (1) we deemphasized cosmetics and magnifying glass mechanical inspections, and (2) we instituted temperature and vibration testing to duplicate the environment that a product would experience between our factory and the customers' acceptance tests. By deemphasizing mechanical inspections, we eliminated an inspection that was already being performed by the production line and that caused a great deal of controversy between quality assurance and manufacturing. The controversy had existed over the definition of rejects and over the interpretation of standards on issues that had little bearing on customer satisfaction. The ongoing controversy had created a credibility gap between the quality assurance and manufacturing organizations — and we were happy to end it. By instituting temperature and vibration testing, we uncovered many previously unseen defects that were causing serious customer problems.

The next part of the procedure established that a corrective action request (CAR) would be generated for each observed failure, and that it would be verified by both the production engineer and the supervisor before sending the product back to production. To find the cause, the engineer and the supervisor would review the product or process and then recommend and implement the changes to permanently fix the problem.

When an individual product exceeded two defects in 100 samples, quality assurance would call a meeting with the responsible management team and engineers to review that product. All previous CARs would be reviewed to verify that permanent fixes had been installed and/or manufacturing had put in place the necessary screens to weed out these problems. It was by mutual agreement that failure to prove that the problems would not recur would be justification for discontinuing shipments of that product until the fixes were installed.

These meetings — attended by the highest levels of management — ensured that a high level of motivation existed for manufacturing to take ownership of these problems and solve them. In the 12 months following the initiation of this procedure, we realized the following measures of success:

- Our early failures declined from an overall average of 3 percent of shipments to 1 percent of shipments — our goal.

- Our warranty defect rate declined by 25 percent (a savings of $300,000 per year).

- We reduced the number of inspection technicians from three to zero.

- Quality assurance has more credibility with manufacturing and has begun to focus its resources on other aspects of customer satisfaction.

Parallel with the emphasis on quality, the manufacturing organization had implemented other changes. They initiated a JIT production system and introduced some additional robotics in key areas. In the two years following the start of this new strategy, manufacturing reduced cycle times and work-in-process inventory to 15 percent of the starting levels. Additionally, the manufacturing cost — measured as a percent of sales — declined by 25 percent and is still declining. The focus of the manufacturing strategy is quality, cycle times, and cost. None of these improvements would have been possible without the commitment to quality.

Manufacturing's experience is truly a success story and provides the motivation to carry these philosophies forward into other functional areas. Each functional area of a business has equal opportunity for success by applying these principles. There isn't anything that the quality assurance department does that couldn't be eliminated if the other functional areas take responsibility for their own quality. This includes reliability and safety engineering, defect tracking and reporting, and inspection activities. Providing the motivation to make this happen is the responsibility of the management system.

Today's Research and Development Environment

R&D is a primary contributor to customer satisfaction and has many opportunities to improve by assuming its own quality responsibility. Typically, a product that is released to manufacturing falls short of meeting customer satisfaction expectations. The justification for its prerelease is always for business reasons, driven by economic pressures to get the new product to the market. The following list of problems is typical of a business where R&D has not taken ownership for its processes:

- The failure rate of newly released hardware products is several times higher than the mature failure rate, which often takes three years to achieve.

- Products are released with many known defects and without support of a warranty program.

- It is acceptable to release new software updates several times a year to make up for shortcomings in the original product.

- Software is often not available for months or even years after its introduction.

- The schedule for product introduction can slip 50 to 100 percent over the development phase.

- The first shipment sometimes occurs several months or years after the marketing release to sell has been issued.

Each of these problems and many others contribute to customer dissatisfaction and manufacturing inefficiencies; yet, we continue to justify them for business reasons. R&D's failure to look at everything it does as a process and to take responsibility for the outcome is the prime contributor to these problems.

Most businesses have quality assurance functions that support R&D activities much the same as they support manufacturing. The quality assurance functions have engineering quality assurance departments with engineers responsible for reliability testing, software quality assurance, and many other functions. Providing for these services means that an R&D function of 50 engineers might have 10 to 15 people in quality assurance to evaluate the quality and reliability of their work. This cost may represent 20 to 30 percent of the development cost. There are many justifications for this inefficiency, but they all seem to indicate that R&D engineers won't predesign quality and that they believe they are too valuable to test their own work.

Individual responsibility for quality is as much an issue for R&D as it is for manufacturing. Some people say that engineers are too familiar with their own designs; they may overlook too many things. Others say that engineers can't be expected to do the mundane task of testing their own work; it's a waste of their time. Any of these excuses, of course, are just that. They reflect the same attitude that has pervaded manufacturing processes. The engineering people also want to do good work and will do good work if given the opportunity. The engineers, just as the production workers, know the most about their products and processes. Therefore, they are the most capable of evaluating their designs if given the tools, the opportunity, and the incentive.

The strategy for bringing this about again relates to motivation. I have read about and seen many occurrences where software designs were introduced so riddled with defects that they were virtually unusable. The users would install the software and the system would crash, over and over, until the supplier finally had to make major design changes and rerelease the software. This is a standard practice in the software business where quarterly releases are not unusual. The motivation for the design team in today's environment is to get the products released as soon as possible to maximize revenue and establish market position. This motivation and the lack of clearly defined release criteria that truly represent the customers' needs work together to cause this problem.

If we look across America today, we can see many instances of this problem: cars that need frequent warranty repair, integrated circuits that have failure rates 10 times higher than our Japanese competitors, and

Japanese software products that have lower defect rates than ours. These differences exist, not because the Japanese are any less motivated to make money, but because they have taken the time to identify their customers' needs and have translated them into meaningful product release criteria. Once established, failure to meet the release criteria rests squarely on the integrity of the managers who make the decision. In Japan, integrity is a critical part of the management system.

Today's Marketing Department

Marketing greatly influences the efficiency of R&D and the manufacturing departments. It provides the knowledge of customer needs to the R&D department to establish the external specifications that must be developed. It provides the forecast that drives the manufacturing schedule. Marketing provides the technical interface between the factory and field sales force to enhance sales knowledge. It provides the documentation that is used by customers and sales people alike to sell, use, and repair products. It provides the training and technical backup to field people in support of post-sales problems. In summary, marketing is responsible for the processes that have the greatest influence on creating and satisfying customer expectations.

Creating false expectations is a leading cause of customer dissatisfaction. Consider the following list of questions as a means to evaluate the quality of the information that the marketing department provides to the business system:

- How often does marketing introduce new products at a show or at a sales seminar and promise them to customers within 12 weeks, only to finally ship them in 20 to 30 weeks?

- How many times does marketing tell R&D that if a product is developed with given features, it will sell 1,000 per month, only to sell 500.

- How many times does marketing sell 2,000 products, only to find out that the manufacturing department does not have the resources to build them?

- How often does marketing ship partial orders that will be of no value to customers until the other parts arrive?

- How often does marketing ship products with inaccurate or inadequate documentation?

These are just a few of the ways marketing may set false expectations and communicate bad information. Here again, this is an ownership issue. Until marketing takes responsibility for the processes and measures of customer satisfaction it controls, there will be no improvement. In the model for the factory of the future, an important element of the performance of the system was the review of customer satisfaction data. Marketing's role is to continuously review the customer's satisfaction with the product, analyze it, and make decisions about required changes. In most companies a big part of this responsibility is given to the quality assurance function, or else it is not measured at all. Consider the following generic product attributes:

- Functionality
- Usability
- Reliability
- Performance
- Serviceability
- Availability
- Price

In this list are probably only two attributes for which marketing has any real measures: price and availability. The measurement of reliability is almost always the responsibility of the quality assurance function; the other measurements become somewhat vague when specific numbers are sought. Yet, they are the most significant measures by which a product's price is established. Ask a marketing manager for the market value of a certain function and he or she can probably tell you what its selling price should be and what the potential revenue opportunity is. Then ask to see his or her tactical goals and strategies and see if there is a specific measure and goal assigned to product functionality. Chances are there are none, even though R&D is expected to design for specific functionality, usability, and serviceability.

When products become more complex, we seem to lose perspective of the specific market value for product attributes. The simplicity of a pen allows us to keep track of the market value of functionality, usability, etc.; but when we increase the product complexity, as in a test system, we lose track of the market value of these measures. How many marketing managers can tell you the impact of specific levels of reliability on orders? How many can tell you what their metric is for usability and what specific impact the level will have on orders? These are the measures marketing managers should be concerned about; as it is, the only thing they know how to measure is the order level compared to a forecast that was extrapolated from order history.

The Japanese approach to product definition has improved on that, but still it is not where it should be. They look at cost versus features, functions, and performance; they do an analysis of the market needs, and subsequently, design for the 80 percent solution. By ensuring that they meet 80 percent of the market needs with products that are lower priced and higher quality, they have assured themselves a dominant share of the market. They still have not developed the metrics to know the specific market value of a given level of functionality and the other product attributes, however. Doing this well is both a challenge and an opportunity.

Training Methods

When training people for TQC, there is a general set of tools that should be taught. These are the methods that were held common by the Deming Award-winning companies, Chrysler, and Harley-Davidson. Although detailed attention will be given to these methods in later chapters, they are briefly listed here for reference.

Quality Teams (Circles)

The training program should teach the basic purpose and functions of quality teams. Specific emphasis should be put on teamwork and group interaction. All aspects of the business' quality philosophy on quality should be emphasized. (See Chapter 8.)

Statistical Quality Control

SQC and SPC are the same and should be emphasized to all employees. Some companies provide different amounts of training to production workers and engineers. At Harley-Davidson, for example, all machine operators receive 20 hours of statistical training, engineers and administrative personnel receive 30 hours of training, and all foremen and managers receive 90 hours of in-depth training (Beels, 1985). (See Chapter 12.)

Common Problem-Solving Method

The common method of problem solving should be taught to all employees. This method can be taught as part of the SQC class. (See Chapter 11.)

Planning and Review

Each business should have a common method of planning and review. The method should be taught to all managers and supervisors in a formal workshop. It is not unusual for a structured planning and review system to require an eight- to 16-hour workshop. (See Chapter 7.)

Vendor Training

Material suppliers should be trained in the methods of SQC and TQC. While many may be large enough and motivated enough to provide their own training, others may be too small and unable to afford the investment required. Each business should understand that it is in its own best interest to provide this training where necessary. (See Chapter 10.)

Training Method

Some companies have found it desirable to take their people out of the plant for extended periods of time to provide this training over two or three weeks. My own experience with this is that the training will be much more valuable and lasting if taught as part of the job. For example, we decided that all people would be trained in these methods over a period of months. After the training material had been developed and the training personnel had been hired (two statisticians and two TQC trainers), most of our managers were trained in off-site workshops. We then decided that all nonmanagerial training would be done in individual work groups as part of a quality team. The time spent in training is the normal amount that each work group is expected to dedicate to quality team activities (one or two hours per week). The supervisor is the quality team leader and is expected to help facilitate the ongoing learning process. Over a 12-week period the quality team learns the quality philosophy, team skills, problem solving, and SQC. When training is completed, the quality team has been through an intense process improvement exercise for their area of responsibility.

Quality Organization

As quality deployment takes place many of the traditional functions of the quality assurance department will start to disappear. Tasks such as inspection will be the first to go and these jobs sometimes make up over half of the quality department. Other jobs such as reliability engineering will begin to decline as R&D takes on responsibility for the quality of their designs. The transition, from today's organization to the factory of the future, will call for significant changes in every aspect of the business.

We can let our imaginations create many scenarios about what these changes may mean to our own business. When all is said and done, however, the quality assurance department will indeed be the most affected because most of its services will no longer be necessary. As each functional area takes responsibility for its own quality, we will see less costly quality improvement in every process than we had previously thought possible.

Conclusion

The changes in the businesses that overcame a survival crisis all occurred because top management understood what needed to be done and did it. Being at the bottom possibly gives a person more courage to take risks. As Iacocca said just before the second oil crisis in 1979, "There was but one way to go and that was up." Today we are not talking about risk. The risk in focusing on quality as the first priority is gone; too many companies have demonstrated that this is the only way to survive in our new environment. Top management's unqualified commitment to quality is the essential motivation for employees to place quality before quantity.

References

Beels, Gregory J. "Strategy for Survival." *Quality Magazine,* April 1985.

Davis, Keith. *Human Relations at Work: The Dynamics of Organizational Behavior.* New York: McGraw-Hill Book Co., 1969.

Deming, W. Edwards. *Quality, Productivity, and Competitive Position.* Cambridge: Massachusetts Institute of Technology, 1982.

Herzberg, Frederick. "One More Time: How Do You Motivate Employees?" *Harvard Business Review,* Jan./Feb. 1968.

Iacocca, Lee. *Iacocca An Autobiography.* New York: Bantam Books, 1984.

Maslow, A. H. "A Theory of Motivation." *Psychological Review,* Vol. 50, 1943.

McGregor, Douglas M. *The Human Side of Enterprise.* Proceedings of the Fifth Anniversary Convocation of the School of Industrial Management. Cambridge: Massachusetts Institute of Technology, 1957.

San Jose Mercury News. May 6, 1987, San Jose, Calif.

American Business Experience with a Quality Team

A quality team was started in our shipping department to address the quality errors we were experiencing in an internal quality report. Before we started, shipping errors were at an unacceptable 3 percent rate.

The team's first efforts were to understand the major errors and determine their causes. We used a simple Pareto chart to track the errors; then we brainstormed to find their causes. The most common problems were: (1) a picklist that was inadequate to include accessories added by shipping, and (2) an inefficient layout in the shipping department. The team then set out to design a picklist that would break down all add-on accessories by part number and quantity. A computer programmer worked with us to design a software program that would automatically print the new picklist from our order processing and shipping systems. The team also worked with a process engineer to design a shipping area that was easier to work in and more efficient. These two changes cut the shipping error rate in half.

With these solutions in hand, we started the TQC process over again, but this time we used the QA audit as our source of data. We analyzed the data and determined that the largest problem was an incorrect product manual exceeding a scrap rate of 50 per month. At this time, we formed a manual task force that included members from component engineering, purchasing, and the shipping quality team.

Using the TQC model, we gathered manufacturing information and internal handling data; we visited the printers and determined a plan of action. Specfications were written and artwork was designed for the three-ring binder. Our suppliers were required to cover the manuals with paper, and we had to inspect them upon arrival; even the shelves in our shipping department were carpeted to protect them. The team's efforts resulted in a dramatic reduction of defective manuals; their scrap rate is now down to almost zero.

We are presently in the next step of our drive toward total quality. We are implementing a bar code verification system that will use the picklist data and verify, with bar codes, all shipping-added accessories. This program was designed by another division and modified by a programmer from manufacturing information systems. With this system, all customer-ordered and standard accessories will be bar code verified prior to packaging. A customer packing list will also be provided, listing the contents of the box.

All the changes and benefits derived in shipping are a result of much hard work and a commitment to quality improvement. The results in the internal quality report show shipping errors are less than 1 percent; the QA audit defects are down from 15 percent to 2.5 percent; and, due to our changes, the shipment integrity report is under the corporate goal of 0.3 percent. Our goal for continuous quality improvement is being achieved through teamwork and a desire to provide the best possible product for our customers.

Five Months Later

I would like to share with you some of our results since we implemented the bar code verification system in the shipping department.

The shipping error rate, based on the corporate shipment integrity report, went from 0.8 percent in September to 0.2 percent in October, and zero percent in November! The internal quality report had only one error in each of the last three months, two of which were damaged manuals. Based on quality assurance's audit of shipping errors, rate of missing and short shipments has dropped from the previous year's high of 10 percent to below the corporate goal of 0.3 percent.

CHAPTER 5

CUSTOMER SATISFACTION

Since customers provide the revenues that represent the lifeblood of the business, achieving customer satisfaction should be the primary focus of business. A customer's buying decision is based on the expectations that are created before the time of sale; these expectations come from many sources: previous satisfaction with your product, experience with competitors' products, and advertising and sales claims about your product. After ordering a product, the customer will be satisfied only to the extent that no disappointments occur. Therefore, the definition of customer satisfaction could be stated as the absence of disappointments or the absence of the elements of dissatisfaction.

In a dynamic, competitive environment it is doubtful that a perfect state of customer satisfaction exists. Customer expectations continuously rise as technology and competitive offerings improve. A business strives to improve as rapidly as its competitive environment improves, but always seems to lag because of the response of the system. Further satisfaction depends on whether the business can improve faster than its competitors, thereby commanding a greater share of the market.

It is virtually impossible for any given company to always be first with new technology. Customers often continue with a name brand, however, if they have confidence in their supplier; this is referred to as customer loyalty. Loyalty is built up over time if customers are consistently satisfied with a supplier's product. Competitors may occasionally offer higher performance or lower cost through new technologies, but most customers maintain name brand loyalty and know that their supplier will respond shortly. Loyalty does not last forever, though, and businesses must always work toward product improvement to ensure an acceptable level of customer satisfaction.

The *acceptable* level of customer satisfaction, however, may be far below the *possible* level of customer satisfaction. For example, a closed economic environment with only a few competitors existed in the U.S. auto industry 20 to 30 years ago. Then, customers were satisfied at an acceptable level with the products that American car manufacturers offered. The styling, the quality, the performance, and the low fuel efficiency fit the expectations of American culture. When the environment changed dramatically — as in 1973 with the fuel shortage — the story changed. The Japanese auto industry entered U.S. markets with more fuel-efficient cars, which the American public desperately needed.

This new need gave the Japanese a foothold in the American market. Once there, the Japanese demonstrated higher levels of quality, performance, and fuel efficiency. They set new standards for customer expectations. The Japanese demonstrated that a higher level of satisfaction was possible. To regain the lost market share, American manufacturers had to do more than improve fuel economy, and only now — 15 years later — are some American auto manufacturers showing signs of recovery.

The Chronology of Customers' Expectations

When customers buy a product, they have a set of expectations for that product. Customers are neither satisfied nor dissatisfied at any one particular time. Complete satisfaction or dissatisfaction is determined over the life of the product and begins when they decide to buy the product. For example, customers won't decide to buy the product if they are not already certain that the product is going to satisfy their needs. This decision is influenced by the level of communication that takes place between them and the seller. The degree of customer satisfaction will be the result of the product being received and used, and then failing (dissatisfaction) or succeeding (satisfaction), over the life of the product. This occurs over a long period of time, referred to here as the customer life cycle. Let's consider some customer expectations over the customer life cycle.

Before the sale:

- The specifications must not be ambiguous; they must relate to the product's intended application.

- The regulatory requirements that the product meets must be clear; i.e., safety and health standards.

- That the product will function correctly in the customer's intended environment must be clear.

- The delivery information must be reliable.

- All product capability must be clear.

After delivery:

- The product was received by the customer when promised.

- The shipment contains everything expected and needed to use the product.

- Operating and setup instructions are clear and complete.

- The product functions as expected.

- The product is received defect free.

- The product use is easy to learn.

After setting up, learning to operate, and ready to use:

- The product meets specifications and stays that way.

- The product is reliable over time.

- There is easy verification of continued conformance to specifications.

As the product ages:

- Preventative maintenance is clear, easy, and economical.

- Product repair is economical.

- Factory or service center repairs are handled promptly.

- Spare parts are easily available and reasonably priced.

- Spare parts are available for the life expectancy of the product.

These are just a few of the expectations a customer may have of a supplier. Each business should modify this list to reflect its customer base and to understand any product shortcomings. Once customer expectations are known, a business must satisfy them by implementing the necessary organizational processes. Where customer dissatisfaction does exist, an improvement process should be implemented to increase the level of customer satisfaction.

Customer Satisfaction Growth Model

Product or customer satisfaction growth modeling is an effective tool for understanding and managing the relationships between customer expectations and product performance. A growth model is also valuable for assessing the appropriate organizational needs and determining measures of customer satisfaction. Figure 5.1 illustrates a model that can be used to satisfy this need. It should serve for most manufacturing businesses, and, with a little imagination, can be adapted to other types of businesses as well.

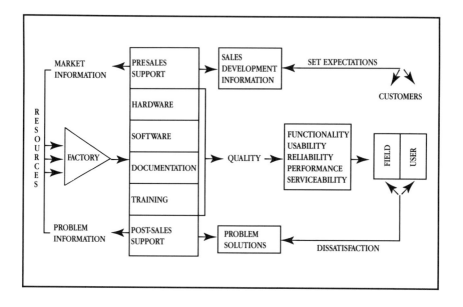

Figure 5.1 Customer Satisfaction Growth Model

Customer Expectations

The customer's expectations are based on needs. If the need exists, the customer will search for a product until it is found. The customer's search is also determined by past experience in the marketplace with similar types of products. Customer expectation is enhanced by known technology changes and by competitors' advertising claims. This set of expectations is relative to the customer's need and will not change unless the need changes or technological progress creates a new customer awareness of product capability.

Presales Support

The presales support function is part of the marketing interface responsibility. It encompasses customer contacts, product advertising, and other communication forms that set customer expectations. The market interface function (marketing) is also responsible for understanding customer needs, customer expectations, and competitive products. The information is collected, analyzed, and forwarded to the design group. The information is then used to define the external requirement specifications (ERS) of new products, thus contributing to a continued product improvement and customer satisfaction.

The Factory

The factory is made up of design, manufacturing, and support processes. All new product information is created in design and is handed over to manufacturing when the design work is complete according to the ERS. Manufacturing will receive all of the documentation, specifications, and tooling required to consistently build and ship the product according to the ERS. This will include specifications for FURPSAP, an acronym for:

- Functionality
- Usability
- Reliability
- Performance
- Supportability
- Availability
- Price

These will be defined in more detail in Chapter 6.

Manufacturing creates the processes to build the product as designed and to alter it as required by the changes in the environment. The changes may come from a number of sources: vendor part performance, part obsolescence, process modifications, or product enhancements. The shipped item may include various elements; for example, a computer product may include needed hardware, special software, or user information

The Product

The elements of a product, as previously defined, represent all or part of the solution to a customer need. When they are provided together as the solution, they collectively represent the product. For example, consider a complex computer product where the solution may involve hardware, software, documentation, and training. A simple product could be defined by only one of the elements.

Quality

The quality of the product is determined by how effectively the entire product meets the customer's expectations. When measuring the quality of a complex product, the FURPSAP measures must be compared to the total product; however, FURPSAP can be applied to an individual element of the product, as will be explained later.

FURPSAP Defined

FURPSAP represents a generic set of product attributes that a customer uses to make buying decisions. They are introduced here to facilitate the definition of the model. This chapter is limited to a discussion of the definitions of FURPSAP and how they apply to customer satisfaction. Chapter 6 proposes some specific ways to measure and evaluate the relative values of FURPSAP.

Customer Satisfaction

Once the customer's expectations are set and the item is received, the product attributes should provide sufficient quality to satisfy the customer. If they don't, a set of dissatisfiers will appear for which compensation must be made. A business generally staffs a support organization to provide prompt response to these problems.

Post-Sales Support

The post-sales support group is normally part of the marketing/customer interface group. This support organization represents the service departments and other customer service groups. It is responsible for providing solutions to the set of customer dissatisfiers; sometimes it does so at great profit by selling its services. This group also collects information about customer problems (dissatisfaction) and passes it back to the factory. The information is then used to identify needed changes to improve the product or processes, therefore improving customer satisfaction.

Closing the Loop

When both the presales and post-sales groups actively pass information along to the factory — and when the factory systematically improves the product — a state of continuous improvement exists for the product. If this product improvement process occurs faster than the customer expectations change, then a state of growth exists for customer satisfaction. It is important to point out that product improvement occuring at the same rate as the change of customer expectations does not result in the growth of customer satisfaction. A business that continuously improves its product can still lose its market share if the improvement process is too slow.

FURPSAP Definitions

As previously defined, a complex product has a set of measures that relates to customer satisfaction; these are the FURPSAP measures. When considering the product (hardware, documentation, or training), it is important to view each part as making a contribution to the whole. A product manual, for example, may stand on its own in some applications (like a how-to booklet sold for profit) and have its own quality measures. But, when taken as part of the product, it must be viewed by the contribution it makes to the effectiveness of the product. This is true for each element of the product. For example, a book has its own measures of quality as a separate product — its functionality, usability, reliability, etc. When considered part of a bigger product, the only important factor is the contribution that it makes to the product's FURSAP attributes. As such, a product manual becomes an extension, or an enhancement, to the product.

Product manuals containing operating instructions and/or installation procedures, have a somewhat universal application and therefore make an excellent example for defining the elements of FURPSAP. In the following definitions, the FURPSAP attributes relate to more complex product information, but they could apply to any product that requires documentation.

Functionality

The function of the product manual is to communicate information about a product. The following is information that documentation needs to communicate:

- Specifications
- Product features, capability, and intended use
- Installation/assembly procedures
- Operation/performance verification tests
- Troubleshooting information
- Operating procedures
- Replacement parts lists
- Repair procedures

Usability

The product manual should be user friendly and easy to read and follow. Typical considerations for usability include:

- Table of contents
- Index
- Glossary
- Prioritization/organization
- Optimum quantity of information
- Correct literacy level (vocabulary relative to intended users)

Reliability

The accuracy of the product manual can affect the perceived reliability of the product if it misleads users on the operation, specifications, and diagnostic information of that product. The reliability of the documentation is determined by the following:

- Typographically correct information

- Diagnostically correct information (accurate identification of failures)

- Correct and validated operating procedures, installation procedures, etc.

- Correct and clear information throughout

Performance

A product manual that does not make a contribution to enhancing the product's use is wasted. As a matter of fact, it should be a challenge to the product designer to design products that are intuitively easy to use and that save redundant information. Areas where a product manual typically saves time are:

- Assembly and installation

- Product learning cycle

- Task accomplishment (productivity of use)

- Diagnostics/troubleshooting efforts

Supportability

User costs to keep products operating and manuals current include those related to repairs, calibration, and preventative maintenance. The elements of the manual that can influence these costs are:

- Type of manual update service provided; i.e., change sheets, replacement pages, new manuals, etc.

- Completeness of service instructions

- Accuracy of parts lists and repair information

Availability

Product manual availability relates to both new and old products. If a producer is in the habit of shipping new products without adequate documentation (preliminary documentation, in some cases), the customer will not get the full benefit of the product. If customers lose old manuals, they need to have access to manuals that reflect their product's vintage, not the new manuals currently available. The opposite is also true; when a product is updated, the manual also needs to be updated.

Price

The product manual makes a definite contribution to the price of a product. In the software industry, it is not unusual for an operating manual to represent more of the manufacturing cost than the product itself represents. The manual also makes a contribution to the customer's total cost of ownership and should not be ignored. For example, if the producer is skimpy with service information, the customer could incur large repair costs over the life of the product. Consideration should be given to the various levels of documentation, the repair strategy, and the customer's total cost of ownership.

Conclusion

Customer expectations are continuously on the rise. A business will be successful to the extent that its product growth rises faster than its customer expectations. This is known as customer satisfaction growth. There are many aspects to customer satisfaction that take years to materialize. Businesses must be organized, with resources allocated to provide for long-term customer satisfaction. The measures of customer satisfaction referred to as FURPSAP represent a generic set of attributes that can be used to evaluate a product's merits relative to its competition. Chapter 6 elaborates on FURPSAP and proposes methods to measure and compare these attributes.

CHAPTER 6

ORGANIZATIONAL MEASURES

Ensuring that everyone in the business focuses on the right things is the primary function of the leadership process. Making certain that the emphasis applies to customer needs will ensure that everyone in the business is treating customer satisfaction as the top priority. This is done through careful selection of our organizational metrics — the measures used to plan for and evaluate the business' effectiveness.

Planning is a critical element of competitive fitness. An effective planning system, however, requires a manager to first identify the elements of the business that are to be improved. Organizational metrics are the measures of the product attributes and the organizational effectiveness. The organizational metrics should be viewed as the structure of the building around which all of the product plans, strategies, and goals will be wrapped. Therefore, it is necessary that this framework be built and bolted tightly together before developing the goals and strategies to be used for improving the performance measures. This chapter develops the definitions for a set of organizational metrics for a manufacturing business, and the next chapter will present a method for planning and review.

Every organization is hierarchical in some way. Viewed from top management, the business plans and measures are defined in general terms — similar to a mission statement — and the definitions for plans and measures become more specific as we proceed down through the organization. A business that is well organized has clear ties both vertically and horizontally in the way the responsibilities are defined for the different functions. Since each of the functions exists to make a contribution to the mission of the business, its measures of performance should be linked accordingly. Building a framework of measures is comparable to building the organizational framework. Similarly, the measures do not change over time; they remain as constant as the mission and the organization of the business. The permanence of the organizational metrics provides management with the incentive to spend more time defining the measures at the beginning of the planning process.

Many efficiency and quality problems can be solved by developing a set of hierarchical metrics. An example of this is the statement made by a R&D manager when attending a project review meeting. He said, "Translating from an external requirements specification to a product definition is still pretty much a black magic process." This common problem results from an absence of clearly defined product attributes that are measurable relative to customer needs. In this situation it is difficult to specify product performance, functionality, and reliability before starting the design. Consequently, R&D will incur considerable rework expense as the product definition changes. Further, some projects may be canceled because the product didn't meet the market's need.

Another example relates to new products that are prematurely released to the manufacturing department. Because of this, the manufacturing department incurs high engineering costs, shipment delays, and poor customer satisfaction. Also, the mature product support (service) department will be burdened with higher costs, eating up valuable resources. This will occur when there are no measures to determine when a new product is ready to release, i.e., when it meets all customer needs. Often, new product release decisions are based on the subjective feelings of managers, whose decisions are strongly influenced by pressure to get the new product to market. This type of criteria is inadequate because most managers will decide in favor of release when there are no objective measures to dictate otherwise. When objective measures are present and goals have been set, product release becomes a matter of management and organizational integrity.

Examples of this nature abound in R&D, manufacturing, and marketing. Eliminating these problems requires definitions for the measures and goals, and the establishment of individual ownership. Someone once said, "When you measure something it gets better; when you measure it and report it, it gets better faster."

The Business System and Its Metrics

When a business is better than its competitors at delivering products with the appropriate attributes, and when it is more productive than the others, it will be the most successful. The task here is to identify the measures and responsibilities for each of these success factors.

There are four categories of metrics. Within these four categories, 18 primary measures make up the framework around which a typical manufacturing business operates. They will form the core for the plans and strategies of the company products, the production processes, and the business markets. These metrics start with revenue growth and profit and develop into measures that contribute toward growth and profit. They are categorized as:

1. Product Attribute Performance (for order growth):

   Measures how effectively a product meets the need of the market/ customer.

2. Market Interface Performance (for order growth):

   Measures how effectively a business interfaces with the market to understand present and future needs, and how effective it is at generating awareness, sales, and distribution of the business' products.

3. Capacity Performance (for shipment growth):

   Measures the production capacity of the business.

4. Process Productivity Performance (for profit growth):

   Measures how efficiently a business uses all its resources in providing for the other performance measures.

Figure 6.1 is a hierarchical organization chart showing a typical manufacturing business with the operational functions of R&D, marketing, and manufacturing. We will use this illustration to identify the measures of performance and responsibilities for the organization at each level.

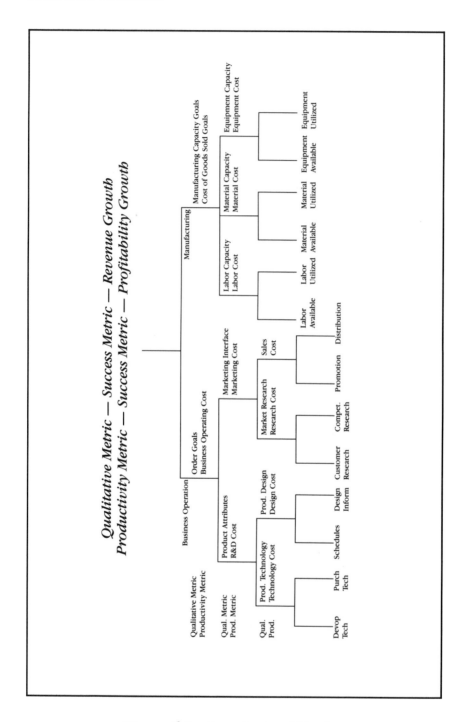

Figure 6.1 Organizational Metrics

Corporate Objectives

Most businesses have a set of corporate objectives or philosophies that describe the business' attitude about customers, employee relations, fields of interest, profit, growth, etc. For Hewlett-Packard, these are known as the seven corporate objectives that were set forth by Dave Packard and Bill Hewlett as operating philosophies early in the development of the company. Through the years these objectives have changed very little; they have stood the test of time as being the embodiment of the founders' beliefs and the foundation of their success. Today they represent the Hewlett-Packard culture, the Hewlett-Packard way, and are the framework for other operating policies. None of these objectives, however, sets forth specific measures or goals for employees to work toward. Such measures are left up to the operating entities, to be defined as part of their intermediate and annual planning cycles.

Business Success Measures

A business' success is traditionally evaluated on its financial merits. Today its financial success is often dependent on its contribution to society in the way it provides for pollution control, fair and healthy work surroundings, as well as other, sometimes expensive, improvements to environmental and social welfare. Business leaders almost always acknowledge a responsibility to society in their corporate objectives, and almost always point out that the best way they can contribute to society is through financially healthy growth. It is through growth and profit that jobs are provided and revenues are made available to stockholders, taxes, and other societal needs. Revenue and profit growth therefore become the primary measures of success at the business highest level.

Revenue growth is determined by order and shipment growth. Orders would have little value if the business did not have the ability to deliver the products; conversely, manufacturing capacity would have no value if we had no orders. Three functions in a business make primary contributions to orders and shipments: marketing, R&D, and manufacturing. Marketing and R&D influence orders most heavily through the design of the product and the effectiveness of the sales programs. R&D and manufacturing influence shipments through the product design and manufacturing's capacity. These are the areas to be looked at first.

Product Attributes (FURPSAP)

As indicated in Chapter 5, product attributes are generically defined as listed below:

- Functionality
- Usability
- Reliability
- Performance
- Supportability*
- Availability
- Price

Functionality

Product functionality is the set of functions and features provided by a product according to market needs. In a simple product, functionality is usually narrow; in a complex product, however, it can become complicated. For example, the functionality of a pencil could be described as a tool for writing on paper with erasure capability; for a typewriter, it might be to permanently print letters, numerals, and punctuation on paper by pressing individual keys on a keyboard; for a word processor, etc. And it goes on and on.

Each product type has some characteristic functionality requirements, and each manufacturer provides different levels of functionality. To gage functionality relative to competitors, an index is needed. The index can be calculated by creating a matrix, as shown in Figure 6.2. In this example a comparison is made of the functionality of the three levels of technology. The matrix specifies the functionality requirements for a market and assigns a number of weighted importance to it; each product is then assigned a percentage of the weight, depending on how well it provides that element of functionality. The totals are added and comparisons are made between the products.

---

*Author's note: The term *supportability* is interchangeable with *serviceability* for products that are service-oriented. For example, computer software: We tend to think of its requirements for support and not service as we do for hardware.

Possible Function	Word Processor	Typewriter	Pencil	Points
Keyboard entry	10	10	0	10
Multiple fonts	9	9	0	9
Easy edit capability	8	2	1	8
Paperless file system	7	0	0	7
Easy reproduction	6	4	4	6
Totals (index)	40	25	5	40

Figure 6.2   Functionality Matrix

More functional aspects exist than are shown here, but the disparity between these three products is obvious. To construct such a matrix, each business needs to know in detail its market and product functionality requirements. When complete, the matrix can be used for making competitive product comparisons, and each new product proposal should have a functionality index goal assigned to ensure its acceptance in the marketplace. To achieve this, a comparison of this type must be made.

Usability

Usability is a measure of the implementation of the user interface, which determines how easy it is to get to the functionality of the product. This includes difficulty of installation, need for user training, and ease of manageability. For example, a black box may be capable of several functions that can be accessed through two different user paths. One is through push buttons on the front panel; the other is by remote access through a digital interface cable. The usability would be different for the two different methods of access. Each method could also vary, depending on the user documentation and instructions provided. Some functions may be easy to implement by pushing a single button or giving a single command; however, others may be difficult, requiring complicated sequences to implement the functionality.

121

The level of usability can be defined in numerical terms that can be used for setting project objectives relative to the customer's needs and the competitor's products. When this is done properly, the progress can be tracked throughout the project and then used as part of the design release criteria. The following formula can be used as a guide for determining usability. The index can be calculated by totaling the cost factors, then dividing the sum by the selling price of the product. This determines the usability cost as a percent of the selling price. Figure 6.3 shows an example of usability.

Formula:

Installation or Preparation Costs + Installation and Operating Manual Cost + Cost of User Training + Average Cost of Time to Exercise a Function ÷ Product Selling Price = Usability Index.

Product Selling Price	$5,000
Installation or Preparation Cost	$100
Installation and Operating Manual Cost	$30
Cost of User Training	$200
Average Cost of Time to Exercise a Function	$5
Total Usability Cost	$335

$$\text{Usability Index} = \frac{\$335}{\$5,000} = .067 \text{ or } 6.7\% \text{ of Selling Price}$$

Figure 6.3   Example of Usability

Reliability

Reliability is a measure of the product's ability to perform to its specifications over a period of time. It is usually a simple calculation, expressed as annual failure rate (AFR) or mean time between failure (MTBF). Unfortunately, it is rarely treated as an important part of the product attribute until it becomes a problem. Many people believe that customers do not care about reliability above a certain level; but when a certain threshold is crossed there is a negative impact on sales. This may be true, but these same people do not have the slightest idea where that threshold is. Varying with the customers and depending on the market norms, it seems to be like many other product attributes that aren't monitored regularly. If we kept close track of sales relative to reliability, a well-defined relationship between orders and reliability would occur that looks like the curve shown in Figure 6.4.

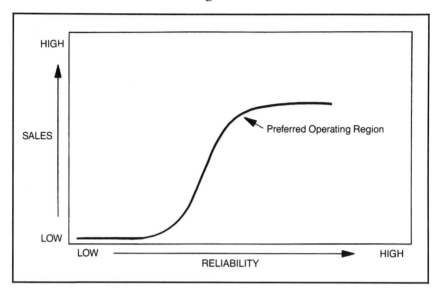

Figure 6.4   Sales versus Reliability

At very low levels of reliability, sales are low and do not increase significantly until product reliability approaches industry norm. At this point sales pick up rapidly until reliability exceeds industry norm; then, sales level off again and do not change much with further reliability improvements. The goal is to operate each product in the knee of the curve — above the norm for a particular industry. This goal requires statistical analysis of the market to determine sales sensitivity in relation to product reliability. It also requires a business to understand industry norms for the reliability of its product type.

Performance

The measures for product performance relate to the product's specifications as they apply to the functionality of the product. Each industry has unique functionality requirements and performance specifications, and they are typically the points of differentiation from competitors. Product performance is usually defined in terms of its accuracy, response, and efficiency. Performance is easily quantified and should be a part of the external requirements specified in the project goals; a performance index can be structured in the same manner as the functionality index.

Supportability

In this example we will use the hardware-oriented form of service. Serviceability is a measure of the owner's cost to maintain the continuous services of the product purchased (sometimes it is referred to as cost of ownership). Several factors go into calculating product serviceability and should be considered as part of the project goals, since they have a direct impact on customer satisfaction and orders.

A serviceability index can be calculated for products as the sum of the costs divided by the selling price. Figure 6.5 shows an example of serviceability.

Formula:

> Cost of Service Documentation + Average Annual Cost of Repair + Average Annual Cost of Calibration or Preventative Maintenance + Annual Cost of Downtime [Annual Failure Rate X (Days to Repair/220 Days) X Selling Price] ÷ Selling Price = Serviceability Index

Selling Price	$5,000
Cost of Service Documentation (sometimes included in selling price)	$30
Average Annual Cost of Repair	$40
Average Annual Cost of Calibration or Preventative Maintenance	$200
Annual Cost of Downtime = .1 X .05 X $5000 = (AFR = 10%) (average repair time = $\frac{10 \text{ days}}{220 \text{ workdays}}$ = .05 years)	$25
Total Serviceability Cost	$295

$$\text{Serviceability Index} = \frac{\$295}{\$5,000} \text{ or } .059 \text{ or}$$

5.9% of Selling Price

Figure 6.5   Example of Serviceability

Availability

Availability applies both to new products under development and current products under production. For the new products, it is the date of release and shipment to customers; for the current products, it is the average delivery time from order date. This is a key attribute that will highly affect the product's market acceptance. New products released a year overdue may have low sales because of new competitive entries. Likewise, current products having long lead times may encourage buyers to seek alternate vendors. Metrics should be assigned and monitored for each product, beginning in the project definition phase and monitored throughout the life of the product.

A measure that can be used to track R&D's timeliness in delivering new products is called the slip factor. At the beginning of each product's design cycle, a completion schedule is set; as the product progresses in its development, it may move ahead or behind its original schedule. The slip factor is the total number of weeks or months that the revised completion date changes from the original completion date. This is expressed as a percent of the original amount of time a product was scheduled to take. The slip factor can be used on individual products or can be used as a cumulative measure for the performance of the R&D function.

The slip factor is a key business measure, since sales are often dependent on the introduction time of new product. The accurate prediction of introduction time could allow a business more insight for better ROI analyses before starting new projects. You may have had personal experience with products that were years late, which you may not have started had you foreseen their delay.

Price

Price is a key attribute that will always affect a product's acceptance. Typically, price-performance measures of a product include a somewhat ambiguous definition of performance. Applied here, price performance relates to the performance of all the previously mentioned attributes. The product definition should clearly spell out the performance expectations for each attribute and state the expected effect each will have on product's lifetime revenue. When all indices for the product attributes have been defined, it is possible to construct a meaningful price-performance curve.

Summary of the FURPSAP Attributes

Specific measures and goals for these attributes are to be established at the beginning of a new product's life cycle; it is then possible to track the product's performance throughout its life. It is also possible to ensure the contributions that different organization members make to these measures; this is done through the planning process. The planning process contributes to product success by identifying each department's role in goal achievement and by assigning responsibility for the measures. This is done by using a product attribute responsibility matrix (Figure 6.6).

Attribute	R&D	Marketing	Manufacturing	Quality Assurance	Finance	Personnel
Functionality	d	d	i	n	n	n
Usability	d	d	i	n	n	n
Reliability	d	d	d	i	n	n
Performance	d	d	d	i	n	n
Serviceability	d	d	i	n	n	n
Availability	d	d	d	n	n	n
Price	d	d	d	n	i	i

d — direct influence   i — indirect influence   n — no influence

Figure 6.6   Product Attribute Responsibility Matrix

During the planning process the business will set specific goals for each of these attributes, based on market needs and competitive analysis. The goals should be applied to each product in development and should be included in the goal set and strategies of each functional area that directly or indirectly influences it. For example, if the goal for usability is to achieve an index of X percent of selling price, it should show up on the goal sets of R&D, marketing, and manufacturing. Each area will have the same goal statement but will have different strategies for contributing toward its achievement. Let's examine the four contributing elements of usability.

1. *Installation Cost.* The installation cost could be significant for a complicated system. R&D usually is responsible for the design of the interfaces; therefore it would also be partially responsible for the installation cost. Marketing, however, also is responsible because it usually is responsible for the determination of the system

integration strategy; i.e., do we integrate the system at the factory, or do we ship it to the customer and let the customer figure it out? The design and integration strategies will also dictate the level of documentation needed by the customer (which is also a separate component of the usability index). In this example, both R&D and marketing directly influence the installation cost, while manufacturing indirectly influences it. Manufacturing's influence is determined by the level of quality achieved in making the products used in the system. Each of these areas should have specific strategies for installation cost as it relates to the usability index goal.

2. *Operating Manual Cost.* The cost of the operating manual has a big impact on the installation cost and the ease of product use. This is true because the manual cost is partially related to the quantity and the quality of the contents. The marketing department traditionally has responsibility for the cost of the manual; the user friendliness design of the product also has an effect on the documentation cost. Since R&D has design responsibility, it should also have cost reduction strategies for the manual. When both marketing and R&D share this responsibility, it can be expected that more integrated designs will be achieved. R&D will think more about the design of the user interfaces and will work toward the elimination of large, expensive operating manuals. This is especially important in the computer industry, where several volumes of manuals are not unusual for a single software product. Therefore, a need exists in R&D for more human interaction and more usability testing as part of the release criteria.

3. *Cost of User Training.* Many products are on the market that require extensive training for the users to become proficient in their operation. The reasons for user training are similar to those for operating documentation — training is the natural extension of the extra documentation needed for more complex, less user friendly designs. Marketing and R&D directly influence the cost of user training; both departments should base their common goal strategies on competitive market information.

4. *Average Cost of Time to Exercise a Function.* This relates to the user friendliness of the product. Complicated procedures, extensive menu changes, frequent setup changes, and poor designs all contribute to this measure. Every product should have available specific metric data to reflect the competitive need. Each of the functional departments has a contribution to make and should reflect it in their plans and strategies.

127

Market Interface Attributes

The product order level is also affected by the marketing interface. The market interface attributes relate to marketing and competititve research, customer awareness, and sales and distribution processes. Each of the business functions contributes to these attributes just as they contributed to the product attributes. We will analyze the market interface attributes and build a responsibility matrix as we did for the product attributes.

Market Research

Market research is intended to collect and analyze information about customer needs, market growth, competitor products, financial data, technology developments, and advertisement and distribution results. It is difficult to define the specific numerical measures of performance needed to compare competitors and trends, but it is possible. By having these measures, you will know whether you are investing properly in this area and whether you are getting the most from the investment. This information can also help you to establish the goals for product attributes, as previously identified and measured.

If you could read your customers' minds, you would be able to understand their buying motivations and their perceptions of your products. The normal lag time between a perceived need and a new product is too long to measure product performance through customer response. It is usually unknown if the market was gaged accurately until it is too late, but one way to improve the interface and judge customer attitudes is through customer surveys. By collecting the correct survey information, it is possible to create indices of buyers' attitudes toward your products; this index provides a gage of market interface performance.

The survey should be constructed so that it reveals the following information:

- Who are the buyers of your product type?

- How many of these products do they buy each year?

- How many of the products purchased are yours versus your competitors?

- Which pro or con factors of your product influenced their buying decision?

The survey can be as broad as you choose to make it. For example, your customers may choose to buy or not buy your product for any number of reasons. The following is a partial list that may represent positive or negative factors for motivating your customers to buy your products:

- Sales force presence
- Product awareness
- Sales force competence
- Past and present compatibility
- FURSAP attributes
- Service support
- Documentation

With this information we can create the ncessary indices to evaluate our present position and to monitor future changes with additional surveys. The indices will reflect the ratio of business lost or the opportunity for gain based on these responses:

- Market size
- Market share for each product
- Total market share for the business
- Largest to smallest influence (from the previous list) on the buyers' decisions

By analyzing this information you may find that you have 20 percent of the market; several of the indices may be predominantly in your favor while one, like reliability, is totally unfavorable. You might also find that 10 percent more customers would buy your product if you improved reliability. This type of analysis will help you to identify the specific actions needed to improve your market share. From here, the information is integrated into the goals and strategies, and the future results are monitored as part of the planning and review process. A responsibility matrix should also be created that ensures that the hierarchical relationships are properly established. The measures included in this category relate to advertising effectiveness (sometimes referred to as marketing communication processes) and the sales and distribution processes.

Figure 6.7 is an example of the responsibility matrix for the market interface attributes. This list of measures may be expanded to suit individual businesses and organizations; an explanation of these relationships follows the matrix.

Attribute	R&D	Marketing	Manufacturing	Quality Assurance	Finance	Personnel
Customer Awareness	i	d	i	i	n	n
Sales Presence	d	d	d	d	n	n
Sales Competence	i	d	n	n	n	n
Responsiveness	d	d	d	d	d	n

d — direct influence   i — indirect influence   n — no influence

Figure 6.7 Responsibility Matrix — Market Interface Attributes

Customer Awareness

Advertising, trade shows, and personal contacts contribute to customer awareness. Should customer surveys indicate that many potential customers are unaware of your products and their capability, you might conclude that either you are not spending enough money here or you are spending it on the wrong things. Marketing directly influences this metric by controlling the organization and the budget responsible for these activities. Other functions like R&D, manufacturing, and quality assurance can influence this metric through customer visits and company exposure through publication of articles in trade journals, etc.

Sales Presence

Where is the salesperson when needed? Standing behind the counter having coffee? Golfing with other clients? Sitting in an office doing paperwork? These are just a few of the reasons you might not find him or her when needed. How many orders have been lost because your salesperson wasn't around when needed? How often do salespersons talk to and call on each customer? Sales presence is an important aspect of competitive position that should be monitored closely. Many people relate Japan's limited success in the U.S. industrial electronics market to lack of sales presence. They have not yet developed the sales force and distribution channels that will provide them with personal access to many of our domestic markets. The marketing organization is directly responsible for this metric; others should have strategies that influence their results where applicable.

130

Some department stores are notorious for the absence of sales people when needed. Conversely, a store like the Seattle-based chain, Nordstrom's, has a reputation for salespeople contacting a customer several times in just a few minutes, each asking customers if they can assist in some way. It is no coincidence that Nordstrom's is the fastest-growing department store in the west. Salesperson presence is an important metric for a small shop, a department store, or a complex sales network that requires remote sales calls. If competent, the salesperson who is there to make the closing sale will always get the most orders.

Sales Competence

How can a bad salesperson ruin a sure sale? Here's an example: My wife and I recently went into an electronics warehouse outlet showroom to buy a microwave oven. There were no less than 25 product models on display. A salesperson approached and asked us what we were looking for; since we were in the middle of the microwave department, I suggested a microwave oven. He pointed out the hottest bargain on the floor and compared its merits to other models. After listening to him for several minutes, I was ready to buy; my wife, though, wanted a demonstration. The salesman stumbled through the instruction manual for several minutes, making a simple procedure look complicated. Finally, my wife suggested that this model was too confusing for her and that we should look around for a while. The salesperson was annoyed and left. While my wife browsed, I read the instruction manual and found out actually how simple it was to operate. I demonstrated it for her, and we decided to buy it — in spite of the salesman's incompetence. We concluded the sale with another, more congenial salesman.

Business is abundant with examples of this nature. Had I not been a persistent optimist, saying, ''This microwave can't be as complicated as he makes it seem,'' I am sure we would not have bought this model. My wife had been so annoyed with the salesman that she wouldn't have bought anything from the store if I hadn't soothed her ruffled feathers. Every business needs a gage to measure its salespeople's competence. This can be accomplished by the suggested survey method or by simply providing customer feedback cards at the point of purchase.

Responsiveness

The president of Hewlett-Packard Company, John A. Young, once reported that he frequently calls Hewlett-Packard sales offices to see what kind of response he gets. This approach to testing responsiveness can be very effective for cursory evaluation, but it does not provide a consistent measure by which the overall responsiveness of the organization can be determined. To do this we need to consistently gage how long it takes to get answers to questions, how long it takes to service a product warranty failure, and how long it takes to make a sales proposal. These are the important elements of responsiveness.

Post-sales support is probably the biggest single contributor to responsiveness and to customer satisfaction in business today. As a customer, I don't want to buy anything from a store that is going to hassle me when I have a problem with one of its products; this includes retail businesses, mail order outlets, and large computer firms. When a product doesn't meet the expectation that was established at the time of sale, it should be handled in a prompt, courteous, and fair manner. Too often we see businesses that will argue endlessly to establish that the product failed due to customer mistreatment. Software manufacturers will tell you point blank that defects are to be expected; that unless you buy an update service, you are out of luck when it comes to getting their help on problems. Almost every electronic and appliance outlet will try and sell you a service agreement that extends the warranty, knowing full well that is profitable business for them and not cost effective for the buyer — unless, of course, they sold you a lemon. For the lemon, manufacturers should extend the warranty without charge — but few manufacturers will do this.

Most businesses have a long way to go in creating the correct level of responsiveness, but those that have found it are proving daily that it is a more profitable way to run a business.

When a business has created products with the correct attributes and has established the market interface attributes, it will be in a position to generate the most orders. Ultimate success will be limited only by its efficient use of resources and by its capacity to produce or supply its products.

Capacity

Capacity is defined as the maximum possible system output. For the manufacturing business, this means production capacity. When I think of how many times I have stood in line to buy something, I usually think of system capacity. When I call a contractor and ask how soon he can do some work for me and he says four weeks, I think of system capacity. When I want to buy a new car that takes 10 weeks to receive, I think of system capacity. Most of us are not fond of waiting to buy what we want and we will find an alternative whenever possible. If not properly managed, capacity can be the limiting factor on a business' revenue growth.

When we make decisions about people to hire, material to purchase, and equipment to buy, we are making capacity decisions. Capacity is something that is bought, and it is a cost of doing business. Efficiency is a measure of capacity utilization. Designs, equipment, people, and procedures determine maximum capacity; but when we choose to operate at less than maximum level, we lower our efficiency. For example, buildings and equipment are capable of operating 24 hours a day, less maintenance time. If we decide to operate our factory for one eight-hour shift a day, we have arbitrarily limited our equipment efficiency to 33 percent capacity.

Three aspects of production capacity must be provided for in the organizational metrics: labor, material, and equipment. A responsibility matrix should be constructed for these elements and their measures, just as was done for product and market interface attributes (Figure 6.8).

Attribute	R&D	Marketing	Manufacturing	Quality Assurance	Finance	Personnel
Labor	d	n	d	i	i	i
Material	d	d	d	n	i	n
Equipment	d	n	d	i	i	n

d — direct influence   i — indirect influence   n — no influence

Figure 6.8   Capacity Responsibility Matrix

The responsibility for production capacity is shared throughout the business. Each area that directly or indirectly influences business capacity must set goals and strategies. The capacity goals will be driven by the expected sales and the established availability. Once these factors are known, the levels for each of the capacity elements can be set.

Labor Capacity

Capacity is the output per unit of time that can be achieved when the production processes are operating in their most efficient state. The amount of labor that is needed to operate at a given output rate will be dependent on the technology, the product, and the labor efficiency. These factors determine the number of people necessary to operate the production processes. Manufacturing typically has the responsibility for managing this production resource, but it will be heavily influenced by product designs, hiring processes, job turnovers, and employee attitudes. Other areas, such as quality assurance, might become bottlenecks if they are part of the inspection process. Each area should look at its plans relative to the volume of anticipated business.

Material Capacity

Material capacity is affected by our ability to purchase, store, pull, and distribute material. The measures that are used here reflect the business' ability to process the material needed in the time required. Traditional approaches to material planning hid many of the material capacity problems by creating large stores of inventory at each stage of the process. The number of back orders could be predicted by the level of inventory at each stage. Supervisors were very defensive of their labor capacity; they would order more material than needed to ensure that their workers didn't sit idle while expediters chased down back-ordered parts. JIT production and the Japanese *Kanban** approach has challenged the nature of these systems.

JIT production requires that everything arrives where it is needed at exactly the right time and right quantity. While this approach can save industry millions of dollars in inventory costs, it also requires a linear procurement system. This puts a greater demand on the material quality, the supplier reliability, and the scheduling process. When a part is back ordered or defective, the entire process may have to be shut down until the problem is resolved. In a linear process, a material's quality, efficiency, procurement, and distribution must be managed at the same level every minute the processes are functioning.

---

*Kanban is a Japanese term for ticket or card and is used to name their JIT system based on the use of pull cards to trigger material deliveries.

While manufacturing again has primary responsibility for establishing the material capacity requirements, other areas are influential in achieving it. Finance pays the bills, and their policies may affect a supplier's attitude about a JIT delivery scheme. Quality assurance may be involved in incoming inspection and vendor qualification and may affect capacity; each influential area should have strategies to enhance material flow.

Equipment Capacity

Machinery, equipment, land, and buildings each has an impact on capacity. Each asset has a maximum capacity to produce that may or may not be achieved, depending on worker reliability, maintenance quality, and use scheduling. Some businesses are moving to a flexible manufacturing environment, where they expect to build a wide variety of products by using the same equipment and labor. Generic work stations are becoming commonplace; these are "test system" work stations that are used to test any number of different products within a day's work. Having this flexibility, they are maximizing their ability to provide a product with short lead times and they are getting the maximum use of their assets.

Providing the right level of capacity may be as simple as providing the correct number of benches for assembly or it could be as involved as building a separate factory for new product manufacturing. No matter what the case, the level must be measurable in terms of output units per day, and the responsibility for achieving it will be distributed jointly among the functions of the business. As shown in Figure 6.1, each element of capacity has a hierarchical relationship within the business, and managers must provide for it in their planning and review activities.

Profitability

We have discussed the measurable elements of products, the market interface performance, the effect on customer satisfaction, and the measurable aspect of capacity on producing and delivering products at the desired sales level. These business attributes combine to establish the future revenue growth for the business. Revenue is not the only measure of success for a business. If it was we would find ourselves trying to buy our way into higher sales by indiscriminately lowering prices until so much money was lost that we could no longer operate. Profit represents the balance to the business equation. Profit and growth together are the final measure of a business' success.

Profit and Productivity Measures

If it were possible to increase productivity at will, a business could control its product's price, volume, and profitability from year to year. The business could look at the changes in material and labor costs, competition and customer need, and regularly make compensating adjustments to productivity. Unfortunately it doesn't work this way; productivity is hard to measure much less control. One of the philosophies implicit in TQC is that measurement of variation is the first step in getting control. Therefore, measuring productivity is the first step in managing it.

Businesses typically do not have good measures of productivity. Managers use profit, output per person, cost of goods sold, or some other set or combination of these measures. Individually they are not true productivity measures because they don't capture all of the elements of productivity. Further, these measures can be influenced by factors other than productivity changes. For example, profit can be influenced up or down by price changes; output per person can be affected by a decision to subcontract more work. A combination of these decisions can allow profit to increase even though productivity has gone down. If this were the case we would have a sense of false security. Eventually our price increases may exclude the business from the market.

Economists tell us that productivity is the ratio of total output to total input. In an engineering sense this is referred to as efficiency. Efficiency however, is normally associated with losses in the system, and therefore is measured as a number less than one, i.e., 90 percent, 80 percent, etc. Productivity of a business, on the other hand, is measured in terms of gain, i.e., we expect to get more out than we put in. Efficiency therefore becomes a component of productivity as discussed in Chapter 3. A useful measure for analyzing decisions from year to year on changes in profit, efficiency, and pricing, or make or buy decisions combines several of these factors. This is a mathematical index that gives you a feel for good or bad decisions. This index is expressed as shown below:

$$\textbf{Year 1} \qquad\qquad\qquad \textbf{Year 2}$$

$$\frac{\text{total cost X total people}}{\text{total sales}} \quad X \quad \frac{\text{total sales}}{\text{total cost X total people}}$$

(1) = Use actual numbers for year 1.

(2) = Use actuals or targets for year 2 that will be compared against year 1.

136

Total costs represent all costs of business that year. This number is equal to total sales minus before-tax profit. *Total people* represent all people in the business required to make it function — direct labor and overhead. *Total sales* include all revenue from goods sold.

The significance of this measure is that it can track several indicators at once. Decisions on pricing, capital investment, and make or buy choices all get aggregated into one index to give the manager a feel for the combined effect on the organization. When the index is a number greater than 1.0, a more productive decision(s) has been made; conversely, the opposite is also true.

Example: A business is in the process of planning for the next year's performance. Many managers are involved in this process. The marketing manager forecasts that sales will be up by 20 percent. The general manager decides that he would like to increase the profit margin by 2 percent and hold back log constant. The manufacturing manager decides to invest $1 million in new machinery and avoid hiring more people; however, one of the major subcontractors of fabrication has increased prices so the manufacturing manager decides to build these parts in house and thus must hire five people anyway. When all this is done costs have risen by 30 percent. What impact do these decisions have on productivity?

Year 1	**Year 2**
total sales = $10 million	total sales = $12 million
total costs = $8 million	total costs = $10.4 million
total people = 100	total people = 105

Ratios

gross margin = 20%	gross margin = 13.33%
output/person =	output/person =
$100 thousand	$114.3 thousand

Productivity Index

$$\frac{\$8 \text{ million} \times 100 \text{ people}}{\$10 \text{ million}} \times \frac{\$12 \text{ million}}{\$10.4 \text{ million} \times 105 \text{ people}} = .879$$

In this example productivity has declined by 12.1 percent. Price increases in material and labor may have contributed to this decline. If the vendor price changes are known it is possible to calculate the absolute effect of the decisions on capital investment and subcontract actions. In this situation it will be possible to reevaluate these decisions before raising prices to offset the decline in productivity.

A similar analysis can be done for each lower level in the organization. The analysis will change depending on the department's output. In some cases, like manufacturing, it is possible to value the output relative to the production volume. For other departments the real value of the output may require further research. Until real values for the output of a department are found, the business' total output must be used as the reference level for calculating the productivity index.

In a real business situation many changes are occurring simultaneously throughout the year: People are constantly being hired, wages and material costs are continuously increasing, and capital investment is constantly on the rise. Using an index as described above may be the only way to gage productivity changes. Measuring it, reporting it, and reacting to it is the only way to manage productivity.

Summary of Organizational Metrics

The metrics discussed here can be used in any manufacturing business to establish a working relationship among its people. When each of the metrics are quantified and distributed according to the responsibility matrix, everyone in the business will be working toward a common objective. The planning and review systems are the next step in this process. It is through the planning system that we achieve the distributed responsibility, and it is through the review system that we ensure continued focus on the goals.

An Example of Measuring Customer Satisfaction

A focus on quality. . . all of us who work in manufacturing have experienced the growing emphasis on quality. Phrases such as total quality control (TQC), outgoing quality level (OQL), process quality measurements (PQM), and quality teams have become a common part of our vocabulary.

In our daily lives we've seen the impact of foreign competition in markets which, at one time, were dominated by the United States. There's a definite perception in the world market that American quality is inferior to foreign competition. No doubt, many of us believe that we can get better quality and pay less money if we buy imported products. This certainly is not the kind of perception we wish to perpetuate!

Customer satisfaction is the primary goal of TQC. An old adage says that beauty is in the eye of the beholder. From this we can learn something: Quality is in the eye of the customer. In the end, the customer defines quality. But how do we know if our customers are truly satisfied? Or if they believe that they have received the best deal for their investment? One way to do this is to provide a means of two-way communication — a feedback loop.

The manufacturing TQC department took an important step in this direction by designing and printing a customer survey card. The shipping department sends one of the cards with every product we ship. Three questions are asked of the customer: (1) Does this product totally meet your expectations for performance and appearance? (2) Was the shipment complete? and (3) Did you run a performance test on this product?

Ample space is provided for the customer to write comments. This, by far, is the most interesting aspect of the project. Cards have been received with comments ranging from, "terrific instrument!" to "I'm very displeased with this product." This is exactly what we want — feedback. But what do we do with it?

If there is a dissatisfied customer, the card is immediately routed to marketing. A customer service engineer calls the individual and offers help; this kind of personal concern can be effective when a customer is displeased.

All the responses from customer survey cards are filed and distributed weekly to all production managers and supervisors. Customer problems are addressed immediately; if customers were pleased, the people who worked on the particular product hear about it; and customers sometimes suggest worthwhile improvements.

Whatever the comments, the customer survey card acts as a vehicle for bringing us closer to the people who purchase our products. The card may never be returned to Hewlett-Packard. Upon opening the carton, however, the customer sees the words on the outside of the card stating, "WE REALLY WANT TO KNOW. . ."

CHAPTER 7

LEADERSHIP THROUGH PLANNING AND REVIEW

Planning and review are important parts of the leadership process, providing the direction and the framework for progress and change. Planning and review are used to ensure that the internal changes to the business are congruent with the needs of the environment. This is accomplished by measuring the needs of the environment, creating a plan to satisfy the needs, implementing the plan, checking the results, and taking corrective action in the business. We have traditionally used various approaches to provide strategic direction, including the practice of MBO. MBO is usually hierarchical in nature and follows the organizational lines of the business; i.e., each level of the organization provides its plans and objectives consistent with the higher level. When completed, the plan serves to guide the business for the coming period; at scheduled times the results are reviewed and corrective actions are prescribed.

The Japanese have demonstrated that traditional approaches to planning and review are inadequate to meet the needs of today's environment. They have found American implementation of MBO to be unstructured. For example, there are too many vague, long-term goals; i.e., they are too generally stated, and specific metrics are not assigned and monitored. Also, the performance measures are not integrated horizontally and vertically through the organization, allowing for deviation without corrective action. Moreover, the review process is rarely structured well enough to ensure that all goals established in the plan are reviewed regularly. Too many deviations are allowed to go unreported; therefore they are not remedied. The lack of structure inhibits the use of the MBO management tool to provide the intended leadership. Therefore, managers are required to practice what is sometimes referred to as "real-time management."

The Japanese have developed what they call *Hoshin,* which can be interpreted as policy. In this use, policy has a very broad meaning: It refers to the course of action that is evaluated, chosen, and pursued by the entire organization to reach its goals. As discussed earlier, *Hoshin* is the adoption of MBO with PDCA applied to it. When PDCA is applied to MBO with the same rigor the Japanese apply to their other processes, MBO becomes a tightly structured planning and review tool. For the Japanese it means (1) that plans are hierarchically formulated, based on customer needs; and (2) they have full involvement of all people and processes, well-defined measures of performance, and regular impartial reviews.

Copying the Japanese implementation of *Hoshin* is difficult because of accurate translation problems; even good translations leave many un-answered questions. The approach presented here uses many *Hoshin* concepts; but it has been tailored to suit an American audience. It allows us to capture most of the benefits of the Japanese system and, at the same time, it clarifies basic concepts to make implementation easier.

To begin, a brief review of the factory of the future is necessary. In this environment, changes come from many directions: the material input, the product design, the process or robot, or the customers' needs. It assumes that change is a constant factor of business and that business must be prepared to react to it.

Some changes may have long-term implications — as would occur when future opportunities are presented by a developing market or when access to new products is provided by new technologies. In these situations, businesses must foresee opportunities and communicate their visions to guide their organization.

As change is detected, it must be analyzed to determine the appropriate response. For large or long-term changes presented by market and prod-uct opportunities, the response may involve a large investment that has an extended ROI. The required analysis is extensive and probably justifies the support of a professional business analyst. For the daily changes occurring in the material and processes, however, the appropriate re-sponse may be a simple adjustment. Real-time analysis is required here and must lend itself to use by everyone in the business.

If a local decision is made in response to a change, it must be cleared with management to ensure that it is consistent with other organizational needs. There are no independent processes, and each one has an influ-ence on the other. Management also should conduct potential problem analysis and should agree on the impact of corrective action. These actions are necessary before implementation can begin.

The implementation process involves making a change to one of the resources, i.e., material, process, or design. In addition, documentation of the process must be updated to ensure that the change is permanent and not lost in subsequent process cycles. After the implementation is started, the results are monitored and compared to the expected results. Any part of the plan, analysis, or implementation could be in error, therefore producing an undesirable result. This error must be detected immediately and corrective action must be taken as soon as possible to avoid unnecessary resource waste. Any new error and subsequent corrective action would begin the cycle over again.

The preceding process improvement cycle is the application of PDCA to MBO. It should be obvious that this type of control is similar to the speed control in a car or the thermostatic control of your home; both of these systems behave the same way. For example, they detect changes in the environment, they analyze them, and then implement compensating changes. They will continue to check and repeat these cycles until equilibrium is achieved. These systems react very quickly and their cycles are continuous. They are so refined that their results are predictable, providing the changes are not too fast or so large that they exceed the range of their system design. The design of the business system also has limits to its ability for responding to changes, and it must be designed accordingly to maximize its ability for reaction to its environment.

It is desirable to have a business system that consistently and predictably responds to change, but the predictability of the system is dependent on the quality of its components. The quality of the system is contaminated when the component reliability varies at random — the response is then difficult to predict. When the system is infested with these independent variables, they must be eliminated or the undesirable effects must be compensated for.

Variables in the hardware and software environment of a computer system are caused by transient signals generated by powerline surges, loose connections, random component failures, or software defects. The occurrence of these variables causes the system to behave in an unpredictable and undesirable way. Consequently, the system may damage the object it is controlling or may waste time because of an erroneous output. To assure operators that the system is functioning as intended, frequent checks and reviews of the data and the performance of the system are necessary.

The business system is also a control system. Since it can experience communication failures and random hardware and software defects, it must also be subject to frequent reviews to avoid unnecessary resource waste and poor quality output. The software of the business is the information that is communicated through the system and must be as defect free as the software in the computer. The hardware of the business is the capital assets and the material that is used within the processes, and likewise, it must be defect free.

People are another independent variable in today's business system. They present additional challenges because of their inconsistency; for example, each person reacts differently to problems — some will underreact and some will overreact to the same situation. People also interpret deviations differently, depending on their backgrounds and experiences. They have different skills and have different ranges of control over which to react — some are wide and some are narrow. Since people are part of the business system, the demands on the management system are indeed great.

The aim of the management system is to eliminate or to neutralize the negative effects of the independent variables as much as possible. The material and equipment must be defect free. The management system must ensure that the instructions, procedures, and plans are defect free and founded on accurate data and good designs. Management must ensure that people understand what is to be done, provide them with the proper training and motivation, and communicate regularly with them. The motivations should line up at each level to ensure that everyone is working toward the same objectives. The internal communication should be defect free to ensure that the people understand the expectations of the system and that the system understands the problems people are experiencing in meeting the goals.

The planning and review system is the vehicle used to ensure that people in the organization are not working at cross purposes. Establishing a clear plan that articulates the leaders' visions, objectives, goals, measures, and strategies for each level ensures that everyone's purpose is mutually reinforced. Communicating the plans, establishing links between the levels, and holding regular reviews ensure that employee motivations continuously seek equilibrium with the business environment.

Implementation

Now that the requirements of the system are defined, the implementation process can be considered. These elements can be divided into the following categories:

1. *Understanding the Environment.* Who are your customers? What products do you want or need to provide? What are the performance expectations? What is my business' performance? What are the unmet expectations?

2. *Selecting Issues.* What is my mission/charter? What is my strategic vision? What are my objectives? What are the measures of performance?

3. *Analyzing the System.* What changes do I need to make? What resources do I have available? What is my organization/allocation of resources?

4. *Planning for Changes.* Specific long-term and short-term strategies, specific measures of performance, specific goals.

5. *Doing the Implementation.* Design products, change processes, etc.

6. *Checking the Result.* Monitor daily performance of processes; conduct regular reviews at appropriate intervals.

7. *Acting as Required.* Make corrective changes through the PDCA cycle again.

These categories can be summarized as the USA-PDCA process. This is the PDCA approach to planning and process improvement, but with some enhancements. The addition of "USA" to "PDCA" is a coincidence of acronyms; this seemed appropriate when it was determined that the added elements helped people understand how these principles apply to the planning and process improvement. The methodology of USA-PDCA will be covered in detail in Chapter 11.

The implementation of the USA-PDCA planning and review system is simple and straightforward; but, just as all planning systems do, it requires a coordinated effort that begins with the organization's CEO/general manager. This is emphasized because if the business charter is not stable, lower level planning will be wasted. If the charter or the mission changes, all planning must start over. When top managers are involved in creating the plan, they better appreciate the purity and the connection of each process. They relate to the changes in such a way that they feel the result of every decision they make, as certainly as they would feel the motion of turning the steering wheel in their car.

The Beginning

The business might start out with a planning and review calendar like the one shown in Figure 7.1. This calendar shows the relationships between the development of the long- and short-range plans, the business targeting cycle, and the reviews. When the CEO adopts this calendar, the CEO and the organization are committed to the first level of structure that will be required, but not the last. Most businesses probably already use a calendar like this, even if it's not so well documented and well organized. Depending on its fiscal year and targeting requirements, the timing of the events will vary with each business.

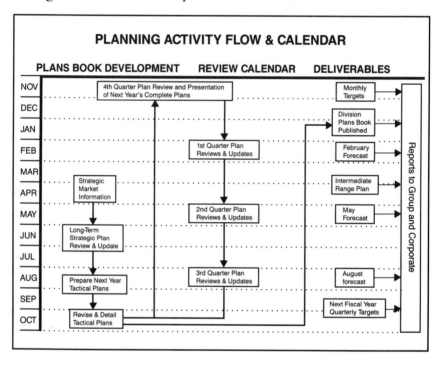

Figure 7.1   Planning Calendar

When the time is right, the CEO's staff will get together and present the calendar. Undoubtedly, there will be various reactions to it: Some may resent any form of structure, stating it inhibits their creativity; others already will be using something similar and will be happy to tie in to a corporate calendar — even if it does mean altering some of their present procedures. Some members of the staff will be ambivalent, thinking to themselves, "Does he really mean it?" or "He'll get over it in time." But the CEO must firmly define the future implementation strategy.

Strategic Council

If he doesn't already have one, the CEO forms a strategic council. This council will be made up of key executives responsible for marketing, R&D, manufacturing/operations, and finance. The function of this council will be to collect, analyze, and summarize key information about the business environment. The following categories of information will be generated:

1. *Market/Customer Information.* Who are the key customers and what are the key markets for our business? What are their needs for products and services?

2. *Competitor Information.* Who are the main competitors? What are the strengths and weaknesses of their products, distribution channels, and business? What is their financial success, market share, profitability, etc.?

3. *Technology Information.* What are the main technologies available or being used? What are the technological costs?

This information should be maintained and updated continuously and used as regular input to the annual planning and review cycle.

Planning

The Planning Cycle

The planning cycle is spread over a six-month period beginning with the long-range plans. Creating the plan must be a participative exercise, encompassing all levels and functions of the business. For this to happen in a timely and consistent manner, everyone must use a common format for planning. The format must (1) provide an adequate framework for each level to express the amount of required detail, and (2) have common definitions. The format will also make upcoming review processes easier to implement. A sample format is shown in Figure 7.2. A three-dimensional model is used because an organization may be involved in more than one business. The cube allows you to segment one dimension into as many businesses as required.

Strategic Planning Model

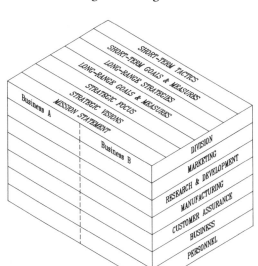

Figure 7.2 Planning Format

Common Definitions

Nothing can be more frustrating than trying to get consensus from a group of managers about the definitions of planning elements. Everyone, through years of conditioning at school, at work, and at play, has internalized their own meanings for the words *mission, objective, goal, strategy,* and *tactics*. These are further complicated by adjectives like *short-term, long-term,* and *intermediate-term*. Nobody seems to speak the same language, and unfortunately, until everyone agrees on common terms, a business plan will be impossible to create.

Integrating plans throughout a large organization requires that everyone uses the same language, not unlike a football team or any other team. Each team and each player has a unique mission, goal, and strategy based on the game and the position played. There are long-term goals and strategies that don't change unless the rules or the environment changes; there are short-term goals and strategies that depend on the play at the time. This means that we should all be using the same game book if we expect to be an effective team.

Using precise planning definitions allows each management level to effectively review the plans for coherence and to effectively communicate any changes. The ever changing, competitive nature of our business environment requires efficient, productive communication of plans to be competitively advantageous.

The following definitions exemplify the level of explanation that should be achieved and accepted throughout the organization:

Mission Statement

The mission statement is an entrepreneurial statement of specific intent, purpose, and reason for an entity, business, function, or process. It explains why it exists and usually makes a statement about the market or customer, the product or technology, the competitive goal, and the investors.

Example: Being the city/state/country/world's leading supplier of chocolate chip cookies and earning an attractive ROI.

Strategic Visions

After the mission statement has been established, it becomes important that management's ideas for future products or services are recorded. Every manager has these visions; but, unfortunately, they are seldom shared throughout the organization. The articulation of these visions in the strategic plan, however, facilitates their communication throughout the business. It is the vision that focuses the goals and strategies for the future.

Example: Devising a cost-effective, computer-aided engineering design system that produces all the necessary information to manufacture a high quality, low cost electrical or mechanical part.

Strategic Areas of Focus

Broad strategic issues where emphasis is necessary to be successful in the given business environment are identified. Specific product strategies are not mentioned here. This can be used for drawing attention to the objectives of the hierarchical priority that is given emphasis at this level. When focus is drawn in this way, it is listed here.

Example:

- Product differentiation through technical contributions.
- Customer satisfaction through cost of ownership.
- Management for competitive fitness.
- Worldwide market interface.

Long-Term Measures and Goals

Specific measures and goals indicate the success of the business in achieving its mission.

Example:

Measures	Goals
Revenue growth	XX percent in five years
Profit growth	X percent in five years
Productivity growth	X percent in five years

Long-Term Strategies

Specific actions taken relative to products, people, organization, and resource commitment for achieving the long-term goals of the business are long-term strategies.

Example:

- Providing a work environment sufficiently rewarding to attract and motivate the highest caliber of employees.

- Managing for continuous improvement in planning, productivity, and adaptability.

- Introducing three products that will cover the existing markets by a given time.

- Investing a percentage of revenues in R&D.

Short-Term Goals and Measures

Specific goals for the current fiscal year are aimed at long-term goals and strategies. The short-term goals and measures should be an identical subset of the long-term goals and measures but should represent an intermediate step toward the long-term expectation achievement.

Short-Term Tactics

Short-term tactics state specific actions to be taken now to meet short-term goals, i.e., resource allocation, controls, etc.

These planning definitions are summarized in Figure 7.3.

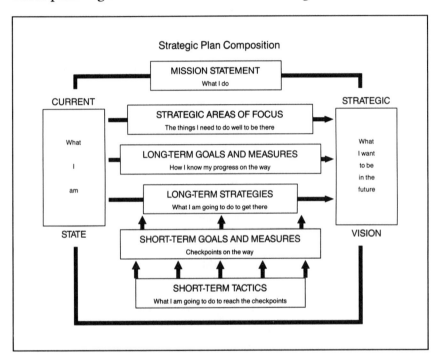

Figure 7.3   Planning Definition Summary

Long-Range Planning

Approximately six weeks are dedicated to completing the business' long-range plans. During this period the long-range plans must be updated and propagated throughout the organization. This will begin with the CEO and his staff who will first meet and review the information from the strategic council. Together they have one week to hammer out any differences that exist between last year's plans and this year's plans. Each level will then have one week to develop its respective plans and achieve consensus with its top organizational manager. It is the responsibility of the top managers to ensure that each of the lower reporting levels is consistent with their own plans. The long-range planning elements to be completed include the mission statement, the company vision, the strategic focus, and the long-range goals and strategies. These elements of the plan should not change significantly from year to year; therefore the time needed to update them should be minimal. Writing them for the first time, however, will likely require each level to dedicate the most part of a week in some hideaway. Groups have sometimes taken two full days just trying to complete a two- or three-sentence mission statement.

Long-Term Goals

The goals and measures are the most significant part of the planning process. It is through the goals that internal polarization of all the people and all the processes will be achieved. Special care must be taken to ensure that the selected measures and goals have special significance to the success of the business; this begins at the top of the organization and cascades downward. Goals should not be set at lower organization levels that do not directly support to the goals of the higher organization levels. When the common goals and individual objectives are clearly defined, the system will be designed to function in its purest form.

The previous chapter discussed organizational metrics. Each business has a generic set of metrics that can be used to set goals to measure performance and to plan reviews. These metrics should now be defined in terms of the goals that were set and should be included as part of the organizational plan.

Figure 7.4 is an example of a business planning table. This short plan identifies all the key measures and responsibilities for the business over a five-year period. After they are collected and combined, it is easy for a department manager to see the congruence achieved by his or her subordinate managers.

BUSINESS PLANNING TABLE

FIVE-YEAR GOALS

Department Name _____ Manager _____ Date _____

LONG-TERM OBJECTIVE	MEASURE	GOAL	STRATEGY
Improve product reliability.	Annual Failure Rate	Less than 1% fail in 1st year; less than .5% fail in 2nd year.	(1) Implement strife testing on all products prior to release to shipment with firm release criteria that relates to customer failure rate. (2) Current failure rate is 3% in 1st year and 2% in 2nd year. Ensure that each new product introduced makes a contribution toward long-term goal.

Example

Figure 7.4   Business Planning Table

Long-Term Strategies

Strategies reflect specific actions for projects, processes, timing, and resource allocation to implement the changes that will make it possible to achieve the goals. Too often *strategies* are offered as *goals.* For example, say you have a goal stated as: "Finish a project by a certain time" or "Train 15 people in TQC by year end." These are *strategies* that make it possible to achieve some goal; otherwise, you would not be doing it. Strategies show action, whereas goals measure business success.

When the goals are stated in terms of measures that are important to the success of the business, the difference between goals and strategies becomes obvious. For example, the goal for reliability (a product attribute) is stated as 1 percent annualized failure rate. All activities to make this possible become strategies. Training becomes a strategy for productivity and achieving product attribute goals; new product development schedules are strategies for increasing revenues.

Short-Term Goals

Each department should have a set of annual goals. The goals should be nothing more or less than an intermediate step toward the long-term goals. Normally these goals tie in directly to the annual targets. When combined, we will have a set of measures, goals, and strategies that will define the activities, investments, and priorities for the coming year. These can be illustrated on a short form similar to the one used for the long-term goals. This form is called an Annual Planning Table (see Figure 7.5).

The timing required for completing the short-term goals is similar to that for the long-term goals. Each level will have about one week to complete its goals; there is an interaction process, however, between the targeting cycle and the goal setting. Usually, not enough money is available to do what we wish; therefore, the interaction is necessary as a reality adjustment.

EXHIBIT 1:   SHORT-TERM TACTICAL PLANNING & REVIEW FORM

DATE: DEPT.:

TACTICS/PROCESSES	MEASURE	GOAL	ACTUAL	COMMENTS/CALENDAR												
				N	D	J	F	M	A	M	J	J	A	S	O	

C = Completion date   — >   = Project pushout   − − − = Working on item
S = Start date   ← −   = Project pull-in

Figure 7.5   Annual Planning Table

Short-Term Tactics

These tactics relate specifically to the elements of control and actions that are planned to ensure that short-term goals are achieved in the specified time period. They should be specific enough that other levels can understand them, but they do not need to be elaborate. They will show up on the Annual Planning Table.

155

Defining the Responsibilities for Creating the Plan

Throughout the six-week planning cycle, different levels in the business will become involved in the process of planning. After the CEO or general manager has completed the plans with staff, staff members will be asked to do the same thing at their level. The plans then will filter down and fan out into all levels and processes of the business. As discussed earlier, each level will have about one week to complete its plans and to reach consensus. After consensus has been reached throughout all levels, the plan is ready to be documented.

Documenting the Plan

One of the challenges for managers who are to create a hierarchical plan is to come up with a method of documentation that allows it to be a living document. The plan book published at the completion of the planning cycle is the medium for storing and communicating this information. To enhance its usability, the book should incorporate three characteristics:

1. Information should be easy to obtain and understand.

2. Information should be easy to change.

3. The plan book should be made visible throughout the organization.

A problem with many traditional plan books is that they not only include the measures, the goals, and the strategies, but also all the related analysis data. The first step in making the information easy to obtain and understand is to eliminate all the analysis data. This will keep the focus of the plan book only on statements that are key to success; the book will be informative but concise.

A plan book that is thick and cumbersome makes mass copying and distribution prohibitive. This hinders the influence that changes in one area have on changes in another area. Books that are not properly updated tend to be of limited use; usually they are shelved and forgotten until the next year.

Modern information systems give us the capability to overcome these difficulties and ensure a long and lasting life for our plan book. If the business has a central on-line management information system, it is possible to create and document the business plan on the system. Using the three-dimensional planning model, a business can assign a code to each element of planning (one to six), to each level of the organization (one to eight), and to each unit of the business (one to four, depending on the number of business units). In this way, an alphanumeric code can be generated to store all the plans of the organization. The use of a spreadsheet format enables a higher level manager to examine plans of a business unit or a functional area thoroughly. Also, it is possible to look at a hierarchical view of all missions, goals, or strategies to see how they tie together.

Reviewing and Updating the Plan

Information systems can also help us to review progress and update plans. If the key measures are identified in the plan and if another data base is set up to contain all of the performance data for each metric, it is always possible to call up the measure of interest and graphically illustrate it in comparison to the business goal. These data could be the basis of regular reviews, easily updating short-term plans in lieu of the annual review.

While information systems may be out of reach for some people, they provide the logic and the structure for considering the use of business plans. With or without information systems, the business plan format should be kept simple, logical, and active. A simple analogy relates to all forms of automation: The repetitive consistency of a robot can produce better product quality than a human being is capable of producing. The robot, however, can't handle too many variables; therefore, to commit a process to automation, the variables must be reduced to a machine-manageable set. There is no doubt that had the variables been eliminated from the human process, quality and efficiency also would have been better; the machine, however, can go on to work five times faster than the human being. The moral of the story: Without information systems we can still improve the quality and the efficiency of our planning process, but our productivity will be better if automation is used.

Review

Review and corrective action are as important to the leadership process as are good plans. When changes occur through the year, the deviations should be visible and corrective action must be taken. The planning is done from the top down; the review process, however, is done from the bottom up. For example, an employee may review his process performance real time, using control charts and hourly or daily inspection. That employee's supervisor may review the individual's work daily or weekly; department managers may review results weekly or monthly; the general manager may review departments quarterly, etc. Simply stated, there is no point in starting these reviews from the top, because the variations and actions are summarized from the bottom and go upward.

These reviews should be tied directly to the measures of performance as identified in the annual planning table. To facilitate this process, a review table can be used to show the plans as set forth in the annual planning table, with results to date shown (see Figure 7.6). Sometimes a discrepancy report can be used, as shown in Figure 7.7. This report is intended to identify the deviation from plan with an explanation and analysis showing recommended actions.

This type of system requires managers to view planning and reviewing as their primary function; they will find that they spend more time than they previously spent on this process. The benefit, however, will come from saving time later. A manager will come to a regular review and will make sure that the people who report to him or her are prepared with the necessary information. When deviations exist, subordinates will have the answers and corrective action already may have been taken. The manager can spend the time reviewing the major projects that offer considerable return — and not spend time "fighting fires." He or she can concentrate on preventing problems and making continued improvement to the processes; as a result, management's effectiveness is considerably improved.

To be successful in this type of environment, a business must adopt a nonthreatening attitude toward performance deviations. The emphasis should be placed on the methods used and the results achieved. By continuously focusing on process improvement and group consensus, managers will learn to trust and help one another. This environment can only be achieved when the CEO or general manager believes in the value of this type of planning and requires it of everyone in the organization.

When the people and the processes are linked through the common metrics discussed in the previous chapter, there is little room for deviation. Where deviation does occur, it is understood and remedied. A structured approach to planning and review eliminates the ambiguity of performance that typically confronts so many managers. When completely implemented, the system will be more successful and the people will be more confident.

TACTICS/PROCESSES	MEASURE	GOAL	ACTUAL	COMMENTS/CALENDAR N D J F M A M J J A S O
Provide Training: Total Quality Ctl.	No. of people trained	*		*To be negotiated with functional managers
Working in Groups	No. of people No. of classes	140 10		Every 4 to 6 weeks
Planning	No. of people	120		To be scheduled
Develop Training: Planning Class				———C For management and supervisors, top-down implementation
Individual TQC				S———C Short class focusing on personal application of TQC tools and concepts
CA Productivity				
Provide Training: Total Quality Ctl.	No. of people	20		All CA departments
Working in Groups	No. of people	30		All CA departments

C = Completion date   —→ = Project pushout   — — — = Working on item
S = Start date   ←— = Project pull-in

Figure 7.6 Annual Planning Table Example

ABNORMALITY REPORT | The *Abnormality Report* forms the "check" part of PDCA. It should be filled out whenever the actual deviates from the plan or whenever a problem surfaces.

Prepared by _____ Date _____
Reviewed by _____ Date _____

Item:
Identify the deviation.

2. Circumstances under which abnormality occurred: Month/Day/Year
Describe the circumstances under which
the deviation occurred.

3. Analysis of causes [analysis method, estimated cause(s)]:

Analysis of the causes of the deviation.
The analysis should be supported by data.

4. Immediate countermeasures and results:

Describe the emergency measures being taken
to alleviate the immediate problem. Were
the emergency measures sufficient?

5. Short-term measures for preventing a recurrence:

Describe the short-term measures being
taken to prevent the problem from recurring
before the root-cause(s) are removed.

6. Plan for removing the root causes(s) of the problem:

Describe the plan for final solution of
the problem: the removal of the root-cause(s).

7. Results of plan and remaining problems:
Monitor the results of the plan for removing
the root-cause(s). Was the plan successful?
Are there any remaining problems?

Figure 7.7   Discrepancy Report

A TQC Look at the Forecasting Process

The financial planning process had some major deficiencies. This conclusion was reached after several difficult planning exercises during FY 1984, including the targeting process for FY 1985. The following are examples of process problems:

- There are too many iterations late in the process that require time-consuming changes to detailed plans.

- Functional area plans are not understood by division manager (or understood too late). The process did not prepare division manager to justify plans upward.

- Internal guidelines are not well communicated or well understood.

- The accounting department spends many hours working through iterations.

- Last-minute major changes to plans make early efforts seem wasted.

- The number of iterations is damaging to morale, commitment, and integrity of financial plan.

- Financial planning process is not defined.

- Management absences make scheduling difficult.

- "Lastminuteism" leads to silly-looking plans.

In order to address these concerns, the forecast quality team focused on defining the financial planning process using some TQC concepts. The next business example is a summary of a presentation made to the division staff prior to beginning work on the February forecast. At that meeting, the staff agreed to implement the approach identified by the quality team for the February forecast.

The forecasting process involves a lot of time from a lot of people, most of whom have other equally important demands on their time. Therefore, because the finance department coordinates this process, we decided that the process needed careful review so that each participant's time was being used efficiently and effectively. This was the basis for the forecast quality team.

The forecast quality team, created in June FY 1984, is made up of the cost accounting manager, the forecast coordinator who prepares the statements, the production analyst who forecasts production cost, the R&D analyst, the administrative support person who assists with statement preparation, and, currently, the statements supervisor. They are the most directly involved people in the forecast process, and are therefore in a good position to make recommendations for improvements.

During the first meeting, the group decided on the scope of the team and determined which subjects would be reviewed. It was quickly agreed that we needed to improve our internal process before we could look outside of our department. To do this, we took a three-step approach. First, we surveyed key forecast players to determine their expectations of the finance department during a forecast. Next, we made a flowchart of the process needed to pull together a forecast, focusing on the role of the finance department. Finally, we looked for ways to improve our ability to produce forecast statements. Our current statement preparation was based around the financial system and was not flexible enough to allow for the many rework and "what if" steps that are needed for an effective forecast.

At this same time, the department was in the process of setting up a personal computer to use as an analytical tool. The team decided that the spreadsheet applications available on personal computers provided the most flexibility, without requiring extra CPU time on the central financial computer or programming effort. LOTUS 1-2-3™ was chosen as the best package because of its ability to combine various files and its macro capability, allowing numerous repetitive keystrokes to be executed in one stroke. We set up statements FPT1-4 for each facility and a worldwide summary. The goal was to have a piece of information entered only once and then let the spreadsheet make all the appropriate calculations. Production cost forecasting was also set up in LOTUS to allow the same flexibility with a minimum of effort.

Once we could efficiently produce forecast statements, we turned our attention to the division as a whole and to the process of putting together our forecasts. We began by identifying the sequence of events that needed to take place and by determining what information was needed at each step. We also identified the routes of rework and the group expectations for our financial plans.

By developing a flowchart of the forecast process, we could identify the potential bottlenecks and the critical information steps. From this, we put together a proposal of what we considered to be the most efficient flow of information, and therefore the most effective process of assembling a financial forecast. This process, and the resulting schedule, was presented to the division staff and received approval; the February forecast was put together using this new process.

The forecast team then turned its attention to evaluating the process and looking for other areas for improvement. The most obvious area needing attention was communication, both within the department and to the rest of the division. One suggestion was to give a kickoff presentation to the division staff before any forecast began in order to review the process and come to consensus on the nature of the forecast. We also better defined the forecast coordinator's role in communicating to the rest of the division. This included holding stand-up meetings, sending weekly messages to the accounting representatives, and giving regular updates to division forecast participants.

CHAPTER 8

EMPLOYEE PARTICIPATION THROUGH QUALITY TEAMS

Quality teams are an integral part of business life in many successful Japanese companies. In Japan, quality teams, called quality control circles (QC circles), are a major part of corporate-wide quality control and TQC. In response to increasing competitive pressure from these Japanese companies, many U.S. organizations began looking for the key factors to Japan's success. What many saw were QC circles. Some viewed this as a panacea for quality or morale problems. Many organizations began promoting QC circles, but the results were generally unimpressive. QC circles, under any name (quality teams, employee participation groups, etc.), did not seem to work very well. Many people rationalized that QC circles were a Japanese cultural phenomenon and would never be effective in the United States.

This is not true, as discussed in Chapter 3. QC circles can only work in an organizational culture suited to participative management. This reason alone does not explain why QC circle programs often fail; the most important reason is simply that QC circles do not function as stand-alone programs. They were never meant to function as such. Davida Amsden, a noted authority on QC circles wrote:

> Circles are too often seen as a way to improve quality at the hourly level without middle or upper management's really believing in, let alone using, statistical quality control and other sound quality control methods. By contrast, quality control circles were the logical outgrowth of the Japanese realization that quality is everybody's job. (Papers, 1983).

When used appropriately within the framework of quality control, QC circles can be an integral and effective means of practicing quality control at every level of an organization.

Quality Teams Defined

A quality team is a small group of employees from the same work area who meet voluntarily to perform quality control activities. The group continuously, and as part of company-wide quality control activities, solves work-related problems, implements or recommends solutions, and improves quality. A team consists of those employees who perform similar functions, generally for the same supervisor (all buyers, all assemblers, etc.), or it can consist of those individuals who, though they do not have similar responsibilities, work together on the same processes.

The reasons for quality team activities, carried out as a part of corporate-wide quality control activities, are to:

- Contribute to the improvement and growth of the organization.

- Show respect for people (develop mutual respect).

- Build a productive and happy working environment (build teamwork).

- Exercise human capabilities fully (satisfy higher order needs).

An organization involved in a QC circle program should be "looking for an environment in which all workers accept the premise that quality is everyone's business" (Ishikawa, 1985).

Since quality teams are made up of people who are familiar with a process, there is great opportunity for synergy when this pool of knowledge and expertise is focused on quality control and process improvement. The benefits derived from quality team activity include:

- Improved quality, productivity, and communication.

- Enhanced problem-solving skills and personal growth of the participating employees.

- Increased job interest and ownership by employees who feel responsible and influential in their jobs.

- Better teamwork and cooperation among individuals, groups, departments, etc.

- Increased commitment to the collegial philosophy fomented by improved employee-management relations and communications.

- More people involved in developing performance measures means that supervisors and managers have access to more data than they could possibly develop without that assistance. This effectively increases the management's span of control by allowing them to manage more processes more efficiently.

- A basis for recognition for employees is provided. Participation in a quality team provides members with the opportunity to make significant contributions and to be recognized for them.

Best Practices

Quality teams began at Hewlett-Packard in 1979. Training materials development and quality team participation grew rapidly through 1981. Beginning in 1982, this growth slowed and commitment and belief in quality teams seemed to wane. This pattern has been rather common in the United States. Many companies have begun QC circle programs modeled after the Japanese; but successful implementation has, in many cases, proven to be elusive. A corporate task force was asked to review the use of quality teams to identify why they had not become a "way of life" at Hewlett-Packard. The task force quality team compared implementation at various divisions to determine what types of activities had consistently led to success and what things had not seemed to garner the enthusiasm that had been expected. The items that the task force identified were consistent with the findings of many of the quality control specialists that have been involved in the U.S. QC circle movement, most notably, Davida Amsden and W. S. Reiker. These items are herein referred to as "best practices" (Walter, 1984).

Best Practices #1

The first recommendation of the quality team task force was that quality teams should not be a stand-alone program, but that they should be a part of a larger quality improvement methodology — TQC. Without an all-encompassing approach to quality improvement, quality team activity was inconsistent both over time and between groups. There was no clear direction given to making improvements. Quality teams alone were not the secret to the success seen in so many Japanese organizations. They were, however, an integral part in the quality TQC programs of those companies. W. S. Reiker, a well-known quality control circle consultant, wrote, "QC circles is not a total quality control system nor a total management system. It is not complete enough to stand alone as a concept or as a society. It direly needs integration into the balance of the company's operations. It needs to be part of TQC." (Papers, 1983).

A basic premise of TQC is that quality is the responsibility of every single member of an organization. Quality circles are used by the Japanese to enhance quality consciousness and to provide a forum for everyone to act on his or her responsibility for quality.

Quality teams are focused on quality control. All the benefits of quality teams presented earlier are the result of people working together in solving problems. That is the one objective that yields all the other benefits. Donald L. Dewar, president, International Association of

Quality Control Circles, wrote, "The pursuit of quality as the number one most visible objective not only will aid in achieving acceptable quality levels but, more importantly, in improving them. Productivity increases automatically follow any improvement in quality. It is a natural and abundant by-product of quality improvement" (Papers, 1983).

Best Practices #2

The second recommendation of the task force was that management at all levels become involved in quality team activity. Originally, quality teams were asked to function without mangement participation. This decreased the importance of quality teams in the eyes of the employees and introduced a measure of inconsistency between the strategic plans of management and the priorities and strategies done at lower levels of the organization. The basis tenet of TQC is that all activities are part of processes. Processes can be improved — even management processes. Participation by management in quality teams can provide a number of benefits:

- The processes that involve management will improve, allowing managers to be more productive.

- Management's dedication to quality teams and ownership of the TQC process will reinforce the importance of these activities at all levels.

- Management does its strategic planning to guide its quality team projects and activities. These plans then cascade down the organization, giving direction to quality teams at all levels.

The authors of the article "Quality Circles: A Managerial Approach" wrote:

When managers are themselves immersed in the circle methodology (previously defined as TQC), they more readily understand what is happening at other levels. . . If lower level management and workers see the problem-solving techniques being applied and decisions made accordingly by upper management, they will be much more amenable to using the problem-solving methodology in their jobs (Papers, 1983).

In his article, "Can Quality Circles Make it in the Western World?", Donald L. Dewar listed three essential characteristics of management support (Papers, 1983):

1. The decision to start and keep the quality team function must come from high up in the organization.

2. Management of each functional area where quality teams exist must fully support the program.

3. There must be considerable depth of management support — not just a couple of managers.

In concluding his discussion on management support he said, "Management support is also demonstrated convincingly to the circle members when managers translate words into actions by doing such things as dropping in during circle meetings and by encouraging circles to make management presentations that describe their activities" (Papers, 1983).

It is impossible to understate the importance of management *commitment* with regard to management support.

> Management support requires that time is provided for meetings, rooms are available, training is done, there are budgets for operating circles, and access to information is provided. Commitment requires that managers become personally involved. Managers attend circle meetings and circle presentations, seriously consider recommended solutions, and encourage the use of problem-solving techniques (Papers, 1983).

TQC and quality teams can only become a way of life if they are implemented at all levels of the organization.

To support quality teams in the manner previously described, management must adopt four basic assumptions:

1. Workers are creative and are willing to contribute to organizational goals.

2. Workers know more about what they do than anyone else.

3. Workers can be taught problem-solving techniques.

4. A quality control circle program will not threaten the importance of managers; existing management structure will be intact.

Best Practices #3

The third recommendation of the task force involved the training quality teams should receive. If all employees are expected to adopt quality team activity as an integral part of their responsibility, they must be trained in the skills they will be expected to use: statistics, problem solving, group work, and team building. The entire TQC methodology process should be covered, and where possible, a real-life sample project should be included. Training is not to be thought of as a one-time event, so materials and resources should always be available to everyone.

One of the original goals of the QC circle program developed in Japan was to provide for the self-development of the worker. Self-development and group development is even included in Japan's QC Circle Headquarters' definition of a QC circle (Juse, 1981).

In addition, all levels of management should receive training in the problem-solving methods and the statistical tools that the quality teams will use, as well as a thorough orientation of the structure and organization of the quality team program.

Best Practices #4

The last recommendation made by the task force was that teamwork should be emphasized for quality teams; people should receive training in group dynamics and experience working together. The TQC focus on customer satisfaction also strengthens teamwork attitudes between departments of a company, but most organizations still have many practices that deter teamwork. Human nature involves looking out for one's self first. TQC and quality team activity take away the blame and the responsibility for problems from individuals and assign them to the processes. When this is understood, especially by management, people are less defensive and are more willing to work together.

Many companies have pay scale and recognition systems that cause people to work individually rather than together. Criteria for evaluating performance should include a heavy dose of teamwork and participation. Everyone should be rewarded for working together for the overall good.

Management is essential to fostering teamwork at all levels; they must encourage teamwork at lower levels through goal selection, project assignment, or whatever is necessary. Even when responsibility and decision making are decentralized, it is important that the separate groups do not feel like separate entities.

Quality Team Structure

A quality team program usually has six key elements. The following list briefly describes the individuals or groups that comprise these elements and states their main tasks:

1. *Team members* make up the primary element of the quality team. They are people who do the same type of work, who generally report to the same supervisor, or who are all involved in the same process.

2. The *team leader* often is the immediate supervisor of the quality team members. This individual guides the direction and process of the quality team. This may be an elected and/or rotated position.

3. The *facilitator* assists the leader and helps make the team more effective. This person should be viewed as a resource to the team who can be an advisor on technical points and group relationships.

4. The *steering committee* consists of several managers who represent key functions in the organization (manufacturing, personnel, quality assurance, R&D, marketing, etc.). They also should demonstrate their commitment and support to the teams by frequently visiting meetings and by being available and responsive to team presentations. This committee acts as an administrative body and will be involved in providing for the needs of the program.

5. The *specialist* is an expert who is asked by the quality team to help solve a problem. The role of the specialist is to teach or help the team define and resolve only those problems for which the team has asked assistance. This person can be a statistician, a technical expert, or any skilled person who is needed to provide insight into the problem.

6. *Nonmembers* are involved employees who are not members of a quality team. This involvement is strongly encouraged. They will have many ideas that can help the team; nonmembers generally are invited to join a team because they are involved or affected by the issues that the team is addressing. These people temporarily are full-fledged members of the quality team. They should feel that it is also their team and should know that their ideas will be considered.

Quality Team Activity

Quality teams meet weekly or biweekly for one to two hours in a place that is conducive to training and discussions. Initial meetings should be dedicated to quality team and TQC training. The teams operate according to a problem-solving methodology consistent throughout the organization.

Kaoru Ishikawa, commonly referred to in Japan as the father of QC circles, calls this methodology the "QC story" and defines it as follows (Ishikawa, 1985):

1. Decide on a theme (establish goals).
2. Clarify the reasons for choosing a particular theme.
3. Assess the present situation.
4. Analyze (probe into the causes).
5. Establish corrective measures and implement them.
6. Evaluate the results.
7. Standardize (prevent slip-ups or recurrence).
8. Consider remaining problems.
9. Plan for the future.

This methodology should be refined and detailed to suit an organization's particular needs. In this book, the methodology is referred to as USA-PDCA. A more detailed discussion of this method can be found in Chapter 11.

Common Quality Team Tools

The quality team can use a great number of tools in the process of problem selection and problem solving. These tools are explained in greater detail in the chapters on USA-PDCA and statistical quality control (Chapters 11 and 12), but the following examples are presented:

- *Brainstorming.* Quality team members address a problem or an issue by submitting as many ideas as possible. All evaluation or criticism is put aside. Unusual, creative, and offbeat ideas are encouraged.

- *Cause and Effect Analysis.* This occurs either in the form of a simple list of problem causes under investigation or in a more sophisticated form called a fishbone diagram. A fishbone diagram is a graphical representation of the major causes and subcauses of a problem or issue.

- *Data Collection.* Various forms of checklists are used. A simple checklist is a tally sheet requiring a tic mark when something occurs. A recording checklist is a more complex listing of all possible problems that can occur and needs to be filled out for each occurrence. A location checklist is a diagram that is used to tally the location of defects that occur by placing a check mark on the appropriate location of the diagram.

- *Data Analysis.* The data are put into a format that can be interpreted easily. The most common formats are the bar chart, the line chart, and the control chart.

- *Pareto Charts.* This is a type of bar chart used to prioritize types of occurrences or problems. It is a visual representation based on the Pareto principle which states that most of the occurrences will be due to a few of the causes.

The Quality Team Review

The result of the quality team's efforts is either an implemented improvement or a recommendation to management. Because the advantages of quality teams include the improvement of employee problem-solving abilities and the provision of a basis for recognition, it is important that the quality team receives feedback on its efforts. The quality team review is an effective forum for communicating necessary information to management and for providing feedback opportunity for the quality team members. This feedback, however, must not be confined to a study of the results.

The evaluation of a quality team's activities should emphasize factors such as the manner in which QC circle activities are conducted, the attitude and effort shown in problem solving, and the degree of cooperation existing in a team. Ishikawa gave the following example of a weighted evaluation method (Ishikawa, 1985):

Selection of the theme	20 points
Cooperative effort	20 points
Understanding of the existing condition and the method of analysis	30 points
Results	10 points
Standardization and prevention of recurrence	10 points
Reflection (rethinking)	10 points
Total	100 points

It is possible to structure quality team recommendations into an employee suggestion system (see Chapter 9). Even when this is done, the quality teams should be given the opportunity to formally present their activities and results. Having this review provides the following benefits:

- Allows the quality team to present project results to management and customers.

- Provides the quality team with the opportunity for recognition.

- Gives management and customers an opportunity to see the project process, understand the recommendation, and ask any questions.

- Legitimizes management's concern and involvement in quality teams and TQC in team members' eyes.

- Allows management to own the TQC process through support of the quality team activity.

- Provides feedback to the quality team on its activities so it knows what areas can be improved.

- Gives good presentation and preparation skills practice to the members of the quality team.

- Helps educate others by seeing what has been done.

Table 8.1 contains the information given to quality teams at Hewlett-Packard LSID. This information describes the purpose and function of the review program developed at LSID for its quality team program.

The purpose of the quality team review is to:

- Allow quality teams the opportunity to let others know what they have accomplished.

- Give recognition for their efforts.

- Help provide consistency throughout the division regarding the application of problem-solving methods.

Periodically, each quality team will be invited to make a presentation of a recent TQC cycle in a forum open to all employees. This presentation should take about 15 minutes, with another five minutes allocated for questions. The quality team should attempt to make the presentation as professional as possible. The majority of the information should be available from documentation of the project. Each team should include information on team member attendance and the frequency and duration of the meetings.

Each presentation will be reviewed to provide feedback on the team's presentation, the team's problem, and the team's application of the problem-solving process. TQC is continuous process improvement, and feedback provides the information needed to determine which areas need improvement.

Table 8.1   Quality Team Review Program

Having a quality team review system consistent throughout an entire division can allow for motivational contests if they are structured enough to allow vastly differing projects to be compared. It also lends some consistency to the quality team efforts throughout the division; continuous recognition for these efforts will help to perpetuate them so that the program can remain active and effective.

Summary

Quality teams provide a great opportunity for everyone to dramatically affect the quality of the processes with which they are involved. TQC is an extremely powerful way of life. Quality teams help to make it successful because of the practical knowledge and capabilities that team members can bring to the problem-solving arena. They can provide important, cooperative benefits; they can instill feelings of pride and accomplishment because of the solutions they help to develop. The collegial management philosophy requires growth opportunity for each individual. TQC and quality teams provide the opportunity for every person to grow in self-esteem by directly and visibly impacting their jobs and by receiving well-deserved recognition for their efforts.

The Quality Team Presentation Feedback Form

The feedback form will be used by the presentation reviewers to record comments on the quality team's activities during the presentation (Figure 8.1). The items listed on this form are divided into three main categories:

1. TQC Process

2. Improvements Resulting from the TQC Cycle

3. TQC Presentation

The first section contains items that should be done in a TQC cycle. The quality team can use this as a checklist to monitor its performance and progress through the TQC cycle.

The team should use the items in the remaining two sections to aid in preparing the presentation so that it meets the listed expectations and contains the appropriate information.

The feedback forms will be returned to the team after the reviewers have made their comments. This gives some insight for activities in the TQC cycle that need improvement and acts as positive reinforcement for their efforts.

Team Name _____

X

I. TQC Process

  A. Issue Selection   —

    1. Customer expectations were used to identify potential issues (or issue was assigned by management). —

    2. Appropriate steps taken to prioritize potential issues. —

    3. Issue clearly stated. —

    4. Issue consistent with department objectives. —

    5. Issue owned by the quality team. —

  B. Analysis

    1. Effective use of flowcharts, cause and effect diagrams, check-sheets, and graphical analysis techniques as applicable. —

    2. PQMs identified and monitored before and after process change. —

    3. Appropriate data collection strategy developed and followed. —

    4. Data analyzed accurately and in a timely manner. —

    5. Major cause(s) identified through stratification. —

  C. PDCA — Solution and Implementation

    1. Solution(s) selected appropriately. —

    2. Implemented process changes clearly documented and communicated. —

    3. Steps in USA-PDCA cycle clearly documented. —

    4. Future quality team plans developed. —

    5. Data collection strategy identified to monitor process. —

II. Improvements Resulting from TQC Cycle

  A. Cost Savings (if appropriate) —

  B. Quality —

  C. Productivity (cycle time, time savings, output, etc.) —

III. TQC Presentation

  A. Presentation easily understood by the listener's item. —

  B. Effective use of visual aids displaying the tools used in the steps of the USA-PDCA cycle. —

Figure 8.1   Quality Team Presentation Feedback Form

References

Ishikawa, Kaoru. *What is Total Quality Control?* trans. David J. Lu. Englewood Cliffs, N.J.: Prentice-Hall, Inc., 1985.

Quality Circle Papers: A Compilation. Milwaukee: American Society for Quality Control, 1983.

Union of Japanese Scientists and Engineers. *Report of QC Circle Activities,* No. 14-1981.

Walter, Craig, Ray Price, and Sandy Mobley. *Quality Team Task Force Report.* Palo Alto: Hewlett-Packard, 1984.

An American Business Example
of a TQC Application

The supervisory staff in the printed circuit hand assembly operation decided they needed a TQC training session so that they could better lead the four emerging quality teams in their area. The request for the pilot class was made to the training coordinator. The training began in mid-June and was completed by the end of July with the results presented to the manufacturing manager's staff.

The TQC process can be described as a procedure for solving problems that will ultimately lead to better customer satisfaction. The techniques and ideas of this class, when used together with a quality team, can contribute to continual process improvement and growing customer satisfaction. The strategies that make up this TQC process and the training cycle we pursued are detailed below:

1. *Understand the effectiveness of the current process.* We began by listing our customers and product responsibilities. As a team we went out and surveyed our customers [assembly and wire (A&W) supervisors], identified their expectations, and identified the areas in which we were not meeting expectations.

2. *Select a problem statement.* We identified a number of problems and, with some guidance from our trainers, picked a problem that was small enough in scope to be solved in class, thereby gaining experience and motivation that comes from a successful solution to a problem. The issue statement was: to reduce the turnaround time for rework on PC boards from A&W.

3. *Analyze the current process.* We used several techniques to aid us in analyzing the rework process on boards from A&W, such as flow-chart, cause and effect diagrams, checksheets (which we used to tabulate the total time that a board from A&W was in our department), Pareto charts, and a run chart showing the average hours/tote for rework time in PC.

4. *Plan the solution and adopt the change.* We decided from the data collected in the first two weeks that our major cause for a high cycle time (sometimes in excess of six hours) was the amount of time it took the boards to reach the individual who was responsible for the rework. The path through the supervisors was taking too much time. We experimented by delivering the boards directly to the rework person. By graphing the run chart for weeks three through seven, it was quite obvious that the change was causing dramatic results. A final process change was made and communicated to our A&W supervisors in late July. Our current average turnaround time for PC rework is less than 0.2 hours. This cycle time is now put into control charts and reported weekly.

In summary, the class effectively defined the problem-solving process for us. It complemented the SQC efforts that we currently use to control our processes. The TQC process ultimately will give all employees who work in manufacturing the opportunity to contribute greatly to production process improvements.

CHAPTER 9

PARTICIPATION THROUGH EMPLOYEE SUGGESTION SYSTEMS

In addition to using quality teams and other participative management techniques (i.e., management by objectives, management by walking around, etc.), an employee suggestion system provides an organization with another way to utilize its employees' potential. A suggestion system is the formal means by which individuals, groups, or quality teams contribute their ideas to the company. There has been a resurgence of the suggestion system in the last 10 to 15 years, but the form it has taken is more sophisticated and structured than before.

Benefits of Suggestion Systems

A properly administered suggestion program can provide many benefits to both the company and the employee. Member companies of the National Society of Suggestion Systems (NSSS) have reported savings of between $5 and $6.50 for every $1 invested in the suggestion program, with a total dollar net savings of over $500 million among some 225 companies. In addition to the monetary advantages, other substantial benefits can be realized from a successful suggestion system:

- Improved communication between workers and managers.
- More team spirit in the company.
- Employees more conscious of productivity.
- Employees more conscious of process improvement potential.

In addition to these organizational benefits, an employee suggestion system can provide substantial advantages to employees:

- Opportunity to earn more.
- Promotional visibility.
- Peer respect and admiration.
- Recognition for accomplishments.
- Increased sense of contribution in the workplace.
- Increased job satisfaction.

The objectives of a suggestion system fit in with the philosophy of participative management. Having a suggestion system indicates that management considers everyone to be valuable. Everyone must work as a team.

Elements of a Suggestion System

A large percentage of the suggestion systems implemented are either discontinued or are never successful. The administration of a suggestion system requires a number of essential activities and features; unsuccessful programs invariably lack or mismanage one of the following vital features of successful systems:

Top Management Support. Complete support by management is necessary for the successful operation of a suggestion system for two reasons. Obviously, management must support the administration of the program; also, management commitment affects the attitude of the rest of the organization toward the system. All management, including first-line supervisors, must be well versed in the program and must support it. Management must not criticize first-line supervision for not providing the suggestion themselves.

Supervisory Support. Supervisors are directly involved with the employees who develop and submit the suggestions. They must therefore be supportive of the program; nothing kills suggestions more rapidly than supervisors who believe the suggestion program is an insult to their supervisory skills. They need to understand the true nature of the program. Management must hold supervisors responsible for the operation of the suggestion system in their own departments; in addition to being supportive, supervisors should provide assistance to employees in preparing the suggestions.

Eligibility Guidelines. Clear policies should be developed concerning suggestor eligibility, scope and type of suggestions, and the way awards are determined. These policies must be structured to provide consistency throughout the company and must be published so that all employees are aware of them. All points of possible confusion should be cleared up to prevent future disagreements.

System Procedures. The processing regimen should be spelled out in detail. This should include not only routing conventions, but also time guidelines, status requirements, and rejection procedures. It is important that submitted suggestions be handled quickly. Lengthy delays in evaluation and feedback significantly dampen the employee's enthusiasm for the program.

Suggestion Evaluation. A consistent and equitable way of suggestion evaluation must be implemented. Guidelines for suggestions must be well defined so that employees know how to write appropriate suggestions. The NSSS defines a suggestion as "an idea that poses a problem, potential problem, or opportunity; presents a solution; is written on the prescribed suggestion form; is signed by the suggestor; and has been received and stamped with the date and time by the suggestion office (or evaluator)."

Promotion and Publicity. Aggressive program promotion is important for the ongoing success of the suggestion system; it keeps the employees up-to-date on what is being done and on what opportunities exist for them. Keeping the employees enthused about the program improves both the quality and the quantity of the suggestions made; a good way to accomplish this is by holding well-advertised recognition and award ceremonies.

Record Keeping. Detailed and accurate records should be kept of the specific suggestions made, the evaluation of those ideas, the implementation of suggested ideas, and the reasons for rejection of suggestions. These data allow realistic reports to be made to management on the performance of the system. It should be understood that a submitted suggestion is a legal contract between the suggestor and the company. The company can be held liable if the idea had been initially rejected but then was later adopted without due credit to the suggestor. Therefore, accurate records of all improvement plans in the organization should be kept to safeguard against this.

Forms. Suggestions should be submitted on a form designed for easy reading and completion. The forms should include enough information to make the suggestion clear and understandable.

Appeals Process. Many suggestion plans have a process whereby a rejected idea can be appealed, allowing a suggestor to include more data or evidence which support the suggestion. It also indicates the willingness of management to consider fully employees' ideas, letting them know that management is not infallible.

Rejection Process. Some suggestions must be turned down, and this must be done tactfully. The best way to do this is to contact the person personally and explain in detail why the idea is not feasible. Care should be taken not to couch the rejection in generalities or euphemisms and

183

not to use the word "rejected." The denial should be as positive as possible; "not accepted" sounds much more encouraging. If the suggestion has already been submitted, or if it is currently being investigated in the company, this should be made known to the suggestor with as much detail as is appropriate. This prevents the suggestor from feeling cheated if it is implemented at a later date.

Awards. The most common award for accepted suggestions is cash, but the amount of the award differs greatly between companies. The NSSS reported that, on the average, the cash awards for cost savings or productivity suggestions was about 17 percent of the first-year savings. The cash awards ranged from virtually zero percent to a full 100 percent of the first-year savings. Studies conducted by the NSSS indicate that there is a large difference in system success when the cash award is higher, having a significant break in perception when the award is above 10 percent of the first-year savings. Individual companies differ and the larger organizations tend to have larger awards. Regardless of the percent, an upper dollar limit should always be set for the award. The largest upper limit known by the NSSS is $250,000; most are in the $1,000 to $5,000 range.

Recognition. In addition to the awards given for accepted ideas, it is important to give the employee recognition for the suggestion; this can be as large a motivator as a cash award. Many programs have special dinners and publish the winners' names in company newsletters or community newspapers.

Job Security. Employees must be sure that no suggestion they make leads to someone losing a job because of an increase in productivity. The best safeguard against this deterrent is to have created a corporate climate wherein the employees do not fear job loss due to increased efficiency.

Sample Suggestion Systems

Figure 9.1 shows a flowchart of a suggestion system presented by Milton A. Tatter (Tatter, 1975). This system is typical of successful programs in existence and incorporates the previously reviewed elements.

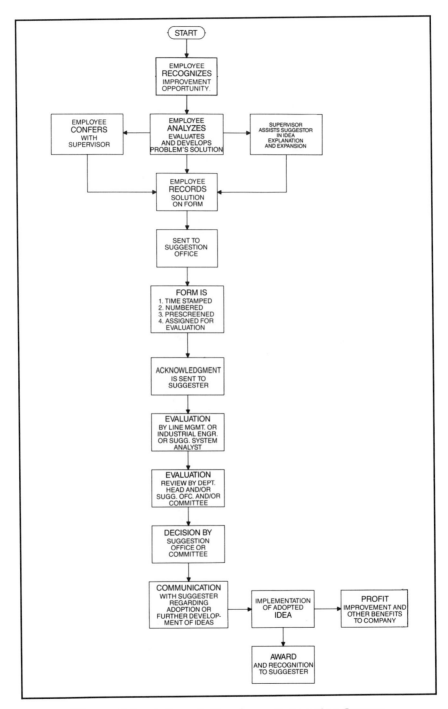

Figure 9.1 A Sample Employee Suggestion System

Employee Suggestion Systems and TQC

TQC strives for customer satisfaction through continuous process improvement, and those process improvements come from suggestions made by quality teams or individuals. The suggestion system is the vehicle whereby these ideas are evaluated and moved to implementation. All individuals or quality teams are expected to implement any change in processes over which they have responsibility. The suggestion system is the mechanism by which individuals or teams present solutions that are not within their own job responsibility to implement.

The workings of an employee suggestion system are consistent with the teamwork spirit and the participative management style fostered in a TQC environment. This type of system, along with an extensive network of quality teams, allows opportunities for the organization to benefit from the employee and allows for the employee to benefit from participation in the program, both psychologically and monetarily.

The following section is a detailed description of ECAP (Employee Corrective Action Plan), the employee suggestion system used by Hewlett-Packard Singapore and by Yokogawa Hewlett-Packard. This system utilizes existing management hierarchy for suggestion evaluation rather than having separate suggestion program administration. They also have an award scale based on a point system rather than on a percent of savings. This program has been successful in these two Far Eastern companies. The cultural differences between the United States and Japan and China may interfere with the assumption that the plan would work as well in the United States without modification.

For this system to work in the United States, the award program would probably need to be modified to reflect what the American worker would consider to be a more equitable compensation for the suggestion. It would also be extremely important to train supervisors and managers to be professional evaluators, since they would be the ones responsible for evaluating the ideas. The no-appeal feature of ECAP would not be acceptable to most U.S. employees because of the perception of subjective considerations in the evaluation process.

The ECAP award system is very sound for noncost savings or for nonproductivity ideas like safety or work environment suggestions. Since these types of ideas are very difficult to quantify, they traditionally carry with them no monetary award — but they do at least provide an equivalent amount of recognition and hoopla.

ECAP Suggestion Scheme

Objectives

- To support the participative management philosophy of the company.

- To allow Hewlett-Packard employees to make logical and practical suggestions for improvement in the work environment; the safety rules; and in the quality and design of systems, processes, products, and services.

- To encourage QC circle participation.

Areas of Concern Applicable to ECAP

- Materials and their flow.
- Design and layout of production floor.
- System or process in general.
- Design of equipment, tools, and fixtures.
- Work environment.
- Safety.
- Product or service quality and design.
- Work procedures.
- Information flow.
- Other (as defined by the operation manager or management equivalent).

Areas of Concern not Applicable to ECAP

- Personnel policies and guidelines.
- Salary and wage administration.
- Personal grievances.
- Human conflicts.
- Job responsibility or work assignment (should be within the direct control of the proposer).

Eligibility

- All Hewlett-Packard employees are eligible to participate in this scheme.

- The suggestion may be submitted either by an individual, a group, or a QC circle. QC circle suggestions will not be assessed under the grading system. All QC circle projects completed in FY 1984 and beyond are applicable to this suggestion scheme.

Rules and Regulations

- Suggestions must be submitted on a standard ECAP form (Figure 9.2).

- All concerns must be accompanied by a suggestion before they can qualify for assessment. Proposers should ask their immediate supervisors for assistance whenever necessary.

Name: _____

Employee No.: _____

Department: _____

Location Code: _____

Date of Submission: _____

QC CIRCLE PROJECT: □YES □NO

PHOTO

(OPTIONAL)

Guidelines:

A. Briefly describe present condition, method or practice.

B. Details of your suggestion for improvement.

C. Please write neatly or type.

D. Use additional sheets if necessary.

PRESENT CONDITION:

_____

_____

_____

_____

_____

_____

_____

_____

YOUR SUGGESTION:

_____

_____

_____

_____

_____

_____

_____   Is your suggestion already implemented?

_____   □ Yes   □ No

_____   If yes, date of implementation: _____

MANAGER'S COMMENTS:

_____   For implementation: Yes/No

_____   Responsible Person: _____

_____   Date of Completion: _____

_____   Net Savings: S$_____
(First year only)

Figure 9.2 ECAP Suggestion Scheme

- The decision of the judges is final.

- The steering committee reserves the right to make changes to the suggestion scheme and its reward system whenever necessary. The steering committee also reserves the right to terminate this suggestion scheme if deemed necessary.

- Accumulation of points is **not** allowed.

Grading System

- All individual and group suggestions will be graded (Figure 9.3) To qualify for assessment, improvement must have occurred as a result of the suggestion. Points are awarded based on the following conditions and criteria.

For suggestions that cannot be implemented:

   - Applicability
   - Idea
   - Effort

For suggestions that will be or already are implemented:

   - Applicability
   - Idea
   - Effort
   - Safety
   - Quality
   - Profit
   - Others

- QC circle suggestions will not be assessed. To qualify for a prize, the suggestion must have resulted from the use of QC circle tools and techniques in circle meetings.

			× 12 =	

(1) No of labor units saved x labor rate (S$ /unit labor/mth) × 12 = ☐

(2) Man-hour reduction (hour/unit × no. units produced/mth × hourly rate (S$ /hr)) × 12 = ☐

(3) Cost savings/unit × no. of units produced/mth × 12 = ☐

(4) Other savings/mth × 12 = ☐

A Total Savings = ☐

(5) Capital investment × depreciation rate/mth × 12 = ☐

(6) Other incremental cost/mth × 12 = ☐

B Total Costs = ☐

| A | Total Savings/yr | − | B | Total Costs/yr | = | C | Total Net Savings/Yr | ☐ |

Criteria	Measures	Grades			Score 1st Assessment	Score 2nd Assessment
Applicability	Possibility of immediate implementation	Cannot be implemented 0 Point	Will be implemented ☐ Already implemented ☐ 10 Points			
Idea	Degree of originality	Negligible 0 Point	Some 8 Points	Significant 15 Points		
Effort	Amount of effort in generating the suggestion	Negligible 3 Points	Some 8 Points	Significant 15 Points		
Net Savings	First year net savings as a result of implementtion	Zero — 0 point 2 points of each nearest $1000				
Safety	Degree of safety improvement	Negligible 0 Point	Some 5 Points	Significant 15 Points		
Quality	Degree of quality improvement	Negligible 0 Point	Some 5 Points	Significant 15 Points		
Others	Additional points could be given for other criteria not mentioned above. In this case give reasons.					

will be or already implemented.

TOTAL NO OF POINTS ☐

Reward System

Total score	0-14	15-49	50-79	>80
Prize value	Nil	$10	$40	$80
Certificate	Thank You	Bronze	Silver	Gold

Date of Final Assessment _____

Figure 9.3 Award Scoring Card

191

Reward System

- For individual and group suggestions only:

Total Score	Prize Value	Certificate
0-14	Nil	Thank You
15-49	$10	Bronze
50-79	$40	Silver
80+	$80	Gold

- For group suggestions: The prize has to be shared among the group members.

- For QC circle suggestions: A flat fee of $10 is awarded to each group leader and circle facilitator. Each department must submit its claim voucher to administration at the end of each month.

Guidelines for All Supervisors and Managers

- The immediate supervisor must decide whether the problem raised by the proposer is within the job responsibility or work assignment. Suggestions for problems within the direct control of the proposer do not qualify.

- Response time to suggestion after submission:

  - One week — suggestion requiring own department to assess.

  - Two weeks — suggestion requiring another department to assess.

- If actual assessment time exceeds the guideline, the responsible supervisor must explain the delay to the proposer's immediate supervisor.

- The immediate supervisor can approve suggestions deserving a $10 prize; the department manager can approve $10 and $40 prizes; the functional manager must approve all $80 prizes.

- No points can be accumulated toward the next suggestion.

- Under the profit assessment criterion, only the first-year savings will be considered.

- The immediate supervisor is responsible for seeking assistance in proposing suggestions pertinent to the department, but beyond his or her area of expertise.

- The immediate supervisor should reject all frivolous suggestions, thus saving both time and effort required in their assessment.

- See Figure 9.4 for an ECAP flowchart

Department ECAP Tracking System

- To assist in monitoring the progress of ECAP suggestions, a tracking system and record form should be used (Figures 9.5 and 9.6).

- In addition, the amount of monthly savings reported to TQC headquarters should be categorized as either potential net savings or actual net savings. Their definitions are:

    - Potential net savings are savings from suggestions yet to be implemented.

    - Actual net savings are savings from suggestions already implemented.

    (These two amounts can be extracted from the recommended record form.)

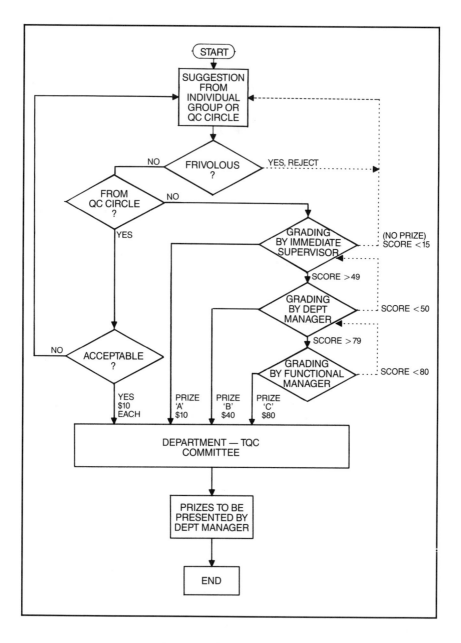

Figure 9.4 ECAP Flow

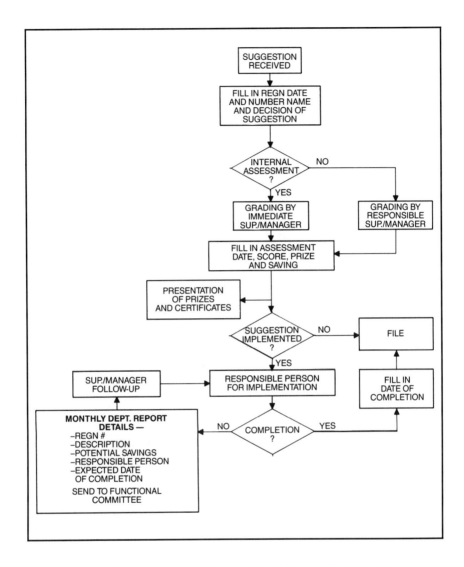

Figure 9.5 Department Suggestion Scheme Tracking System

ECAP SUGGESTION SCHEME
RECORD FORM

| Regn. # | Name(s) of Proposer | Description of Suggestion | Date of Regn. | Assessment | | | | Date of Prize/Cert Presentation | To be implemented? Yes/No | Responsible Person | Date of Completion |
				Date	Score	Prize	Net * (1st yr. Savings Only)				

* To be filled only if a suggestion will be or already implemented.

Note: This form should be kept for inspection during the TQC Audit.

Figure 9.6 Record Form

Reference

Tatter, Milton A. "Turning Ideas Into Gold." *Management Review,* March 1975.

CHAPTER 10

VENDOR PARTICIPATION

Customer focus is essential in a TQC environment. The use of TQC methodology throughout an organization provides customers with quality products and better services; production costs also decrease, allowing the business to be more price competitive. Customers deserve to have their expectations met — they deserve quality.

Every company is also a customer. A business benefits greatly when its vendors provide products and services that consistently meet expectations. The higher the quality of input to a manufacturing process, the higher the quality of the manufactured product. An integral part of TQC is the management of the customer-vendor relationship, assuring that perfect parts are received.

Benefits of Vendor Involvement in TQC

Vendors that use TQC to improve their own manufacturing process are better able to provide their customers with high quality parts, outstanding services, and unbeatable prices. Vendors who improve the input to their processes have a greater opportunity to improve the process itself. Table 10.1 compares the beneficial changes that typically occur in a business when its vendors use TQC for quality improvement.

Present Situation	Desired Situation
Parts seldom arrive on time.	Parts arrive on schedule.
Quantities received are often incorrect.	Parts arrive in the right quantities.
A portion of the parts are defective.	All of the parts are good.
Many parts must be tested prior to use.	No need for incoming inspection.
Some bad parts reach production and must be screened by inspection and replaced by rework.	No component-related rework.
High safety stock to cover part failures, unreliable receipts, unacceptable shipments, and unknown rework quantities.	Little or no safety stock.
All items either are counted and verified in the receiving department, or their quantities are assumed to be correct.	No need to count items to verify shipped quantities.
Confirmations made by purchasing staff in an effort to ensure delivery.	Little or no need to confirm deliveries.

Table 10.1   Present Situation versus Desired Situation

The actual, achievable level of quality probably lies somewhere between these two extremes. Still, the closer a business can get to the desired situation, the greater the improvements and savings in its own processes. The objective is to get rid of activities that exist to "inspect in quality" or to create "just-in-case" inventory.

The expense created by incoming, low quality vendor materials can be measured by totaling the costs of in-house quality inspection activities — necessary because it is too late for the vendor to rectify the problem. These costs include but are not limited to:

- Incoming inspection.

- Rework to replace failed components.

- Servicing a higher warranty rate.

- Handling discrepant material.

- Carrying higher safety stock inventory in case bad parts are received.

- Lost sales and customer dissatisfaction due to faulty components or product failures.

Late or early delivery from vendors can also be costly. This is measured by totaling the costs of all the steps that were taken to compensate for parts not arriving on time. Also added to the total are the cost effects of not having the parts when they were needed. These costs include, but are not limited to:

- Carrying higher safety stock inventory to prevent parts shortages before the arrival of the next shipment.

- Rescheduling direct labor and losing productivity due to absence of needed parts.

- Losing sales due to customer dissatisfaction because of back-ordered parts and delayed shipments.

- Carrying more work-in-process inventory to allow production rescheduling alternatives and to complete work with missing parts.

- Obtaining a replacement part through alternate sources.

A business cannot expect to maximize cost reduction through its own TQC efforts alone; it must depend on its vendors as well. No matter how much internal success is achieved, the success will be limited if the business does not receive the right parts, on time and defect free.

Vendors' Customer Expectations

Quality is defined by customer expectations. The vendor must think of your business as its customer; to provide you with quality parts and services, the vendor's definition of quality must be identical to your expectations. If these expectations have not been communicated explicitly, a vendor is likely to assume that they are similar to these traditionally acceptable levels of performance:

- Parts should be delivered before the due date.

- Early parts delivery is acceptable — even if it's by a few weeks.

- A certain percentage of defective parts below a standard limit will be acceptable.

- Prices will be comparable to those available elsewhere. The parts need to meet a set of specifications on a drawing to be acceptable.

Accepting the traditional level of performance leads to inspection and rework. Even if a vendor is doing better — giving the right part, at the right time, in the right quantity — holding to traditional expectations would still result in wasteful inspection and testing activities. Compare the traditional expectations to the following TQC-derived expectations:

- Parts must be delivered by the due date — and no more than two days early.

- Parts must meet all requirements — zero defects allowed.

- Prices should be lower (and if the vendor is using TQC, probably will be) — but price is not more important than quality and delivery.

- Vendors must prevent problems before the problems affect our processes.

- Vendors must provide documented proof of process control using control charts of previously agreed PQMs.

- Vendors are expected to assist customers with technical expertise wherever they can help products or processes.

- Parts should meet all specifications, whether explicit or implicit.

Since these expectations will need to be met constantly, it will be absolutely necessary for companies to work closely with their vendors.

Vendor/Customer Teamwork

Working with a vendor during the product planning stages for design and manufacturing offers many benefits. Customer support in areas like quality control and technical assistance makes it easier for the vendor to understand and meet expectations; this level of involvement requires a great deal of coordination between vendor and customer functions. Figure 10.1 shows a model for vendor communication channels; it compares traditional purchasing with TQC integrated purchasing (Juran, 1974).

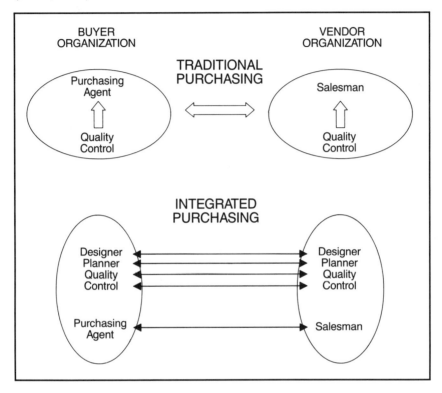

Figure 10.1   Traditional versus Integrated Purchasing Models

Involving vendors allows them to use expertise developed through practice. Vendors should be able to recognize potential improvement opportunities such as:

- Over-specification for the use of the product.

- Emphasis on original price versus cost of usage over the life of the product.

- Emphasis on conformance to specification, not fitness for use alternate designs or specifications that could improve performance or producibility.

203

Vendors must be informed in detail about the process in which their product is involved and exactly how it is expected to perform. The most important specifications a product must meet are the performance specifications.

The vendor must know not only the expectations of the product, but must also be aware of delivery and process performance documentation requirements. The object is for the vendor to build quality into the product by verifying the process. Quality measures applicable to the vendor process should be chosen and should be mutually agreed on; sampling methods should be specifically defined. As confidence is gained in the vendor's process, this documentation can formally replace incoming inspection.

Even after the product is designed and is being delivered satisfactorily, it is important to maintain a vendor/customer team attitude. Any changes to the performance specifications or to the customer expectations should be discussed with the vendor as soon as possible. The vendor should be utilized as a vital resource to design quality into products.

Communication and information sharing are vital elements to this type of vendor/customer relationship. This level of communication cannot come about overnight. The vendor and the customer must trust each other; each must firmly believe that the other will never use any information in a deleterious way. This level of trust can only be built through experience. A great deal of effort must be made by both parties, but the potential benefits are well worth it.

It is important to realize that it is not always necessary to develop a relationship to this degree with every vendor, but it is certainly advantageous if the vendor supplies critical or high-cost volume parts. The level of interaction must be a function of the derivable benefits of success. As Deming said in his book, *Quality, Productivity, and Competitive Position,* concerning standard, easily available, and technically unsophisticated materials,". . . hardware should be brought as hardware." This does not mean, however, that vendors of insignificant parts would not be told our expectations or that they would be excluded from any vendor training opportunities. The questions should always be: Are the available benefits worth the effort? Are the benefits commensurate with the dollars spent on the part, its production criticality, its substitutability, its uniqueness, its technological complexity, and its current quality? Is the level of vendor interest and the process improvement devotion that can be developed in the vendor company high enough to justify the effort?

Getting Vendors Involved

TQC means change, and change is not always welcome. At first, vendors may have difficulty accepting increased expectations. If they are not already involved in a TQC effort, they may see these expectations as unrealistic and impossible; this preception could very well be true of their existing processes.

To keep a company's business, a vendor may reluctantly agree to use TQC; but this attitude must change to adopt the TQC philosophy successfully. The vendor must be reassured that TQC utilization is not expected to take place immediately, that it occurs over time and is a dual effort between customer and vendor.

A huge effort on the part of the customer may be required to help vendors progress through TQC, therefore the customer must already be using TQC methods. Not only is example the best teacher, but extensive application of TQC methodology provides better definitions of the processes and more readily identifies those areas that vendors can influence, thus allowing specific and accurate communication of expectations to the vendors.

The company should provide training in SQC and TQC to vendors, but deciding who in the vendor organization should receive the training depends on the situation. As a general rule, the higher the level of management that can be involved, the better. This rule should be tempered with the practicality of providing TQC training to management or personnel drastically removed from the relevant vendor processes. The objective of the training is to introduce the vendor to TQC and SQC and to provide motivation and guidance in implementing their use throughout the entire vendor organization.

TQC training should start with formal lectures and seminars, but should evolve into a forum for practical application. It is a good idea for vendor training programs to contain the same information as the business' internal training programs. This reduces duplication of effort in material preparation and lends consistency to terminology and application between the vendor and the customer which aids in communication between the two.

Vendor motivation can be difficult to attain, but it is not impossible. Vendors must realize that if progress is not made toward meeting customer expectations, the customer will look for alternate sources. Quality is required — it is imperative. A team effort is mandatory, so vendors need to know that you will not abandon them if they put forth their best effort. They must also realize, however, that if their effort is not forth-coming other teammates will be found to replace them.

Vendors should understand that TQC is a long-term commitment — on the customer's part as well as theirs. Their participation leads to them benefiting from TQC advantages and also ensures them continued and increased business.

The first successes can lead to more involvement. This is true not only within one vendor's organization but throughout the active vendor base. When a vendor applies TQC with successful results, that project should be made known to the rest of the vendor's company, rewarding those who participated and motivating others. Success with particular vendors should also be shared with other vendors (only with the vendor's approval and always with care not to reveal any confidential or sensitive information). This can be accomplished in various ways: newsletters sent to all or selected vendors, personal contact made with buyers, or vendor days, where several are invited in and awards are given.

Another good motivator for vendors to get involved with the TQC process is the opportunity to become certified in TQC.

Vendor Certification

Vendor certification is a means of certifying that a particular vendor is meeting or is satisfactorily progressing toward meeting expectations. It means that the vendor is actively working on process improvement using TQC, can provide evidence of process control and improvement using control charts, and has reached minimum qualification levels for certification.

A vendor certification plan should "put the burden of producing quality components primarily on the vendor — where it belongs anyway" (Juran, 1974). The certification process should be demanding; if certification is to be meaningful to the vendor, it must be accomplishable — but not without effort.

Certification is done on a part/vendor or part-class/vendor relationship. It does not mean that a vendor is certified for all products; rather, it indicates that a part of a part-class is considered certified for that vendor.

The goals of a vendor certification program are to:

- Improve the quality of incoming parts.
- Provide positive feedback to vendors.
- Develop vendor performance to a level where incoming inspection is unnecessary.
- Provide recognition to vendors for accomplishments.

An example of a vendor certification program is shown in Figure 10.2, describing its development and implementation at Hewlett-Packard Singapore.

Vendors and TQC

The philosophy of purchasing in a TQC environment is to create a situation in which the vendor is expected to perform in the same way as an internal process. Following the principles of JIT purchasing, the parts would be delivered directly to the production line in just the right quantity and just in time to be used. This situation is set forth as an ideal. It is not always achievable, but the closer it can be approached, the greater the advantages.

The goals of JIT purchasing are, among others, to:

- Reduce lead times as much as is feasible.
- Reduce order quantities as much as is feasible.
- Reduce/eliminate purchased parts inventory.
- Increased response to engineering changes.
- Reduce paperwork.
- Reduce/eliminate incoming inspection.

An excellent discussion of JIT purchasing can be found in Schonberger's book, *Japanese Manufacturing Techniques* (1982).

Summary

Vendor involvement in TQC can lead to phenomonal process improvement. Vendors should be treated as extensions of the customer organization and should be expected to perform as such, requiring an environment of teamwork and cooperation. The importance of vendor/customer interaction cannot be overstated, because process improvements lead to higher quality and lower costs for everyone involved. Therefore, the TQC process presents no disadvantages in its use.

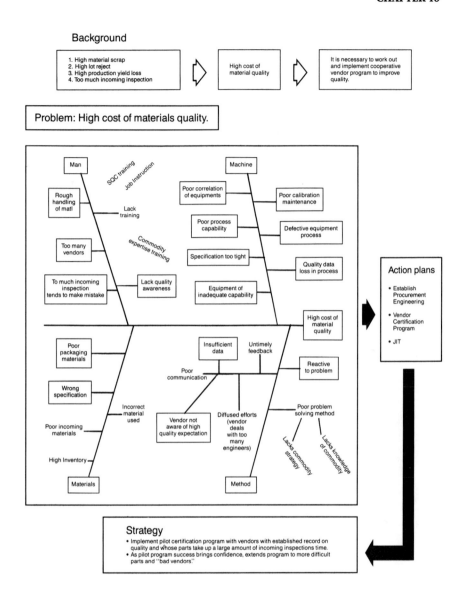

Figure 10.2 Vendor Certification Program

209

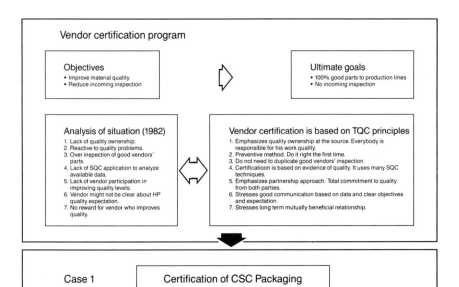

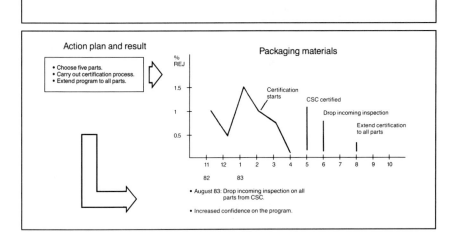

Figure 10.2 (Continued)

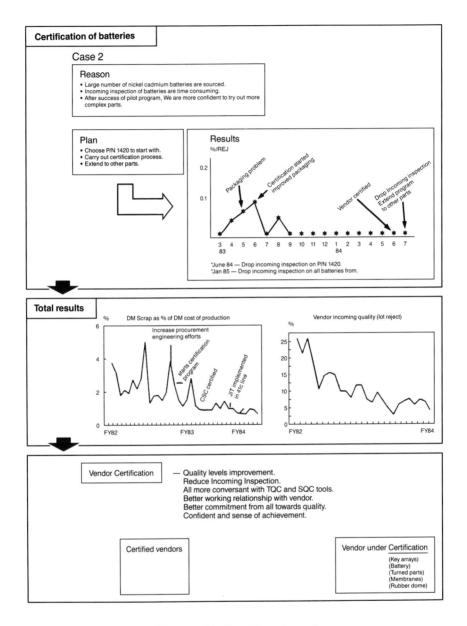

Figure 10.2 (Continued)

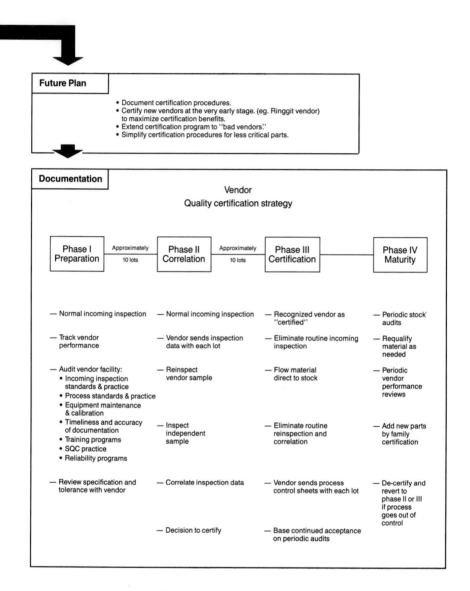

Future Plan

- Document certification procedures.
- Certify new vendors at the very early stage. (eg. Ringgit vendor) to maximize certification benefits.
- Extend certification program to "bad vendors."
- Simplify certification procedures for less critical parts.

Documentation

Vendor
Quality certification strategy

Phase I Preparation	Approximately 10 lots	Phase II Correlation	Approximately 10 lots	Phase III Certification	Phase IV Maturity

— Normal incoming inspection

— Track vendor performance

— Audit vendor facility:
  • Incoming inspection standards & practice
  • Process standards & practice
  • Equipment maintenance & calibration
  • Timeliness and accuracy of documentation
  • Training programs
  • SQC practice
  • Reliability programs

— Review specification and tolerance with vendor

— Normal incoming inspection

— Vendor sends inspection data with each lot

— Reinspect vendor sample

— Inspect independent sample

— Correlate inspection data

— Decision to certify

— Recognized vendor as "certified"

— Eliminate routine incoming inspection

— Flow material direct to stock

— Eliminate routine reinspection and correlation

— Vendor sends process control sheets with each lot

— Base continued acceptance on periodic audits

— Periodic stock audits

— Requalify material as needed

— Periodic vendor performance reviews

— Add new parts by family certification

— De-certify and revert to phase II or III if process goes out of control

Figure 10.2 (Continued)

References

Deming, W. Edwards. *Quality, Productivity, and Competitive Position.* Cambridge: Massachusetts Institute of Technology, 1982.

Juran, J. M., ed. *Quality Control Handbook,* 3rd ed. New York: McGraw-Hill Book Co., 1974.

Schonberger, Richard. *Japanese Manufacturing Techniques.* New York: Free Press, 1982.

CHAPTER 11

SYSTEMATIC PROCESS ANALYSIS: USA-PDCA

To make the goals of TQC a reality requires process improvement at all levels of the organization. Waste in the form of long cycle times, huge inventories, scrap, and rework must be reduced as much as possible. Every job — whether engineering design, product assembly, or cost accounting — must be studied to find opportunities for improvement. The systematic approach to process analysis described here is a method that can be applied universally to identify those improvements.

First, recognize that every activity in an organization is a process. A process is a repeatable series of tasks that produce a product or service. For example, the assembly and test operations in manufacturing are obviously processes. But what about nonmanufacturing areas? Accounting closes its books every month by using a definite process; personnel handles employee benefits according to a process; marketing follows a process when responding to calls from the field; and R&D follows a process for designing a new circuit. Every department in the organization depends on its processes to reach its goals.

Each department depends not only on its own processes but also on the services provided by other departments. The next process or department (your customer) also requires a quality product or service; so people within the organization who depend on your product are internal customers. The entire business is composed of producers and receivers, with each department playing both roles.

The business as a whole must be concerned with the ultimate customer, while every department within the business is focused on the needs of the next process. The process analysis method presented here is customer focused — the assumption being that the process exists to serve the customer and that nothing is more important than providing a better product to that customer.

The process analysis method is known under many names: TQC cycle, Deming Wheel, or PDCA cycle. The cycle used here is the USA-PDCA cycle. The model begins by focusing on customer expectations and proceeds with an ordered set of process analysis tools.

The goal is to focus your effort on items that are most important to your customer. Begin by understanding your customer's expectations for product and service quality. Do this by following the stages of the USA-PDCA cycle:

Understand

To understand, ask yourself the four customer questions:

1. Who are the customers of the process? Which people depend on your product to perform their job? Technicians test the product that assemblers build, but both depend on the quality of design from R&D. Field engineers depend on marketing engineers to answer their calls quickly and accurately. Marketing people depend on the finance department to provide accurate cost studies. As previously stated, many levels of suppliers and customers exist within one business.

2. What products or services does the process supply? Are they instruments, parts, designs, reports, forms, references, information, or what?

3. What are the customer's needs? What needs are the product or service trying to meet?

4. To what extent does the product or service meet the customer's expectations for quality? How completely has the product or service met those customer needs? Are there any unmet expectations?

Select

Any difference between your product's performance and your customer's expectations constitutes a problem that you need to resolve. Select a single problem for analysis from those identified in the *Understand* stage. A simple statement, clarifying exactly what is to be done, is then developed from the problem — it is called a problem statement.

To aid your selection of the right problem, compare all of the possibilities with regard to:

1. How much ownership or control your team has over the problem.

2. The urgency of the problem.

3. The trend of the problem. (Is it worsening or improving?)

The problem statement specifies what is to be changed, the direction that is desired, and the process that is involved. The problem statement is the objective to be gained by doing the rest of the process analysis.

Analyze

This stage of the USA-PDCA cycle uses analytical tools to study the process and to identify methods for improvement. The two analytical tools used by industrial engineering, statistical quality control, and other disciplines are:

1. Current process analysis
2. Cause analysis

Begin the current process analysis by developing a flowchart of how the process presently works. Start at the macrolevel and develop additional detail as necessary. Sometimes a cause for a process problem becomes apparent during this step; if it does, skip on to the *Plan* stage of the cycle and make the improvement.

It is often useful to do some "imagineering" by drawing a flowchart of the ideal process. Comparing the ideal process to the actual process shown in flowchart can be an eye-opening experience. Many people are surprised to find out just how many steps are encompassed in their process. After the flowchart is constructed, identify the quantitative measures of the process quality to assess the effects of the action taken. A control chart is the ideal tool for tracing process quality measures. If the measurements cannot be taken during the analysis cycle, a before-and-after study is recommended.

Finally, consider setting a goal for the quality measures. Perfection may be your ultimate goal, but it is fun to set and achieve intermediate targets.

The search for problem causes probes progressively deeper into the analysis process. The tools that are used include: cause-and-effect diagrams, data collection check-sheets, scatter plots, Pareto analyses, and Kepner-Tregoe cause analyses. To isolate the fundamental cause, this step may also include several iterations of cause and effect, data collection, Pareto analysis, and stratification.

Plan

Once a factor or set of factors is identified as being the cause of a process problem, brainstorm the possible solutions. Choose a solution from your list and plan its implementation.

Do

Implement the solution. If possible, try the solution on an experimental basis rather than throughout the entire process.

Check

Confirm that the solution had the impact intended. Check your PQMs on the control chart or do a before-and-after study. If the results are favorable, go on to the *Adopt* state. If the solution did not work, loop back to the *Analyze* or *Plan* stages.

Adopt

Once an improvement is demonstrated, incorporate it permanently into the process. Take care of all the details that sometimes handicap a good solution; update the documentation, conduct the necessary training, install the new tools, and explain the reasons for the change to everyone. Document the problem-solving process that led to the change, so that you can review it later should the need arise.

This stage of the cycle is also a time for review. Assess where you are and where you have been. Has the process reached the goals that you set for it at the outset? Are there additional causes for process problems you have not yet addressed? You may want to move back to the *Plan* or *Analyze* stages to develop and implement further process improvements. Repeat the *Plan, Do, Check,* and *Adopt* cycles as many times as is necessary to achieve your quality goals.

Summary

Figure 11.1 shows a model of the USA-PDCA analysis method just presented, emphasizing the cyclical nature of process analysis.

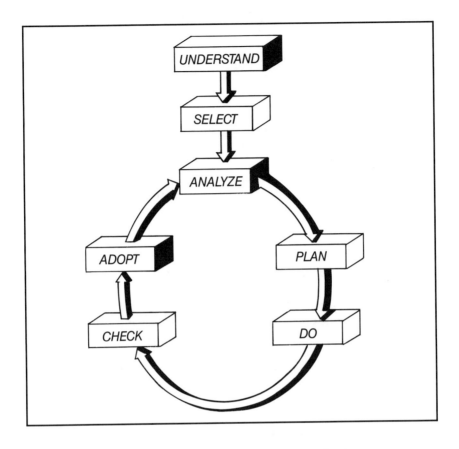

Figure 11.1   Process Analysis Method

A common phrase in TQC literature is, "Do it right the first time!" This does not mean that process changes should be expected to work as anticipated the first time they are implemented. Inevitably, adjustments are required to get the bugs out of the system. Doing it right the first time refers to the goal of a perfect process that produces products without scrap or rework. We may not be able to implement our solutions correctly the first time, but after detailed analysis and experimentation, a business should find that its processes are, for the most part, doing it right the first time.

Process Improvement Using USA-PDCA

The balance of this chapter is intended as a practical, working reference for people who want to learn USA-PDCA to improve their processes and to achieve higher product quality. The key elements of this strategy are listed as follows:

1. *Customer satisfaction* (i.e., quality) is the bull's-eye at which TQC aims.

2. *Management commitment* means that management acknowledges that quality improvement is the fundamental goal of the business and provides the leadership and resources necessary to implement TQC.

3. *Total participation* means that everyone in the business operates in, and benefits from, the TQC framework.

4. *Common process improvement framework* means that process improvement efforts are more efficient because quality teams know they will be using the TQC framework and can spend minimal time deciding what to do next; and that separate but related work groups can communicate their strategies and progress more easily.

5. *Statistical quality control tools* are techniques for understanding how a process works and where problems are occurring within it.

The USA-PDCA Cycle

The USA-PDCA cycle is a framework used to improve a process, and a process is a sequence of tasks that achieve a desired result. In an industrial or business context, more processes are (or should be) repeatable. Repeatable processes can be improved, because problems identified during one cycle of the process can be eliminated or diminished on subsequent cycles. Virtually everything we do is part of a process.

The four main segments of the USA-PDCA cycle are:

1. Understand

   • Who are the customers of the process?
   • What are the products of the process?
   • What do the customers expect of the product?
   • How well does the product meet the customers' expectations?

The differences between the customers' expectations and the product's performance are called problems.

2. Select

   Of the differences between the customers' expectations and the product's performance, which one will be addressed during this cycle?

3. Analyze

   • How does the process really work?
   • What is the current level of quality performance?
   • What are potential causes of the problem?
   • What are the actual causes of the problem?

4. PDCA

   • *Plan.* Device a way to eliminate the cause(s) of the problem.
   • *Do.* Try the plan experimentally.
   • *Check.* See if the plan worked as expected.
   • *Adopt.* If it worked, incorporate the solution permanently. If not, start the cycle over.

Although the model shows the general order in which the steps will occur, a real process improvement cycle will have some "rework loops," especially in the PDCA portion. That's fine, as long as all the steps are completed and the process is improved in the end (Figure 11.2)

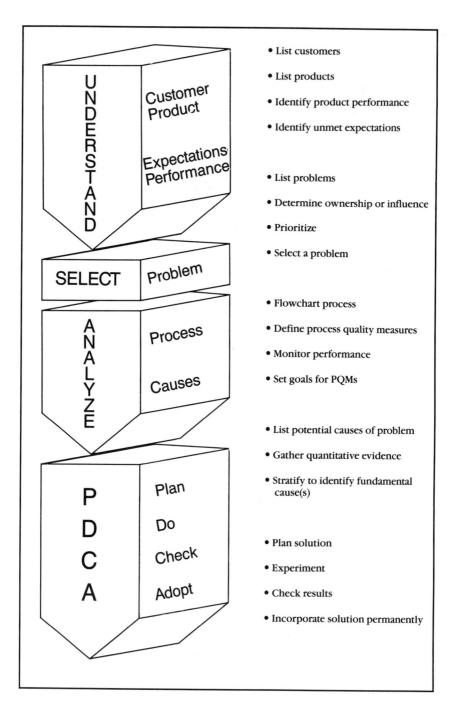

Figure 11.2   The USA-PDCA Process Flow

Mission Statement and Objectives

A review of the team's mission and objectives will help keep the TQC cycle moving in the right direction. If the quality team is composed of an established work group, statements of the group's mission and objectives probably already exist. When a work group doesn't understand its mission statement, it is prone to identify problems that are unrelated to the group's activity. The mission statement will focus its activities. If the team is an *ad hoc* task force, it should understand the mission of the task force or it will never achieve its objectives.

Mission statement. Defines in general terms why the group exists. It usually mentions the products, the customers, and the scope of the group's activities.

Objectives. Define in more specific terms what the product is and how, when, and where it will be produced. What is the objective to be accomplished?

For more details on mission and objectives refer back to Chapter 7.

UNDERSTAND
CUSTOMER EXPECTATIONS
CUSTOMER SURVEY INFORMATION

CUSTOMER	PRODUCT OR SERVICE	CURRENT EXPECTATIONS	PERFORMANCE	NEED MET?

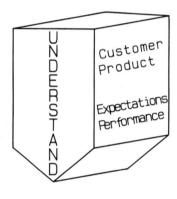

Tools and Hints

Customers	Who are they?	• Identify and list
Products	What goods or services does your process provide to your customers?	• Review your department mission statement
Expectations	What specific expectations do your customers have of your products?	• Customer interview • Customer survey • Be as quantitative as possible
Performance	How well do your products perform as compared to your customers' expectations?	• Be as quantitative as possible
Issues	What customer expectations are not met by your product's performance?	• Each "gap" between expectations and performance is a potential issue

Fill out the milestone document for the understand segment.

Figure 11.3   The TQC Cycle — Understand

224

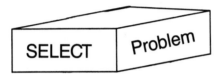

- Any difference between your customers' expectations and your product's performance is a problem. A problem statement is a simple description of how you plan to change your process to reduce that difference. The objective of this segment is to select one problem to work on, and then write a problem statement for it.

- A quality team will normally be able to identify several problems. Until a team has had a substantial amount of experience with the TQC cycle, it makes sense to address just one problem at a time. In the end, the selection of an issue to work on will largely be a judgment call, but consideration of the following factors may help:

  -How much ownership or control does the team have over each problem?
  -How urgent are the various problems?
  -Should the team choose a relatively simple problem just to gain the experience and the motivation that comes with a quick success?

- To generate a problem statement, answer these questions:
  -What kind of change will it be?
  -What needs to be changed?
  -Where will the change take place?

		1.	2.	3.
Marketing	→	reduce	errors	in-service manuals
Admin	→	reduce	hold time	during telephone transfers
Board Test	→	increase	turn-on rate	of 3582-01 board
A&W	→	decrease	scrap rate	of 3325 bezels
R&D	→	increase	accuracy	of new product costing

- Use the milestone document for this section to list all the problems, prioritize them, choose one to work on, and write a problem statement for it.

Figure 11.4 The TQC Cycle — Select a Problem

225

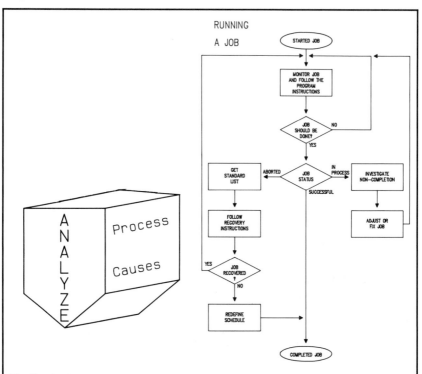

The "analyze" segment of the TQC cycle is broken into two parts:

- Process Analysis. Understanding how the process works generally.
- Cause Analysis. Sifting through the workings of the process to find the primary cause of the selected problem.

The primary tools of process analysis are the process flowchart and process quality measures:

- The process flowchart is a schematic, or picture, of how the steps in a process fit together.
- The process flowchart helps the team develop a mutually agreed on view of how the current process works before even talking about how to improve it. Flowcharts always take a long time to develop, especially in a group. In the end, a good flowchart will not only save time, but also prevent a lot of frustration and disappointment.
- The process flowchart is made up of:
    - Rectangles that show activities or operations, such as' "load parts"
    - Diamonds that contain questions, such as: "Is the part defective?"
    - Arrows that show the order of activities and questions.
    - Ovals that show input and output materials or information.

- As you generate the flowchart, ask the following questions:
    - What are the main activities or operations in my process?
    - Which ones always occur? Which ones happen only some of the time?
    - Under what conditions do the "sometimes" activities or operations take place?
    - In what order do the activities or operations take place?

Figure 11.5   The TQC Cycle — Analyze the Process I

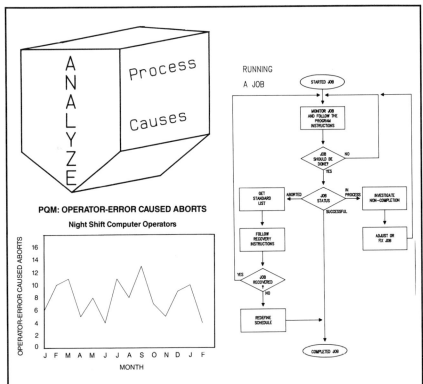

Process Quality Measures (PQMs):

- Are quantitative indicators of how well a process is performing.
- Should measure those aspects of your process' performance that are most important to your product's success in meeting your customer's expectations.
- Usually measure rates, such as:
  - Percent defective
  - Units completed per day
  - Monthly production dollars per square foot
  - Scrap dollars per month
  - Missing parts per board
  - Average time for purchase order acknowledgment
  - Customer complaints per month
  - Turnaround time for repair

- To generate and evaluate PQMs in your process:
  - Define PQMs for your process by asking, "What measurements of my process best predict the quality of my products?"
  - Collect data on the actual values of each PQM to see how well your process is currently operating.
  - Plot your PQM data on appropriate charts. These could be run charts, control charts, etc.
  - Set target values for your PQMs. These are the values that you think your process needs to operate at in order to produce a satisfactory product.

Figure 11.6 The TQC Cycle — Analyze the Process II

227

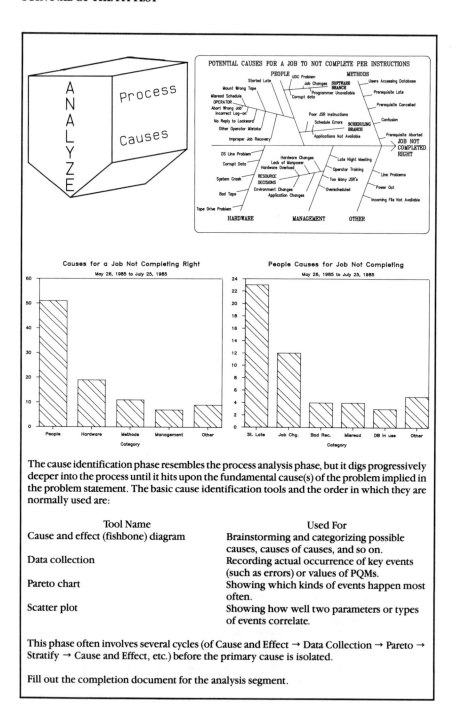

The cause identification phase resembles the process analysis phase, but it digs progressively deeper into the process until it hits upon the fundamental cause(s) of the problem implied in the problem statement. The basic cause identification tools and the order in which they are normally used are:

Tool Name	Used For
Cause and effect (fishbone) diagram	Brainstorming and categorizing possible causes, causes of causes, and so on.
Data collection	Recording actual occurrence of key events (such as errors) or values of PQMs.
Pareto chart	Showing which kinds of events happen most often.
Scatter plot	Showing how well two parameters or types of events correlate.

This phase often involves several cycles (of Cause and Effect → Data Collection → Pareto → Stratify → Cause and Effect, etc.) before the primary cause is isolated.

Fill out the completion document for the analysis segment.

Figure 11.7   The TQC Cycle — Analyze for Primary Cause

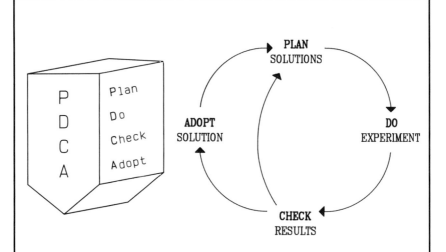

→ Plan → Do → Check → Adopt → Plan → Do → Check → Adopt

The start of the P-D-C-A phase marks the transition from looking at and thinking about the problem to actually doing something about it. The P-D-C-A sequence ensures that the final solution really works as anticipated and that it is incorporated into the process permanently. The team might have to go through the P-D-C-A sequence several times before achieving a substantial improvement in the process.

Plan
- Brainstorm possible solutions. If the cause analysis was done thoroughly, at least one solution should be evident.
- Select a solution.
- Set success criteria. What values would your PQMs have to run at to make you think the solution was successful?
- Generate a timeline showing who will do what and when.

Do
- Implement the solution on a small, experimental basis.

Check
- Confirm that the results of the experiment satisfy the success criteria.
  If they did, go on to "adopt."
  If they did not, go back either to "plan" or "analyze."

Adopt
- Update process documentation, material documentation, and training materials.
- Conduct update training.
- Install new tools, tooling, and fixtures.
- Modify data collection and analysis procedures.

Fill out the completion document for the PDCA segment.

Figure 11.8 The TQC Cycle — PDCA

229

Writing Problem Statements

A problem statement is a statement that indicates the intended result of intervention in the process. It is composed of three parts:

1. An indicator of change and direction:
   - Increase
   - Improve
   - Eliminate
   - Reduce
   - Remove

2. An indicator of quality in a service or product based on customer perceptions:

   - Errors, mistakes, breakdowns
   - Production yield
   - Turnaround time
   - Delivery rate
   - Durability

3. A process or operation:

   - Production line
   - Typing a memorandum
   - Order processing
   - Communication between ABC and XYZ departments
   - Translation of training manuals

Example of a problem statement: (R&D) Improving the forecasting accuracy of software design manpower requirements.

Self-check questions:

1. What is the intended result of dealing with this customer's concern?

Problem: Write a problem statement based on the answer to this question.

2. What is the end result of this problem statement?

3. Does the end result of the problem statement directly match the intended result?

Process Quality Measure

PQMs are the quantitative indicators of the quality of a process. The components of PQMs are:

1. The quality indicators of a process. Most quality indicators are further delineations of the following quality characteristic groups:

   - Effectiveness
   - Accuracy
   - Efficiency
   - Timeliness

2. The unit of measure:

   - Percentages (e.g., percent of items that fail a test)
   - Individual counts (e.g., number of typos in a memo)
   - Ratio (e.g., number of man-hours per function performed)
   - Rates (e.g., requisitions processed per month)

Writing PQMs:

1. Identify the problem statement and the quality indicator of your process.

2. Determine the quality characteristic group(s) in the problem. The quality indicator should be a specific example from that group.

3. Decide what unit of measure you will use to quantify the quality indicator.

Data Collection Planning Worksheet

Q1: Why are we collecting these data?

- What is our purpose?

- Is this purpose the same as our problem statement? If not, revise the problem statement or purpose.

Q2: What data do we need?

- Which PQMs will be studied? (Limit to three or less.)

- Make sure each PQM has two parts: the quality indicator and the unit of measure.

  PQM1:
  PQM2:
  PQM3:

- Classify each PQM as:

  -Qualitative (QL), quantitative discrete (QD), or quantitative continuous (QC).

  -What are the operational definitions for each PQM?

  -Include rule or description.

  -Include method of measurement.

  -Which possible related factors have been selected?

  -Which variables have been chosen for stratification?

  -Are there prior data on PQMs, related factors, or stratification variables on which to draw? If so, describe.

Q3: Where in the process will data be collected?

- Refer to your process flow diagram.

- Consider collecting data at the output and input of the process. If you do this, which data will you collect?

- Is time involved in your PQMs or related factors? If so, do you plan to collect time-related data at holding steps or loops? Describe what you will collect.

- Describe where data will be collected on your potentially related factors and stratifying variables.

- Indicate on your process flow diagram where all data will be collected.

Q4: How will the data be collected?

- What is the population of interest? Describe.

- Will the data collection be a census or a sample? Why?

- If sampling is chosen, which random sampling design will be used? List its advantages and disadvantages.

- If sampling is chosen, which random sampling aid will be used?

- Write a brief description of how your selected data collection methods will be carried out.

Q5: Who will collect the data?

- Who is responsible for the data that will be collected for each PQM selected?

  PQM1:
  PQM2:
  PQM3:

- Who is responsible for the data on the related factors and the stratifying variables?

Q6: How much data should be collected?

Review your answers to Q4, then ask:

- How much variability is present in our PQMs?

- What precision is needed in the answer?

- What level of concern is there about the correctness of the answer?

- What are the resource constraints?

- How many items will be measured before analyzing the data? How many variables (PQMs, related factors, stratifying variables) per item measured?

Q7: How long should the data be collected?

Review your answers to Q4 and Q6, then ask:

- How often do data become available? Does the process have a long or short cycle time?

- When do you plan to analyze the data?

- How long can resources be allocated to continue to collect the data?

- How many data (number of items measured multiplied by the number of measurements) will you have at that point?

Q8: How will the data be recorded?

Use the checksheet design process flow diagram to develop the checksheet(s) needed to complete your data collection plan. Then ask:

- What type of checksheet is being used?

- Is a single checksheet being used to record data across time? If so, what time period?

- Will data on potentially related factors appear in the header, in the format, or in both? Describe.

- If data were available now, would the checksheet help you to analyze the results?

Q9: What limits exist for the data collection plan?

- Review the answers to each of the eight key data collection questions. What constraints have been imposed? What assumptions have been made?

- What could go wrong with the plan? Is there anything you could do differently to prevent problems?

- What will be done with "bad" or "unusual" data?

- Finally, what would you do with the data if you had them now?

An Example of the USA-PDCA Process Improvement Model as Applied to the Printed Circuit Board Process

Now that you have reviewed the USA-PDCA process analysis model, an example of the approach as it applies to a specific process should help clarify how it works. The next several pages show the completion documents from a quality team of printed circuit (PC) assembly supervisors working to improve the PC board repair process. In order to make an easy connection with the preceding discussion of the TQC cycle, the documents are labeled with the appropriate stage of the USA-PDCA model.

An example follows these steps:

1. The team identifies reducing turnaround time as the major problem by collecting customer information.

2. Next, the team defines the process by using a process flowchart and by taking data on their process quality measure — turnaround time.

3. They stratify the turnaround time data and construct a Pareto chart to identify the major contributors to the problem.

4. A cause and effect diagram is used to summarize the results of a brainstorming session regarding possible causes for unacceptable turnaround times for repair.

5. From this diagram, the team selects the most likely reasons for unacceptable rework times and lays out a plan for resolving the problem.

6. After implementing the solutions selected, the results are assessed by updating the time series plot of turnaround time.

7. Since the process changes proved to be beneficial, a new process flowchart is constructed and details are taken care of to ensure a successful transition to the new process.

No two applications of the USA-PDCA cycle look exactly alike, but all should follow the same general pattern. Projects do not all require the same analytical tools, but they do share the common activities of prioritizing issues based on customer input, current specifications, problem analysis, and solution experimentation.

Customer: _____

Work Group: _____

Date: _____

Needs	Expectations & Measures	Met? (Y/N)	Own or Influ?	Sit. Anal.*		
				S	U	T

Issue Statement: _____
_____

*Kepner-Trego Situation Analysis
Seriousness: High, Medium, Low
Urgency: High, Medium, Low
Trend (if left alone): Increase ↑, Decrease ↓, Steady →

Figure 11.9 The TQC Cycle — Customer Survey Information

Customer: _____

Work Group: _____

Date: _____

Needs	Expectations & Measures	Met? (Y/N)	Own or Influ?	Sit. Anal.* S	U	T
Hand-loaded PC boards	Correctly loaded	N	O	M	L	→
	Delivered on time	Y	I			
Response to problems	Quick response	N	O	L	L	→
	Appropriate response	N	O	L	L	→
Repaired boards	Good turnaround time	N	O	H	M	→
	Proper repair	Y	O	L	L	→

Issue Statement: _____
_____

*Kepner-Trego Situation Analysis
  Seriousness: High, Medium, Low
  Urgency: High, Medium, Low
  Trend (if left alone): Increase ↑, Decrease ↓, Steady →

Figure 11.10   Understand and Select — Customer Survey Information

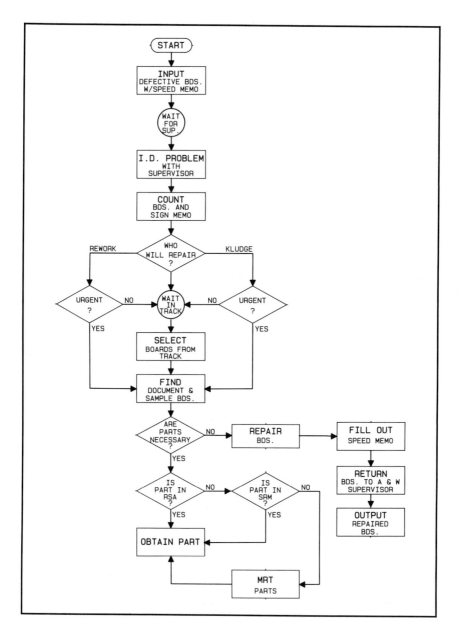

Figure 11.11 PC Repair Process

238

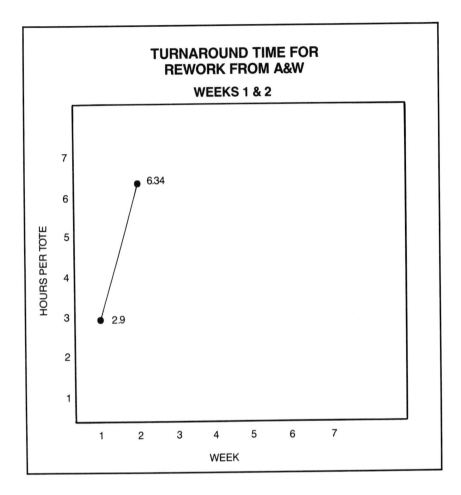

Figure 11.12 Process Analysis

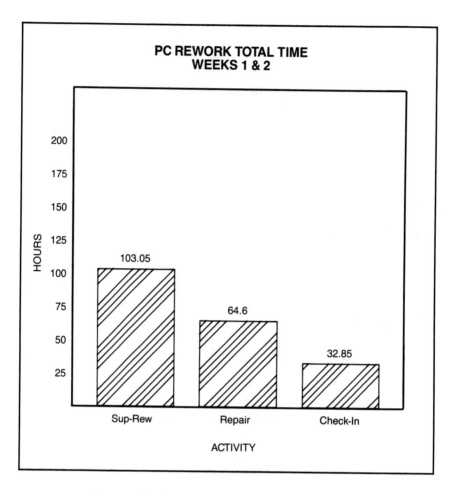

Figure 11.13 Cause Analysis — PC Rework

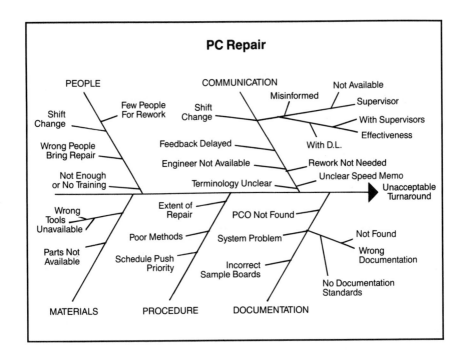

Figure 11.14   Cause Analysis — PC Repair

Goal for PQM: _____

Major Causes	Possible Solutions	Solution Selected
Time needed for supervisor check-in	Eliminate both steps	Eliminate both steps
Time needed to go from supervisor to rework	Reduce both steps	

Who Did	What	When
Joan & Eileen	Contacted A&W about new procedures	June 3
Bob & Cammy	Took over operation	June 3
Four new people	Assigned to do rework	June 3

Figure 11.15   Plan-Do Chart

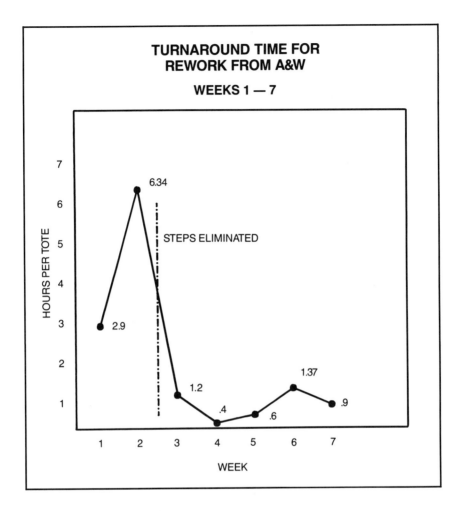

Figure 11.16   Check Rework Turnaround

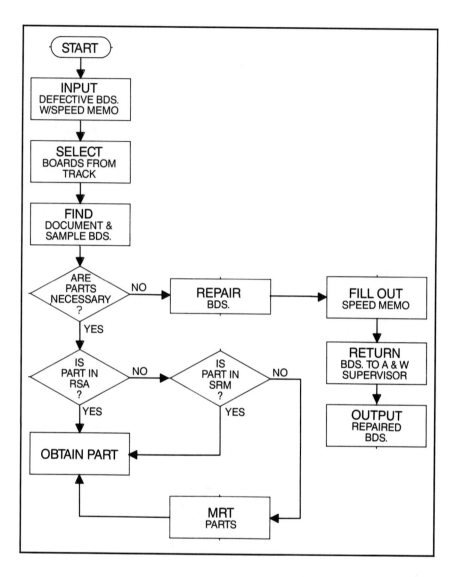

Figure 11.17   Check Flowchart

To eliminate unwanted time added to the total rework cycle, we would like to implement a new routing process for all A&W rework to PC.

Beginning Monday, all rework should be routed directly to the two appointed rework statons so those boards in question will be top priority and reduce cycle time back to A&W. If questions should arise, please direct them to the area supervisor.

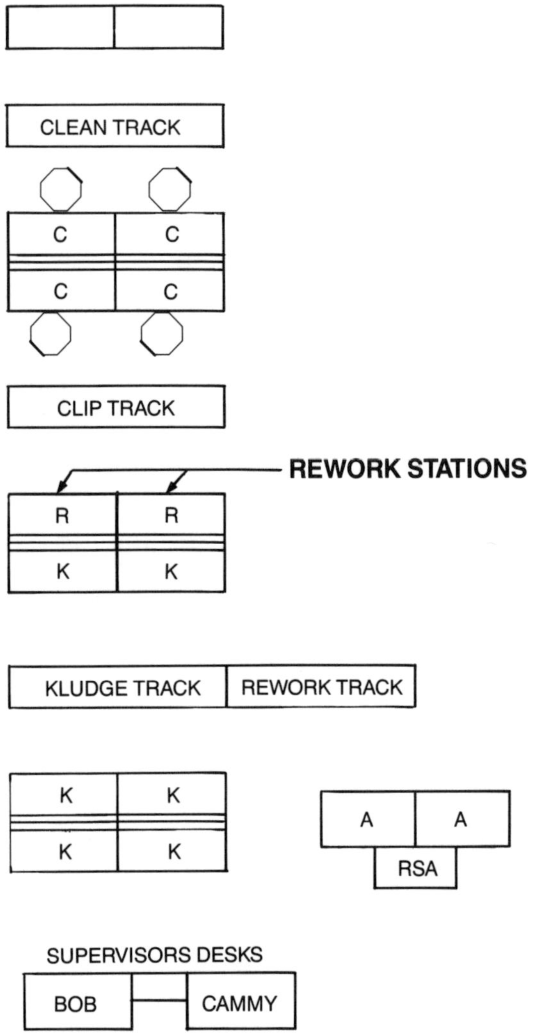

Figure 11.18 Rework Station Chart

245

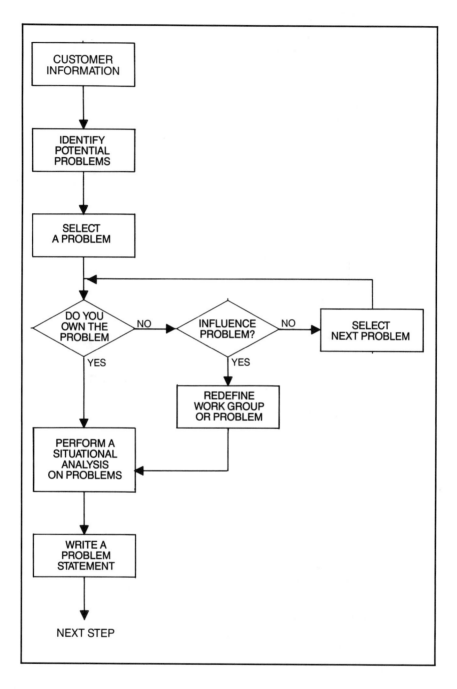

Figure 11.19 Problem Selection Process

CHAPTER 12

QUANTITATIVE ANALYSIS: SQC

The term statistical quality control causes anxiety for many people. The prospect of expending effort to interpret data and to apply statistical formulas is not inspiring to most practical-minded employees. Computers have assumed the burden of the mathematical calculations, so part of the trepidation associated with statistical methods should be eliminated. To some degree this is true, but often the complexity of calculations is not the reason SQC tools are left unused. The major obstacles tend to be the mastery of the fundamental concepts and the difficulty of data collection.

The goal of this chapter is to help the reader understand the practical application of statistics to the USA-PDCA process. Many reference books on SQC treat the subject with greater detail than is presented here. Our focus is only on the essential tools, simplifying the information so that nontechnical employees can grasp the concepts.

Statistical Theory

Our aim is to produce a product that is pleasing to the customer every time it is used — today's product, tomorrow's product, and next year's product are to be of good quality. For our purposes, the definition for quality is that the product meets the customer's expectations. Quality means fitness for use.

The customer expects perfection. This statement does nothing more than reword the definition for quality just given. The term "perfection" may seem unrealistic, but it does make it clear that no deviations from expectations are to be tolerated. Customers do not want to hear excuses. A new car that leaks oil is defective, period. The buyer does not care whether the problem is a design flaw or an assembly error; perfection is expected.

The term "perfection" is used for a second reason: Taken literally, it is impossible to attain. No human endeavor is capable of producing a product wherein every unit produced is identical to all the previous units and all units to follow. Some degree of variation always exists. This inevitable variation in quality casts serious doubt on a producer's ability to provide the customer with perfection. Statistics is the study of variation and the first tool available for analyzing these problems.

When you define the phrase "fitness for use," you find it to mean "conformance to specifications," whether these specifications are expressed in inches, pounds, smoothness, shininess, distortion dB, color intensity, picture clarity, reply time, etc. The customer's expectations eventually come down to a set of specifications that must be met. The customer does not remain equally satisfied, however, regardless of where the quality characteristic falls within the particular set of specifications.

Acceptable versus Quality

In 1979 a comparison of the color density of television sets made by Sony-USA and Sony-Japan showed that the Sony-USA sets were distributed uniformly over the tolerance interval (Phadke, 1982). This was achieved by quality control through screening. The sets produced in Japan, however, had a color density distribution which was bell shaped and centered at the target value; this was due to Japan's deliberate effort to come as close to the desired specification as possible. The cost of ownership was significantly less for the Sony-Japan televisions because of lower repair costs related to color density problems (Figure 12.1).

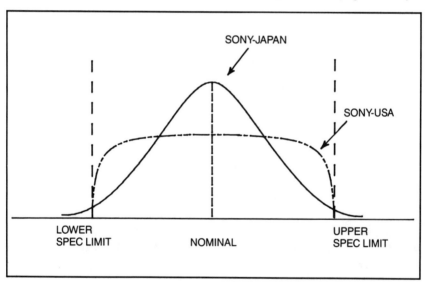

Figure 12.1   Distribution of Color Density in TV Sets

Building a product that is fit to use does not mean simply satisfying tolerance limits. To be competitive, a distribution must be achieved for every quality characteristic that is centered at the desired mean value and has the smallest economically justifiable variance. This distribution typically falls within the normal, bell-shaped curve. SQC is the science of developing a process whose product's quality characteristics are distributed around the nominal value with the smallest economically justifiable variance.

Consider a process that produces units whose performance characteristics fall within the normal distribution range. Monitoring the individual units while they are being produced would show that their performance varies. It would be impossible to predict exactly what the performance of the next unit would be; but it is statistically possible to predict that the next unit would fall within certain bounds. This constitutes statistical control — the variation among units is random about a known average value with a known amount of deviation — and the quality of the next product produced can be predicted based on past performance. To restate this, the distribution of product quality is stable over time; the shape of the distribution curve does not change from week to week. This is an advantageous position for a manufacturer to be in because future quality can be predicted with confidence.

Now consider a process that produces units with an unstable distribution of performance. In this case, the performance of individual units varies unpredictably. The products produced this week perform quite differently from those produced last week. The process is out of statistical control; it is almost impossible to predict the quality of the product in future runs, but statistical theory can help gain statistical control.

Variation

There are two types of variation that may be present in a process: random and nonrandom. Random variation is always present because no two items, processes, or circumstances are precisely alike. Nonrandom variation may or may not exist. A nonrandom deviation in product quality may be due to a vendor change, a new employee, an uncalibrated instrument, etc. Nonrandom variation can be tracked down, the cause can be eliminated, and the process can be improved. This is not the case for random variation.

Consider a manager who is unaware of the two types of product quality variation. The current month's scrap report is up from the previous month, due entirely to random causes, and our hypothetical manager demands an explanation from the responsible production supervisor. What could be said? Or — just as bad — this month's results are better than last month's and the manager seeks out the supervisor to offer praise. Again, what could be said? If the system was under control, the supervisor could at least take solace in the knowledge that, over a long period of time, praise would come as often as criticism without the manager understanding SQC.

The first objective of SQC is to identify the causes for nonrandom variation in product quality and to eliminate them, thereby bringing the process under statistical control. Nonrandom variation may be either beneficial or detrimental; the elimination of its cause may mean adopting an improvement procedure or discarding an inefficient step.

Achieving a stable distribution of product quality is not an end to itself; doing so does not guarantee that the product meets specifications. The goal of SQC is to improve product quality and specifications through the process of identifying and fixing the detrimental, assignable causes of the system variation.

Definition of System

The term "system" (Deming, 1982) is defined to be all of the elements that make up the current process: people, environment, procedures, materials, tools, documentations, rankings, etc. It is the interaction of all these elements in the system that produces the random variation observed in the product quality. If the present distribution of product quality is unacceptable, one or more of the elements of the system must be changed. Three major vehicles to accomplish this are management, engineering, and statistical experiment design. The last two vehicles are inseparably intertwined.

An example of the potential that management has for improving the system will help explain the concept. Suppose the manner in which employees are evaluated causes them to work individually rather than as teams, emphasizing quantity above quality. Due to customer dissatisfaction, a system such as this could eventually cost the company millions of dollars in lost productivity and reduced sales. Yet, it would likely manifest as random fluctuation in the performance of the system. Only management is in a position to correct such problems.

250

An engineer is often faced with the task of improving a new product design or process method. Improvement, in any specific procedure, means changing some set of quality measures to more desirable values. Examples of such measures regarding product design are accuracy, smoothness, distortion, reliability, or intensity. Measures of process quality may include cycle time, work quantity, material scrap, or defect rate. Improving one or more of these quality measures translates into shifting their average, reducing their variability, or doing both.

Numerous variables often exist which the engineer could consider changing for product improvement. Engineering knowledge may exist about the relationship between the quality measures and some of the independent variables — but not all of them. Even if a physical relationship is theorized, the strength of that relationship under all conditions may not be known. In any case, some level of experimentation is necessary.

Statistical Design

The contribution of the statistical design of experiments is a scientific approach to analyzing the direct effects of several independent variables on one or more dependent variables. To test product designs or processes by holding all variables fixed while changing one, allows variable interactions to cloud the results. Well-documented designs (such as factorials, fractional-factorials, blocked designs, nested designs, and response surface designs) enable the researcher to test the effects of variables both singly and in combination with other variables.

Statistical designs recognize experimental error to be ever present and provide a means of testing the significance of effects against the experimental error by the analysis of variance procedure. Through analysis of variance, variables which do not influence the quality characteristics may be separated from variables which do, even in the presence of random error.

Having identified the key variables influencing the quality characteristics under study, response surface designs enable statistical models to be constructed which provide a map of the response variable(s) over the experimental region. From these maps, regions of maximum or minimum can be identified. Contour plots of several response variables can be overlaid to see the operating conditions that optimize several quality characteristics simultaneously.

Taguchi design methods focus on separating independent variables that influence only the mean of the response, those that influence only the variability of the response, and those that influence both (Taguchi, 1980). Furthermore, these designs use a minimum number of experimental runs to test for effects by assuming interactions to be negligible. For this reason, Taguchi techniques have received some criticism; but in situations involving a prohibitively large number of independent variables, there may be no other practical solution (Box, 1985). Good experimental practice means following limited screening designs with experiments capable of detecting interaction among variables found to be of significance in the initial Taguchi experiment.

In summary, experimental designs enable the engineer to separate the important variables from those having little or no impact upon the quality characteristics of interest. Furthermore, the effects of these variables can be modeled and mapped to discover optimal operating conditions. Experimental designs may be bold, covering a wide range of the possible operating conditions; or they may be evolutionary, varying the independent variables over a small range so as to control the possibility of producing a defective product while conducting an experiment on the process. By identifying the variables that have little or no impact on either the process mean or variability, wide tolerances can be set for these variables and cheaper materials can be used. Variables that affect the process mean but not the variability can be used to keep output within specifications despite changing conditions in the process. Finally, appropriate nominal and tolerance limits may be assigned to those variables affecting both the quality characteristic average and variability.

The Tools of Statistical Quality Control

Control Charts

The principal tool for evaluating the process' state of control is the statistical control chart. The control chart, simple in construction and operation, consists of an ordinary run chart. It is enhanced by the addition of a center line drawn at the process average and lines drawn at the tails of the distribution such that if the process is under statistical control, 99.7 percent of all observations fall within the limits. A history of 15 to 30 samples is required before a control chart can be constructed. This is necessary to arrive at a reasonable estimate of process average and process variability.

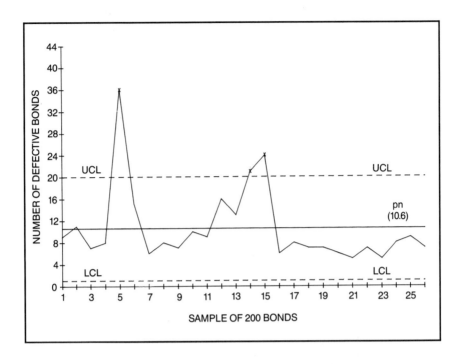

Figure 12.2 A Control Chart: Number of Defective Bonds
per 200 Attempts

Four common problems in applying control charts:

1. Selecting samples from the process.

2. Knowing when to recalculate the control limits.

3. Not using the chart real time (plot results often).

4. Confusing specification limits with control limits.

The selection of appropriate samples for plotting is essential to the usefulness of a control chart. The samples should be tied closely to the actual working process; they should represent batches, days, shifts, machines, or whatever is pertinent in the situation. Do not select samples during a time in which there is a likelihood of process disturbance.

253

Recalculating the control limits with every sample is probably the most common error in the application of control charts. Once enough samples have been taken to calculate the average and to set the control limits, project them over time and continue to plot the data on the chart without adjusting the average or limits. In the special case where sample sizes fluctuate, the control limits can vary with each sample but the average should remain fixed. The process average and control limits should only be recalculated after an assignable cause of variation has been eliminated or a change has been made in the system itself, making the control chart out of date.

Do not defeat the usefulness of this tool by failing to evaluate the most recent occurring sample (real time). It may be difficult to track down the reason for nonrandom behavior immediately, but it is even more difficult if incomplete or inaccurate data are used.

Unfortunately, computers have contributed to the last two problems by negatively affecting control charts. It is easy for software programs to recalculate the control limits with every sample, thus invalidating a chart. Also, electronic data bases are wonderful places to dump data for retrieval next week or next month, when it is too late to do anything. The very act of penciling in the day's point on the control chart causes a person to evaluate the chart for unusual evidence and to decide action.

Finally, confusion over the difference between control limits and specification limits defeats the entire purpose of control chart analysis. Specification limits are set by customer expectations for quality. Control limits are probability limits set by the past performance of the process; however, the two are not related. It is for this reason that a process can be under statistical control but still may not meet specifications.

A common question regarding the application of control charts concerns the implications of a process that is out of statistical control during the time the first 15 to 30 samples are taken. If the process is under statistical control at that time, then the estimates of both the process average and the process variability are accurate. The resulting control chart accurately reflects the long-term process capability.

On the other hand, if the process is unstable at the time the initial samples are taken, the average and limits calculated are not an accurate reflection of the process capability. In fact, the average and limits may, when drawn on the data, look quite inappropriate. If this is the case, look for the cause(s) of the variation immediately. If a shift in the process occurred just prior to recording the data, the control chart may demonstrate statistical control — but at a false average. In this case, the control chart does not detect the fact that the shift has occurred until the process shifts back again.

Histograms

A histogram is a bar graph of the process distribution. You may think of collapsing the control chart over the time axis to generate a histogram. Note that if sample averages are plotted on the control chart, the distribution of individual observations has a wider spread than the distribution of sample averages. By drawing the specifications on the axis, the histogram clearly shows the position of the process relative to the desired performance. It is clear what is needed: a narrowing of the distribution, a repositioning of the distribution, or both. Remember, a histogram says nothing about statistical control; only a control chart does that.

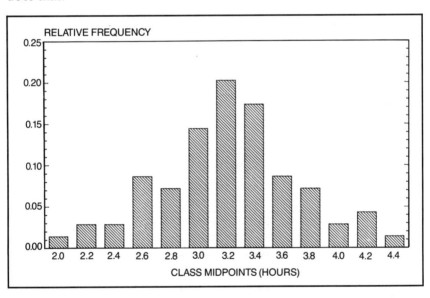

Figure 12.3   Relative Frequency Histogram

Scatter Diagrams

This is the familiar X-Y (or correlation) plot. Whereas both the control chart and the histogram plot a single quality measure, the scatter diagram requires a potential cause variable to be plotted against the quality measure.

By using various plotting symbols, scatter diagrams can be enhanced by differentiating subsets of the data. Stratification of the scatter plot may turn up associations within subgroups that are quite different from the overall picture; this is only one way to make a simple scatter plot more useful. There are as many alterations to the basic scatter plot as there are people to plot them.

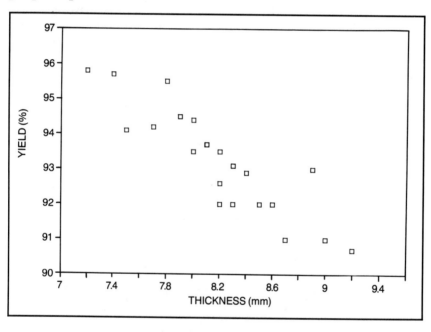

Figure 12.4   A Scatter Diagram: Wafer Thickness versus Yield

Pareto Charts

The common Pareto chart is a simple way of graphically displaying the relative contribution several factors make to the process under study. It is a bar chart with the bars arranged from left to right in descending order;

this tells at a glance which factor is the biggest contributor, second biggest, and so forth. Care should be taken when choosing the criteria for ranking the categories, however. A Pareto chart of causes for rework might be based on frequency of occurrence, dollars, or time lost. The biggest problem might well depend on how one chooses to measure it.

The Pareto principle states that 20 percent of the problems drive 80 percent of the impact to the process quality. Pareto analysis then focuses attention on the vital few rather than the trivial many.

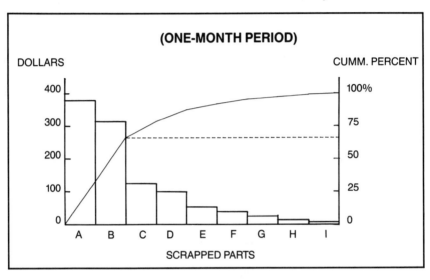

Figure 12.5   Pareto Diagram Showing Cost

Cause and Effect Diagrams

Seldom in any analysis is there just one or two variables that are likely candidates for explaining the observed variation in the process quality. The cause and effect diagram is a good organizational tool for grouping and showing the relationships among the factors brought out in a brainstorming session. The diagram is often helpful in designing a data collection strategy.

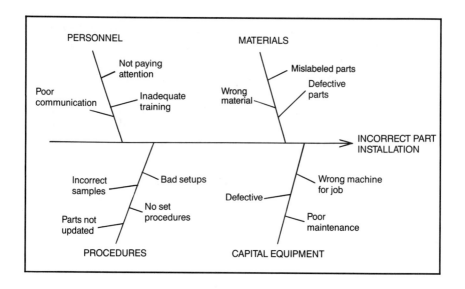

Figure 12.6   Cause and Effect for Incorrectly Installed Parts

Checksheets

The checksheet is the principal tool for data collection. A thoughtful layout of the factors taken from the cause and effect diagram can make data recording quick and simple. In fact, good planning can turn data recording and data analysis virtually into the same step. For example, a histogram can be constructed from the hash marks made on a checksheet. By using a matrix layout and marking the checksheet with symbols rather than hash marks, multivariate data can be recorded in just one step.

Good planning in the layout on the checksheet can benefit both the quality and quantity of the data collected. Collecting data can be a bothersome task that is prone to error and neglect. Making the job easy reduces the chance of a data recording error and lengthens the time people are willing to devote to the effort.

CHECKSHEET

PRODUCT: __03314-66503__   DATE: __April 1, 2001__

PRODUCTION AREA: __Board Test__   DEPARTMENT: __8460__

TYPE OF DEFECT: __Open trace, lifted trace, warped__   INSPECTOR: __John Smith__
board, internal short, other.

REMARKS: __New test bench installed today.__   NO. SAMPLED: __500__

DEFECT TYPE	CHECK	SUBTOTAL
OPEN TRACE	卅 卅 卅 //	17
LIFTED TRACE	卅 卅 /	11
WARPED BOARD	卅 卅 卅 卅 卅 ///	28
INTERNAL SHORT	////	4
OTHERS	卅 ///	8
	GRAND TOTAL	68

Figure 12.7 Checksheet

Data Gathering

We have already touched on some principles of data gathering during the discussions of control charts and checksheets. Now we'll study the process of collecting data in more detail.

All data are the product of a measurement system. This system is composed of seven elements:

1. The concept of the measurement being taken. Initially, someone must identify the measurement and its interpretation. As an example, before you can measure the length of something, you must understand what it means for an object to have length. While this may seem trivial, it becomes more challenging when talking about kinetic energy of an object or kurtosis (the relative degree of curvature near the mode of a frequency curve, as compared with that of a normal curve of the same variance) of a distribution.

259

2. Theory of measurement. All measurement techniques are based on a theory of why they work. This theory may be basic or complex. A simple method of measuring the length of an object is by comparing it with a standard, such as a meter stick. On the other hand, measuring the height of a tree cannot be done so easily. By using a stick of known length and walking out from the tree until, when held at arm's length, the stick appears to be of equal height as the tree, the height of the tree may be calculated by using trigonometry.

3. Equipment used. The equipment used is a variable in the measurement system. Variations in the equipment cause variations in the resulting data.

4. Environment under which the measurement is taken. Imagine a forester measuring the heights of trees using the method described above. If the day is dark and rainy, the measurements taken might be different than if the day were bright and sunny, with snow on the ground, to give a sharp image of the tree.

5. Manner of data recording. Consider two inspectors taking the diameter measurements of a machined part. One takes the measure, then stops to record it with a pencil on a data collection sheet. The other uses a special tool that electronically sends the measurements to the data base. The second method obviously would be preferable, since the first presents opportunities for error in data recording.

6. People taking the measurement. Would two foresters measuring the same tree get the same height? It is unlikely. Data are dependent on the person who took the data. Even two technicians using electronic tools for measuring the diameter of push rods must decide where along the length of the push rod the diameter is measured and how tightly the calipers are applied to the rod.

7. Manner of taking the measurement. The measurement technique, whether done carefully or haphazardly, affects the accuracy of the data gathered.

Change any one of these elements of a measurement system and the data changes, too. It is important that everyone involved in a data collection effort has a common understanding of the measurement system being used. Deming uses the term "operational definitions." Such definitions of measurement assure the same meaning for everyone both today and next week. An operational definition implies many details and questions.

It gives meaning to words like length, uniformity, and distortion — words that have no meaning until expressed in terms of the measurement system.

Plan the Data-Gathering Strategy

It is apparent that good data come from good planning. A good place to begin is by asking what one hopes to accomplish by collecting data. How, exactly, will the data help to resolve the issue? Try to be as specific as possible. It is not too helpful to answer with, "If a bunch of data is taken, something should turn up."

Data-gathering strategy:

- What data are needed? Which quality measures? Which related causal factors?

- Do a thorough job of setting operational definitions.

- Decide where in the process data should be collected. Use a flow-chart of the process to guide you.

Having established the data-gathering strategy, settle on a sampling scheme. Due to limited resources, sampling is usually better than 100 percent inspection. Statistical theory applied to sample data yields results reliable enough to make inspection of every piece unnecessary.

A decision must be made on how much data to gather. This depends on the precision desired in the results and the expected random variation in the process. It is wise for you to collect an adequate amount of data; this enables you to draw some initial conclusions before doing a technical sample size calculation for later studies.

An issue related to sample size is the time period over which the data are gathered. This depends, to a large extent, on the process cycle time.

Specify how the data are to be recorded. Checksheets are an excellent tool for manual data collection efforts.

Decide exactly who will be responsible for each area (data collection, data processing, reaction planning, etc.) before you begin to collect the data.

Conclusion

It is easy to refer to data as quantitative information and to lose sight that, in reality, data are missing washers on subassemblies or instruments that fail distortion tests. When the situation is in front of you, it is easy to believe that the most important action to be taken is to replace those missing washers or to fix the failing instruments. Of course, it is important to do these things. The most important action to be taken, however, is to fix the process so that all the washers are in place and the instruments pass the distortion tests. This is the goal that turns a missing washer into a data point.

The ultimate goal of SQC is total conformance to customer expectations. Sometimes businesses will conduct cost/benefit studies to justify the expense of making further quality improvements. These studies, in themselves, are additional costs of quality that are against the TQC philosphy; i.e., all productivity improvements must come through improvements in quality. Such cost analyses are often incomplete, overlooking the new customers and increased market share that improved quality brings. As one business convinces itself that the improvement in quality is not worth the cost, another decides otherwise and captures the market. The quality potential must not be underrated; the quality first policy should be adopted without reservation.

SQC Tools

The preceding discussion was intended to give the novice quality team member a basic understanding of SQC principles. The following discussions will describe each of the SQC tools most commonly used in the USA-PDCA process improvement cycle. Each tool is described under three headings:

- *What?* — Gives the definition of the SQC tool.

- *Why?* — Explains the purpose of using the SQC tool.

- *How?* — Describes the procedure for constructing and interpreting the SQC tool.

Sufficient information is given about each SQC tool to assist quality team members in using it appropriately in the process improvement cycle. Any previous knowledge or experience in using SQC methods certainly increases the understanding and use of the tools listed in this section. For further information, see the references listed at the end of this chapter.

Brainstorming

What? — Brainstorming is a technique used to get a group of individuals to generate many different ideas on a single topic.

Why? — Groups often get stuck on one idea or one person dominates the discussion. Brainstorming can be used to open up the discussion by involving all members, stimulating their thinking so that many ideas are generated and a variety of perspectives are gained.

How? — Make sure everyone knows the topic or the focus of the brainstorming session. For example, "What are the reasons for wrong shipments?"

Then move into the three phases of brainstorming:

Phase 1: Idea Generation

As a group, brainstorm as many ideas as possible while someone lists them on a flipchart. Follow these rules:

- All ideas are permitted; the more fanciful and free-wheeling the better. One person's imaginative suggestions can trigger another's good ideas.

- Evaluation and discussion are postponed until later.

- Ideas already listed should be adapted or expanded.

- Questions should be asked only to clarify ideas for flipchart.

Phase 2: Clarification

Clarify the items on the list to make sure everyone understands each idea. Add to the list any new ideas that result from your discussion.

Phase 3: Evaluation

Evaluate and condense the list.

Cause and Effect Diagram

What? — A cause and effect diagram shows the relationship between an effect and its possible causes.

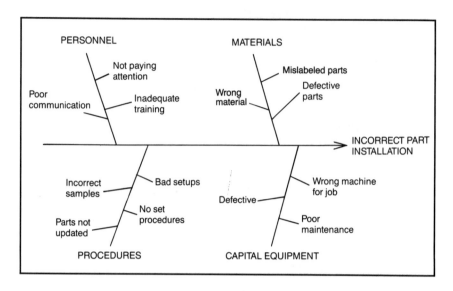

Figure 12.8 Cause and Effect for Incorrectly Installed Parts

Why? — Groups often jump to conclusions, assuming they know the true cause of the effect before a full analysis is done. Defining the relationship of the effect to each potential cause helps the group identify and define the true cause.

A cause and effect diagram is used to identify possible causes of an undesirable effect (i.e., a problem), and to identify factors that contribute to a good process.

How? — Construct a cause and effect diagram:

1. Use brainstorming to list possible causes for the effect. Also, ask other experts to contribute to the list of causes.

2. Review the list and look for interrelationships. Define three to six major categories that the causes may be divided into and categorize the list of causes.

    Four standard categories are:

    - Materials
    - Machinery
    - People
    - Methods

3. Within each category, look for subgroupings based on relationships among potential causes. Continue this hierarchical development of subgroups until satisfied.

4. Write the effect on the right side of the paper and draw an arrow pointing to it.

5. Draw major arrows to the arrow just drawn and label them with the selected category names. Add the potential causes under each category, showing the relationships among them by nesting the arrows.

6. Evaluate the causes based on the group's experience. Select the most likely cause(s) and circle them on the diagram.

Checksheets

What? — Data should be collected on carefully designed checksheets. A checksheet is a form prepared to efficiently gather, organize, and evaluate data.

Why? — The checksheet should be designed to enable you to gather the most information with the least effort. Many different forms of helpful checksheets are available. Before designing a new checksheet, see if you can use one that is readily available.

How? — Use checksheets similar to those shown in Figures 12.9 and 12.10.

CHECKSHEET

PRODUCT: _03314-66503_   DATE: _April 1, 2001_

PRODUCTION AREA: _Board Test_   DEPARTMENT: _8460_

TYPE OF DEFECT: _Open trace, lifted trace, warped_   INSPECTOR: _John Smith_
board, internal short, other.

REMARKS: _New test bench installed today._   NO. SAMPLED: _500_

DEFECT TYPE	CHECK	SUBTOTAL
OPEN TRACE	~~THL~~ ~~THL~~ ~~THL~~ //	17
LIFTED TRACE	~~THL~~ ~~THL~~ /	11
WARPED BOARD	~~THL~~ ~~THL~~ ~~THL~~ ~~THL~~ ~~THL~~ ///	28
INTERNAL SHORT	////	4
OTHERS	~~THL~~ ///	8
	GRAND TOTAL	68

The recording checksheet is used when recording data about types of defects found in manufactured products. List the types of categories, and make a mark each time the particular defect is found in the sample. Count the total number of checks made for each type of defect. Include other information such as date, process, data collection point, etc.

Figure 12.9   Recording Checksheet Example

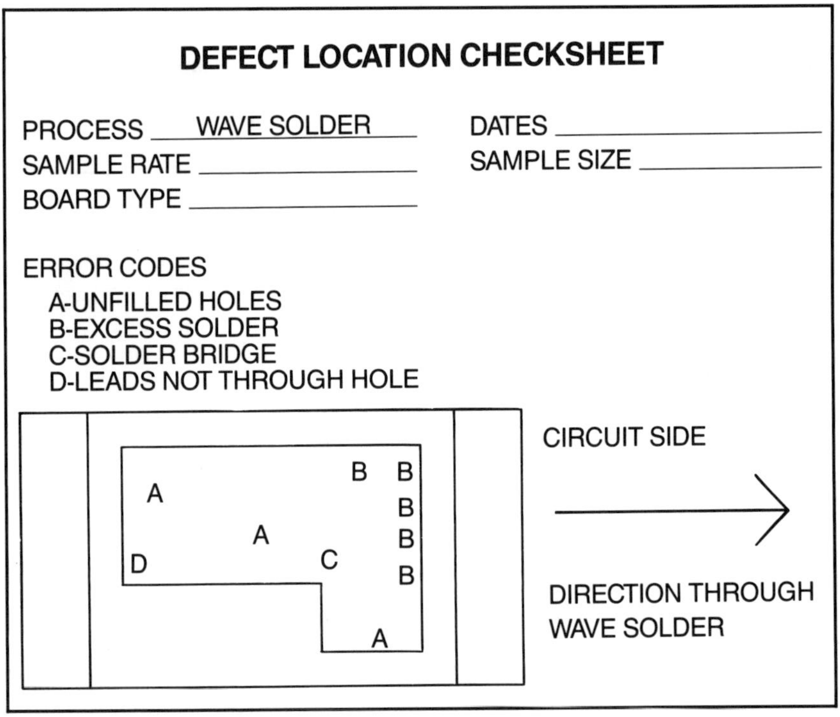
DEFECT LOCATION CHECKSHEET
PROCESS WAVE SOLDER
DATES
SAMPLE RATE
SAMPLE SIZE
BOARD TYPE
ERROR CODES
A-UNFILLED HOLES
B-EXCESS SOLDER
C-SOLDER BRIDGE
D-LEADS NOT THROUGH HOLE
B B
A
B
A
B
D
C
B
A
CIRCUIT SIDE
DIRECTION THROUGH WAVE SOLDER

The location checksheet is a diagram showing where and how often a particular defect or problem occurs.

Figure 12.10 Location Checksheet Example

Control Charts

What? — A control chart is a line graph that indicates how a variable changes over time (Figure 12.11).

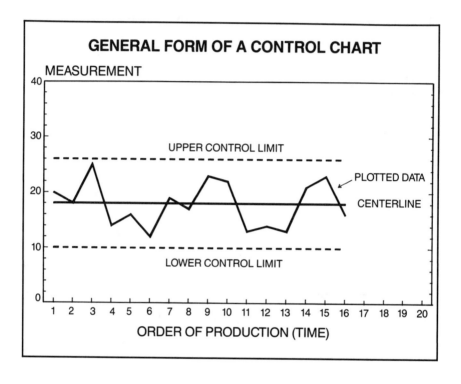

Figure 12.11 Control Chart Example

Why? — A control chart is used for:

- Monitoring a process for consistency over time.

- Identifying assignable causes for variation.

- Comparing processes.

How? — Several types of control charts may be used, but they all must have the following characteristics:

- Heading

- Horizontal time axis

- Vertical measurement axis

- Plotted and recorded data

- Centerline

- Upper and lower control limits

Control Charts

Discrete data are the result of an experiment where there are a finite number of possible outcomes.

- Proportion charts
  -$\bar{p}$ chart
  -$n\bar{p}$ chart

- Count charts
  -c charts
  -u charts

Continuous data are the result of an experiment where the possible outcomes can have any value within some range.

- $\bar{X}$ charts (average)

- R charts (variability)

- X charts (single measurement)

Proportional Charts for Discrete Data

p Chart

Purpose: Monitors the proportion of outcomes that are *defective.*

Sample Size: No restrictions but equal-sized samples (of size *n*) are preferable.

Classify: Each outcome as either *defective* or *not defective.* Graph the proportion of *defective* outcomes observed in each sample.

Centerline:

$\bar{p}$ = total number of *defectives* in all samples divided by the total number of units in all samples.

Control Limits:

$$UCL = \bar{p} + 3\sqrt{\frac{\bar{p}(1 - \bar{p})}{n}} \qquad \text{or 1, whichever is smaller}$$

$$LCL = \bar{p} - 3\sqrt{\frac{\bar{p}(1 - \bar{p})}{n}} \qquad \text{or 0, whichever is larger}$$

Comments:

1. Upper and lower control limits vary with *n*.

2. Multiply observations and control limits by 100 to change from proportion to percent.

3. For samples of unequal size, control limits are often based on the average sample size when the relative change in sample size is small.

pn Chart

Purpose: Monitors the number of outcomes that are *defective.*

Sample Size: Equal-sized samples (of size *n*).

Classify: Each outcome as either *defective* or *not defective.* Graph the number of *defective* outcomes observed in each sample.

Centerline:

$n\bar{p}$, where the definition of $\bar{p}$ is the same as shown for the *p* chart.

Control Limits:

$$UCL = n\bar{p} + 3\sqrt{n\bar{p}(1 - \bar{p})} \qquad \text{or } n, \text{ whichever is smaller}$$

$$LCL = n\bar{p} - 3\sqrt{n\bar{p}(1 - \bar{p})} \qquad \text{or } 0, \text{ whichever is larger}$$

Count Charts for Discrete Data

c Chart

Purpose: Each unit can exhibit any number of defects or other characteristic. Monitor the rate at which this characteristic occurs.

Sample Size: Equal sample sizes (*n*).

Sample Statistics: Graph either the total number of *specials* observed in each sample or the total number of *defects* observed in each sampled time period.

Centerline:

$\bar{c}$ = total number of *defects* in all samples divided by the total number of samples *(k).*

Control Limits:

$$UCL = \bar{c} + 3\sqrt{\bar{c}}$$
$$LCL = \bar{c} - 3\sqrt{\bar{c}} \qquad \text{or } 0, \text{ whichever is larger}$$

271

u Chart

Purpose: Each unit can exhibit any number of characteristics such as defects. Choose a characteristic of interest and monitor the rate at which it occurs.

Sample Size: Unequal sample sizes (n).

Sample Statistics: Graph either the total number of *specials* observed in each sample or the total number of *specials* observed in each sampled time period.

Centerline:

$\bar{u}$ = total number of *defects* in all samples divided by the total number of outcomes in all samples, etc.

Control Limits:

$$UCL = \bar{u} + 3\sqrt{\frac{u}{n}}$$

$$LCL = \bar{u} - 3\sqrt{\frac{u}{n}} \qquad \text{or 0, whichever is larger}$$

Three Charts for Continuous Data

$\overline{X}$ Chart

Purpose: Each outcome is a continuous measurement. Monitor the average value of the measured characteristic.

Sample Size: k equal-sized samples of size two or larger.

Sample Statistics: Observe n observations X_1, X_2, . . . X_n in each sample. Graph the average for each sample.

$$\overline{X} = \frac{X_1 + X_2 + \ldots + X_n}{n}$$

Centerline:

$$\overline{\overline{X}} = \frac{\overline{X}_1 + \overline{X}_2 + \ldots + \overline{X}_k}{k}$$

Control Limits:

$$UCL = \overline{\overline{X}} + (A_2 \times \overline{R}) \text{ where } \overline{R} \text{ is defined under R chart}$$

$$LCL = \overline{\overline{X}} - (A_2 \times R)$$

Comments:

1. Use Table 12.1 to find the proper value of A_2. A_2 depends on the value of n.

2. Special cases may restrict lower control limit to be greater than or equal to zero.

3. Adjustments are available for unequal sample sizes.

4. Control limits are not specification limits.

5. The $\overline{X}$ chart is used in conjunction with the R chart and is referred to as the $\overline{X}R$ chart.

$\overline{R}$ Chart

Purpose: Monitor the variability of the measured characteristic.

Sample Size: k equal-sized samples of size two or larger.

Sample Statistics: Observe n observations $X_1, X_2, \ldots X_n$ in each sample. Graph sample range $R = $ largest X_i − smallest X_i.

Centerline:

$$\overline{R} = \frac{R_1 + R_2 + \ldots + R_k}{k}$$

Control Limits:

$$UCL = D_4 \times \overline{R}$$

$$LCL = D_3 \times \overline{R}$$

Comments:

1. Table 12.1 provides values of coefficients D_3 and D_4 for different values of n.

2. The R chart is used in conjunction with the $\overline{X}$ chart and is called the $\overline{X}R$ chart.

n	A2	D3	D4
2	1.880	0	3.267
3	1.023	0	2.575
4	0.729	0	2.282
5	0.577	0	2.115
6	0.483	0	2.004
7	0.419	0.076	1.924
8	0.373	0.136	1.864
9	0.337	0.184	1.816
10	0.308	0.223	1.777
11	0.285	0.256	1.744
12	0.266	0.284	1.716
13	0.249	0.308	1.692
14	0.235	0.329	1.671
15	0.224	0.348	1.652
16	0.212	0.364	1.636
17	0.203	0.380	1.621
18	0.194	0.391	1.608
19	0.187	0.404	1.596
20	0.180	0.414	1.586
21	0.173	0.425	1.575
22	0.167	0.434	1.566
23	0.162	0.443	1.557
24	0.157	0.452	1.548
25	0.153	0.459	1.541

Table 12.1 Equation Constants

X Chart

Purpose: Each outcome is a continuous measurement. Monitor the value of the measured characteristic.

Sample Size: k samples of size one.

Sample Statistics: Graph the individual observations $X_1, X_2, \ldots X_k$.

Centerline:

$$\overline{X} = \frac{X_1 + X_2 + \ldots + X_k}{k}$$

Control Limits:

$$UCL = \overline{X} + (2.66 \times \overline{MR})$$

$$LCL = \overline{X} - (2.66 \times \overline{MR})$$

where $\overline{MR} = \dfrac{\left| X_1 - X_2 \right| + \left| X_2 - X_3 \right| + \ldots + \left| X_{k-1} - X_k \right|}{k - 1}$

Comments:

1. X charts are often referred to as moving range charts.

2. $\overline{MR}$ is the average of the differences between successive observations.

3. Special cases may restrict the lower control limit to be greater than or equal to zero.

Interpretation of Control Charts

(Control limits are not spec limits.)

Natural pattern (in statistical control) — most points near center, a few near control limit, rarely outside of control limits.

Unnatural patterns (changing system) — three equal width zones between centerline and control limit — consider top or bottom half separately, label A, B, and C from limit.

——— UCL
A
———
B   1. Single point outside control limit.
———
C   2. Two out of three successive points in Zone A or
——— Center   beyond.
C   3. Four out of five successive points in Zone B or
———   beyond.
B
———   4. Eight successive points Zone C or beyond.
A
——— LCL

Other unnatural patterns:

1. Stratification — 15 consecutive points in Zone C above or below centerline.

2. Mixture — eight consecutive points — none in Zone C above or below centerline.

3. Systematic variable — a repeating, predictable pattern.

4. Chart following — two charts which move in unison indicate relation.

5. Trends — consecutive or alternate points trending in one direction.

6. Level shift — abrupt change in level.

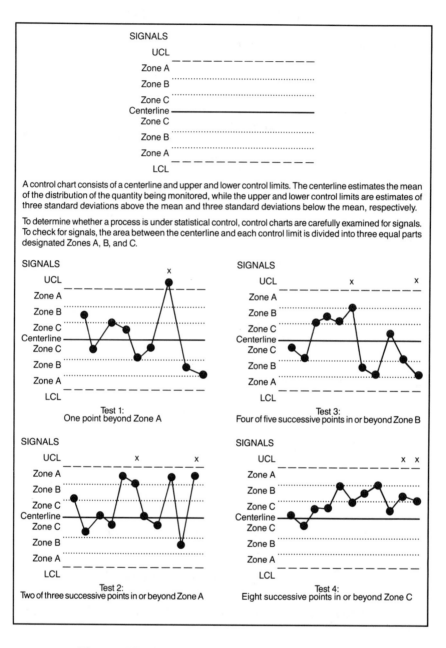

A control chart consists of a centerline and upper and lower control limits. The centerline estimates the mean of the distribution of the quantity being monitored, while the upper and lower control limits are estimates of three standard deviations above the mean and three standard deviations below the mean, respectively.

To determine whether a process is under statistical control, control charts are carefully examined for signals. To check for signals, the area between the centerline and each control limit is divided into three equal parts designated Zones A, B, and C.

Figure 12.12   Interpretation of Control Charts

Data Collection

What? — Data can be defined as "factual material used as a basis especially for discussion and/or decision." Data collection is an information-gathering tool where facts about a process are collected in the form of numbers, pictures, words, etc.

Why? — Groups sometimes assume they know the answer based on instinct or a single piece of evidence. At other times, it seems the person who argues convincingly or has the most influence unduly influences a group that has inadequate data.

Data can be collected for the following reasons:

- To assist in understanding the current situation.
- For analysis.
- For process control.
- For acceptance or rejection.
- For inspection of products.

How? — The importance of a concise, coordinated data collection plan cannot be overemphasized. Consider the following steps:

- Identify the specific purpose of collecting data. No measurements should be taken until you understand how data will be used.

- Identify correct data to be measured. Agreement should be reached on data to be gathered before beginning.

- To determine the reliability of data, examine the techniques and equipment used to collect them.

- Data should be gathered by those individuals most familiar with the process. They should be properly trained in data collection techniques and should be provided adequate time and resources.

- Determine whether data will be monitored on a continuous basis (100 percent) or on a sampling basis. Frequently, resource restrictions of time, cost, and personnel limit the amount of information that may be gathered. Decide on a sampling procedure.

- Develop appropriate checksheets for data collection.

- Decide on how data will be analyzed or charted.

Data should be collected and analyzed in a timely manner, with the results quickly communicated to all concerned. This allows problems to be detected as early as possible so that prompt action can be taken to minimize their negative effect.

Flowcharts

What? — A flowchart is a picture of a process in a step-by-step sequence (Figure 12.13).

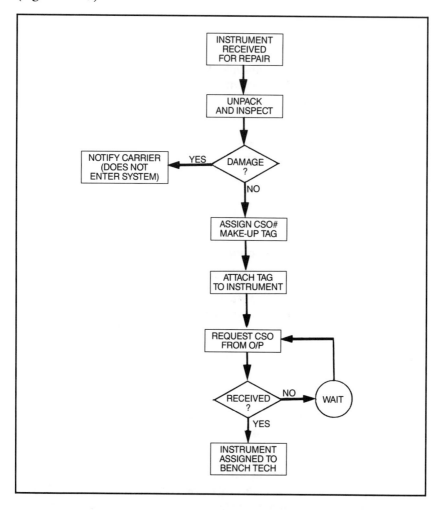

Figure 12.13   Flowchart Example: Assigning Repair Work

Why? — Documenting each step in a process is vital to understanding the overall process.

Flowcharts can assist in:

- Identifying problem areas and simplifying the process.

- Defining an ideal process.

- Identifying where to investigate and where to collect data.

- Documenting and standardizing the process.

How? — The flowchart process:

1. Start by identifying the first and last steps in the process; i.e., write the input and the output steps in an oblong shape.

2. Next, fill in major steps and decision points in your work flow. Keep each step separate. Break complex steps into individual parts.

   Use rectangles to illustrate steps and diamonds for decision points.

   Remember to include:

   - Every operational step — it will help in defining your process.

   - Feedback loops (rework loops) — they are indicators of the quality or possible inefficiency of your process.

   - Open-ended branches — they show areas where the process is not clearly understood. They can also serve as educational tools, but should eventually be resolved.

Pareto Chart

What? — A Pareto chart is a bar graph that displays, in descending order, the number of times events have occurred in each category (Figure 12.14).

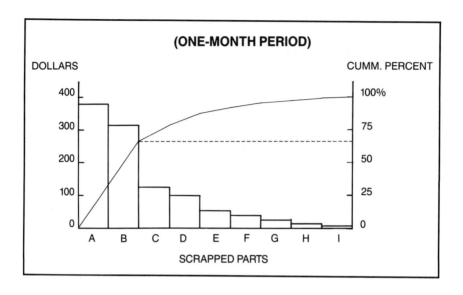

Figure 12.14 Pareto Diagram Showing Cost

Why? — Groups are often faced with a variety of problems, causes, or improvements. These charts enable the group to choose the problem, the cause, or the improvement that will have the greatest payback for time, energy, and resources.

Pareto charts may be used in the following cases:

- Determining which process needs work.

- Determining the major cause of a problem.

- Showing whether your improvement produces the desired results.

How? — Pareto diagram construction

1. Decide how many categories you want illustrated; use one bar for each category.

2. Draw horizontal and vertical axes. The vertical axis displays frequency, time, or money. The horizontal axis displays categories. Label the axes.

3. Total the number of occurrences for each category.

4. Draw bars all having the same width. The height of each bar will correspond to the value on the vertical axis — tallest to shortest.

5. Prepare a legend for the chart that includes: title, date, data source, and your name.

Sample and Sampling Techniques

What? — A sample is a set of units selected from the total units. A good sample is one that is selected without bias or preference. A complete set of units from which the sample is selected is called the population.

Example:

Population	Sample
All registered voters in the country	Any 100 registered voters in the county
All items produced by a company	Any 10 items manufactured by a company

Why? — A sample selected from a population is measured and analyzed.

If the sample is selected correctly, information can be gathered about the population based on the sample findings. Sampling, therefore, is a fast and easy method of collecting information about a population.

Data are collected about the sample because:

- Population is too large (a complete set of data is too big).
- Not enough time is available.
- Resources are not available (money, facilities, people).
- Destructive testing is required.

Therefore, the advantages of sampling are:

- Saves time and energy
- Easier
- Costs less
- Greater accuracy

A good sample must be free of bias. Bias in sampling occurs due to:

- Improper sampling procedures.

- Faulty measuring device.

- Inconsistent measurements from those collecting data.

How? — Three sampling techniques:

1. Simple Random Sampling

    Simple random sampling (selecting n units out of N such that every unit has an equal chance of being selected) is generally free of bias or preference and accurately estimates population parameters. Methods for random sampling are:

    - Rolling dice.

    - Generating random numbers using a calculator/computer program.

    - Drawing cards or names from a well-mixed pile.

    - Using a spinner.

2. Systematic Sampling

    This can have known or unknown bias and preferences if the measure has a systematic nature to it in the population. Methods of systematic sampling are selecting every tenth or fifteenth unit, for example: data collecting on a particular day of the week or a particular week of the month may always be biased by things that only happen on that day.

3. Stratified Sampling

    First, the population is divided into several subgroups or strata. Then independent random samples are taken from each subgroup.

    Example: Selecting sample of instruments for audit.

    Subgroups: types of instruments. Select n random samples of each type of instrument.

Scatterplot

What? — A scatterplot is a chart that shows the relationship between two variables (Figure 12.15).

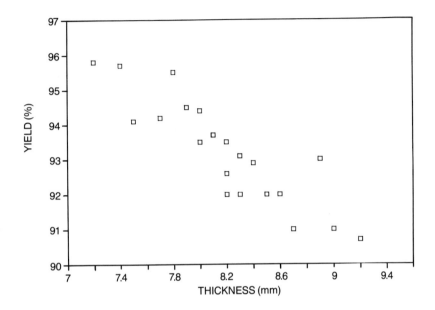

Figure 12.15   Scatterplot Examples

Why? — A scatterplot can be used for:

- Determining if there is a relationship between the two variables.

- Determining the strength of the relationship.

How? — A scatterplot has four elements:

- Heading
- Horizontal axis
- Vertical axis
- Data points

Procedure:

1. Collect at least 25 paired samples of data whose relationship needs to be investigated.

2. Draw the horizontal and vertical axes. Choose the scales for the two axes so all the data points will fit.

3. Plot the data points.

4. Label the axes and write the heading.

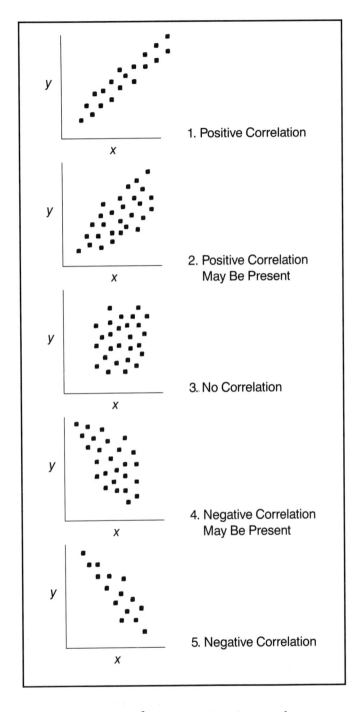

Figure 12.16   Interpreting Scatterplots

287

Time Lines

What? — A time line is a planning tool that can be used by a group to organize the various activities that are needed to reach a goal (Figure 12.17).

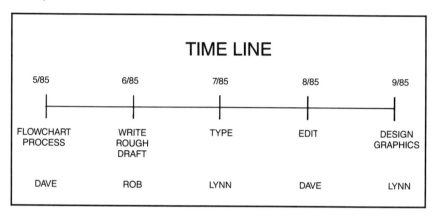

Figure 12.17   Example of a Time Line

Why? — Since a decision has been made by the group, most members feel the real work is done. Many decisions do not get implemented, however, because the group fails to do the detailed planning necessary to ensure success.

A time line can be used for:

- Planning an entire project to allocate time for each task.

- Working to a predetermined deadline.

- Developing an implementation plan.

How? — Making a time line:

- Write a goal statement and the estimated date of completion at the end of the time line.

- Determine and make a list of what must be done, who is responsible, and when it is due.

- Give everyone a copy of the time line. Review and display at every meeting.

Time Series Graph

Run Chart

What? — A time series graph is a line graph that is used for monitoring a particular process quality measure (defect rate, backorder, etc.) over a period of time (Figure 12.18).

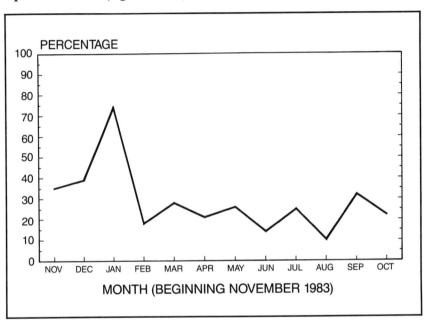

Figure 12.18   Example of a Time Series Graph

Why? — Before trying to determine the cause of the problem, the quality team should perhaps try to analyze the current performance of the process. A run chart can assist in this analysis by:

- Identifying how the process quality measure fluctuates during a given period of time.

- Indicating any trends, shifts, or cyclic nature in the process.

- A run chart can be used for setting PQM goals.

289

How? — Making a time series graph:

- Decide on the PQM to be monitored. Generally, one or two major PQMs are monitored by using the run chart.

- Label time on the x-axis and the PQM on the y-axis.

- Collect data according to plan; plot the points on the graph.

- Join consecutive points on the graph with a straight line.

References

Box, George E.P. "Off-Line Quality Control, Parameter Design, and the Taguchi Method." *Journal of Quality Technology,* Oct. 1985.

Deming, W. Edwards. *Quality, Productivity, and Competitive Fitness.* Cambridge: Massachusetts Institute of Technology, 1982.

Deming, W. Edwards. *Quality, Productivity, and Competitive Position.* Cambridge: Massachusetts Institute of Technology, 1982.

Phadke, M. S. "Quality Engineering Using Design of Experiments," Joint Statistical Meetings of the American Statistical Association, Cincinnati, 1982.

Taguchi, G. and Y. Wu. *Introduction to Off-Line Quality Control.* Central Japan Quality Control Association, 1980.

Additional Reading:
Statistical Quality Control

Deming, W. Edwards. *Quality, Productivity, and Competitive Position.* Cambridge: Massachusetts Institute of Technology, 1982. (A book on managing quality which has some good examples of using SQC tools to improve quality and productivity.)

Duncan, A. J. *Quality Control and Industrial Statistics.* Homewood, Ill.: Irwin Inc., 1974. (Focuses on control charts, sampling plans, inspection, and simple experimental designs.)

Grant, Eugene L. and Richard S. Leavenworth. *Statistical Quality Control,* 5th ed. New York: McGraw-Hill Book Co., 1980. (Focuses on control charts with some acceptance sampling procedures.)

Ishikawa, Kaoru. *Guide to Quality Control.* Asian Productivity Organization, 1976. (A comprehensive book on SQC tools.)

Juran, J. M. *Quality Control Handbook.* New York: McGraw-Hill Book Co., 1974.

Shewhart, W. A. *Economic Control of Quality of Manufactured Product.* New York: D. Van Nostrand Co., 1980. (Emphasizes advantages gained from control of quality, presenting data graphically, and the use of control charts.)

Statistical Quality Control Handbook. Western Electric Company, ITT Publication, 1956. (Written in nontechnical language with emphasis on control charts, inspection, and process capability studies. Describes simple experimental designs.)

INDEX

Statistical theory, 247-248

Subsystem, business as a, 22

Support:
   post-sales, 110
   presales, 109

System:
   automated, 29
   definition of, 250-251
   operating characteristics, 30
   people in, 30-32

Systematic process analysis, USA-PDCA, 215-218

Systems approach to management, 28

Technology advantage, 10

Time lines, 288

Time series graph, run chart, 289-290

Total quality control (TQC), 39, 40
   contribution, opportunity for, 50
   efficiency, 45
   flexibility through efficiency, 46
   market leadership through efficiency, 46
   methods, 43
     traditional, 49
   model, 44
   philosophy, 43
   presidential review, 51-52
   problem-solving method, 57-61
   process, 45
   productivity through quality, 42
   quality circles, 53
   quality, efficiency, and productivity, 44
   reward system, 49
   results, short-term, 49
   rewards, short-term, 40
   success, group, 50
   success, individual, 50